Photo credits

Page 6: © Siteman, 1983, Jeroboam / p. 38: © Alper, Stock, Boston / p. 54: © Preuss, 1977, Jeroboam / p. 90: © Siteman, 1980 EKM-Nepenthe / p. 127: Bermack, Jeroboam / p. 159: Bellak, Jeroboam / p. 187: © Cannefax, EKM-Nepenthe / p. 213: © Wood, Taurus / p. 242: Vilms, Jeroboam / p. 278: Rothstein, Jeroboam / p. 305: Bailey, Jeroboam.

W9-CKJ-983

Sponsoring Editor: Louise Waller
Project Editor: Brigitte Pelner
Cover Design: ARCON
Text Art: Fineline Illustrations, Inc.
Photo Research: Mira Schachne
Production: Jeanie Berke
Compositor: ComCom Division of Haddon Craftsmen, Inc.
Printer and Binder: R. R. Donnelley & Sons Company

Organizational Communication

Library of Congress Cataloging in Publication Data
Wilson, Gerald L., 1943–
    Organizational communication.

    Includes bibliographies and indexes.
    1. Organizational behavior.   2. Interpersonal communication.   3. Communication in organizations.
I. Goodall, H. Lloyd, Jr.   II. Waagen, Christopher L.
III. Title.
HD58.7.W55 1986   658.4'5   85-8723
ISBN 0-06-042387-0

85 86 87 88 9 8 7 6 5 4 3 2 1

ORGANIZATIONAL COMMUNICATION

GERALD L. WILSON
University of South Alabama

H. LLOYD GOODALL, JR.
University of Alabama, Huntsville

CHRISTOPHER L. WAAGEN
University of Alabama, Huntsville

1817

HARPER & ROW, PUBLISHERS, New York

Cambridge, Philadelphia, San Francisco,
London, Mexico City, São Paulo, Singapore, Sydney

CONTENTS IN BRIEF

CONTENTS

PREFACE

Recently colleges and universities have become increasingly aware of student needs to solve communication problems in organizations they will join after graduation. At the same time organizations have come to recognize that human relationships exist at the heart of every business activity. The technological setting of our society also increases the complexity of the communication problems students will encounter.

The quality of relationships, and indeed the managing of human resources within such organizations, depends on people's ability to communicate in a broad range of settings. Some experts suggest that an organization *is* its communication, that organizations would not exist without the flow of messages that hold them together. Guiding an organization and managing human resources, both must be understood as communication activities.

As we see it, the broad goals of an upper level undergraduate course in organizational communication are twofold. First, students planning careers in organizations must be educated in theories of organizational behavior and leadership so that they can understand and use a language indigenous to organizational operations. Because the focus of the course should be on *communication,* the instructor must strive to link existing and emerging theories of organizational behavior and leadership to theories of human communication in interpersonal, small group, and presentational or public contexts. Second, the course should strive to make these theories practical by pointing out how understanding a language of organizational communication can help students communicate more effectively in business settings.

The purpose and scope of this book is to provide careful treatments of the theoretical bases for communication activities in organizations, and at the same time demonstrate how to apply those theories to real organizational settings. Our hope is that we have met these objectives in a timely, relevant, and clearly written manner, and that the book will appeal to those persons who are interested in organizational or business communication, management, administrative communication, and human resources development.

Specific Features of the Text

First, we set out to meet the needs of students. We found through our experiences as teachers that no one current text in organizational communication contained theories of communication and organization that satisfied the complex and varied situations shown to us by our experiences in organizations as trainers, consultants, and employees. For this reason, you will find that we advocate no one theoretical position, but instead provide insight into how several theoretical bases can be combined usefully when describing, analyzing, and adapting to organizational settings.

A second feature of this text is our attempt to explain clearly these theoretical perspectives. Our feeling is that most texts provide competent theoretical discussions, but that too often these discussions are rendered in a language that confuses students. The result is that students may learn how to pass examinations about the theories, but they seldom are able to apply them. Because we want students to see theories as useful and to be able to apply them, we use examples and illustrations drawn from organizational experiences.

Third, our text incorporates what we believe is a holistic approach to organizational communication. What we mean is that we include material drawn from recent advances in interpretive and experimental research. Our objective here was to provide a synthesis of what previously had been competing, if not adversarial, theoretical paradigms. We feel that this is the obvious direction of our disciplines, and that students can benefit equally well from empirical and field studies.

Fourth, we explain a variety of diagnostic tools and instruments useful in examining and solving organizational communication problems. In addition to standard communication audit techniques and measures, we provide guidelines for using Robert Bales' SYMLOG and other instruments that do not require the use of a computer. We believe this will be useful to instructors who want to introduce students to various capacities of diagnostic tools.

Finally, and perhaps most importantly, we wrote the text for students who may not have a background in communication or organizational studies. You will find that we do not "assume" *a priori* knowledge about any topic we cover. We believe this makes our text more useful to the individual needs of instructors and programs.

Design of the Text

Organizational Communication is designed to meet the needs of students and instructors by presenting a systematic approach to the study of organizational communication topics. This approach is adaptable to a variety of teaching methods and course plans. Chapter 1, "The Bases of Communication in Organizations," introduces readers to the essential elements of the communication process in organizations, and defines key terms and theoretical perspectives used throughout the book.

Chapter 2, "Understanding Human Behavior in Organizations," presents discussions of the four primary perspectives on how and why humans behave as they do in organizations, and introduces readers to methods for assessing human behavior from five influential theoretical camps.

Chapter 3, "Organizational Resource Development, Motivation, and Communication," describes how attitudes and values about work and about human performance provide ways of assessing motives and goals relevant to message analysis.

Chapter 4, "The Process of Communicating in Organizations," develops a theoretical perspective about communicating in organizations based on the principles of exchange and equity. Using this perspective, the chapter then shows how levels of meaning are attained, the functions served by messages in organizations, and discusses a variety of communication problems typically encountered in organizational settings.

Chapter 5, "Communication Between Persons," examines one-to-one exchanges of communication in organizations. The nature of interpersonal communication in organizations, levels of analysis for interpersonal relationships, and conflict management are described and analyzed.

Chapter 6, "Communication in Groups," explores how groups in organizations function. In this chapter we discuss the role of groups in organizations, the needs of individuals in groups, making and adhering to agendas, and the resolution of conflict.

Chapter 7, "Public Organizational Communication," presents what we believe to be a cogent treatment of the relationship between public information and organizational communication. This chapter examines the role of publicity, public communication intervention strategies, and models that reveal methods to assess public communication strategies with various publics.

Chapter 8, "Assessment of Organizational Communication," investigates various methods of evaluation. This chapter begins with a discussion of types of questionnaires and instruments, and then explores in detail the use of the ICA Communication Audit and SYMLOG.

Chapter 9, "Communication and Organizational Change," is designed to appeal to those persons interested in analyzing and developing training programs for organizations. It describes how a human resource developer operates, and discusses various training option designs, and the ethics of being a trainer.

Chapter 10, "Designing Successful Communication Training Programs," introduces and explains the Wilson/Goodall/Waagen Assessment Instruction Plan. This plan, based on a five-year research and testing program, provides a step-by-step method for analyzing and designing a communication skills training program for organizations.

Chapter 11, "Organizational Communication Career Development," analyzes how a person should choose and develop a career within any organization.

Using theoretical perspectives derived from human resource management, industrial psychology, and career planning, this chapter shows students how to use
organizational communication understandings and skills in their careers.

Acknowledgments

We are especially indebted to those persons who gave careful critical attention
to the manuscript in the review and revision process: Charles Bantz, University
of Minnesota; Beverly Davenport-Sypher, University of Kentucky; Sue DeWine,
Ohio University; Cal Downs, University of Kansas; Fredric M. Jablin, The
University of Texas at Austin; Walter G. Kirkpatrick, Memphis State University;
Angela Laird, University of Arkansas at Little Rock; Michael L. Lewis, Abilene
Christian University. Their suggestions helped us refine and polish our work.

We also thank those people at Harper & Row who have devoted countless
hours to this project. We are especially grateful to Louise Waller, our editor, who
was generous with her time and exceptional expertise. Louise is one of the finest
professionals we know in the writing/editing field, and her support of us during
this project meant a great deal more than these simple words can convey. We also
appreciate Brigitte Pelner's work in expertly guiding our manuscript through the
production process. She was enormously helpful to us.

Finally, we are indebted to our families. We thank them here for their
consistent understanding, patience, criticism, and encouragement throughout the
writing. We dedicate this book to them with gratitude and love

Gerald L. Wilson
H. Lloyd Goodall, Jr.
Christopher L. Waagen

one

COMMUNICATION AND ORGANIZATIONAL BEHAVIOR

chapter 1

The Bases of Communication in Organizations

DEFINING THE COMMUNICATION PROCESS

Communication: Intentional Behaviors / Communication: Process and Relationships / Communication: Evolution and Culture

THE FUNCTIONAL COMPONENTS OF THE COMMUNICATION PROCESS

The Source(s) / The Channel(s) / The Message / The Receiver(s) / Feedback/Responses to Messages / The Physical and Cultural Environment / The Effects of Communication

DEFINING ORGANIZATION AND ORGANIZATIONS

A Basic Definition / General Systems Theory Definitions / A Managerial Definition / The Cultural Performance Definition / Summary of Definitions

COMMUNICATION IN ORGANIZATIONS

The Organization as a Productive Communication Environment / Communication Is Evolutionary and Culturally Dependent / Learning Organizational Communication

Consider the word *communication*. Probably the word conjures up diverse images in your mind. Communication is talk between and among persons and the various problems associated with understanding what talk means. Communication is physical action, such as how you move through space, or how someone else's eyes fix on yours or avoid contact with you. Communication is a concept, an idea, sometimes used to connote what you wish you could do or to cover what you wish you had done. Communication is a technique, a method for attaining goals, a way of reaching an agreement, resolving disputes, handling difficult moments, or working through conflict. Communication is entertainment, a means of spending time, making thoughtful observations or sharp commentaries, engaging in humor, or telling stories. And communication is, well, somehow "mysterious," the unspoken answer to unutterable questions, something someone else does better than you can for reasons you can't figure out, a quality of being enacted in public and private performances that is almost magical, and often powerful. Communication is all of these images, and then some.

Now consider the word *organization*. Again, what images form in your mind? An organization is a place, a physical environment, in which work is done. An organization is also people, those who do the work with more or less efficiency, who interact formally and informally, who move through corridors with purposes that shape everything from financial statements to national defense, and who give and receive instructions, explanations, and reports. An organization is as well an idea, a concept of order from which dreams are turned into work, profits, losses, and memories. And, an organization is, when considered by a prospective employee or a judicious auditor, a kind of mystery, a puzzle to be solved, an understanding to reach something larger and more powerful than we are because it could go on without us. An organization is all of these images, and potentially even more.

Now put *communication* and *organization* together. What happens? In one sense the terms seem nearly synonymous—after all, you can't conceive of an organization without communication, and communication is meaningless without some form of organization. Yet in another sense the terms are separate intellectual categories. After all, you can study communication in college without ever studying organizations, and vice versa. And in a third sense the terms are equally separate and distant from your own experiences. Communication is something you hope to learn how to do, whereas organization is a way to express where you will probably spend the rest of your working life, and in this odd third sense both terms seem worlds apart and virtually incomprehensible.

The mind, when left to imaginings like those just discussed, plays tricks on you. Words are powerful suggestive symbols, capable of inducing cooperation or mutually assured destruction and of making sense and nonsense out of ordinary experiences or grand ideas, and perfectly willing to mean, as Humpty Dumpty puts it, "anything I want them to mean." So, when you confront two words that are as suggestive as *communication* and *organization,* the mind tends to wander into dangerously abstract territory, usually known as *confusion*.

This chapter is designed to alleviate that confusion. It considers both communication and organizations, and its purpose is to make these abstract words less perplexing.

To begin our discussion, we first define communication, identify its components, and show you how to think about it as an evolutionary, culturally dependent process. Second, we define organization, and show you how to think about it as a manageable communication environment. Third, we combine the terms communication and organization, and show you how to think about the two productively, practically, and profitably. Finally, we review the major claims advanced in this chapter and provide some questions for you to consider alone and discuss freely with others.

DEFINING THE COMMUNICATION PROCESS

Communication is a complex, sometimes confusing term. This section is designed to help you understand what the term *communication* means. We could present a simple definition, but any simple definition of communication would be naive. Communication *is* complex. It requires more than a definition from a single theoretical perspective. For this reason, we believe communication must be defined as (1) intentional behaviors, (2) a process that creates and constitutes human and technological relationships, and (3) an evolutionary, culturally dependent system of assigning meanings to symbols.

Communication: Intentional Behaviors

First, communication refers to a host of *intentional behaviors*. Specifically, these behaviors are called *speaking* and *acting*. We *speak* when talking to ourselves, with others, and to groups of varying sizes. When speaking we use *symbols* to represent what we think, feel, and believe. Usually we communicate in words, although in many organizations today acronyms and numbers are heard at least as frequently as words.

We *act* when we behave without words, or simultaneously with the words we speak. We act when we wink at someone we know, shake hands with a new acquaintance, walk rapidly toward an appointment or slowly toward a door, or grimace at a bad joke or smile knowingly at a familiar adage. Whether we act with or without speaking we are displaying *nonverbal communication,* and as you probably already know, nonverbal communication is at least as suggestive and powerful as verbal communication. In some cases the old saying, "actions speak louder than words," attains a literal truth; however, it is also true that nonverbal actions can be misread or distorted.

Together our speaking and acting are the primary sources of information others have about us. From the choices we make as to what we say and do, particularly in the presence of others, our *identities* evolve.[1]

For example, in an organizational setting managers are known in part by their ability to give and evaluate work assignments. Usually these assignments are communicated and evaluated personally by the manager. Words are spoken, eyelids are raised, smiles and frowns are expressed on the face, gestures are made, a stance is taken, and questions are asked. Through these sources of communication, employees learn what they are to do and, later, how well or poorly they did

Communication refers to a host of intentional behaviors.

it. Conversely, how well the manager communicates during these episodes often directly determines how employees respond to the person *as a manager.* She or he may be the boss, but as Max Weber pointed out nearly 90 years ago, the legitimate authority of hierarchical position does not necessarily mean the person in that position will be treated as the legitimate authority.

For this reason, we conceive of speaking and acting as *performances.* Performances are messages we give to attentive audiences and listeners who in turn evaluate the effectiveness of our performances to arrive at judgments about who and what we are. One rule that you will find consistently emphasized in this book is the rule of intentional behavior in organizations: *The more intentional your behavior is, the more influence you exert over its outcomes.*

Communication is intentional in a real and ironic sense. As many communication scholars have pointed out, communication is intentional because it is goal-oriented behavior. We speak to accomplish purposes; we act to convey meanings associated with those purposes. However, we aren't always conscious of our purposes in communication. We may say something that we later regret, or forget to say something that we later wish we had said. Sometimes we "just talk," to feel included in a conversation or to express an opinion. This is why communication is intentional in an *ironic* sense: During those times when we speak without being conscious of a purpose, others usually act as if we *did* have a reason. The bottom line is simple. Because we treat communication as intentional behavior, we expect people to mean what they say and to say what they mean. When they claim they didn't say what they meant, we become suspicious. When they say they didn't know what they were saying, we tend to doubt them. The irony of intentional communication is that we are inclined to expect more from others than we do from ourselves.

Thus, communication refers to intentional behaviors, even when the degree of intention is questionable. These deliberate behaviors are performances we give to others, and the quality and range of our performances shapes our identities in organizations.[2] However, communication is more than the sum total of our intentional behaviors. The term communication also references a process that creates and constitutes human and technological relationships.

Communication: Process and Relationships

Communication is the substance of all human relationships. We carry on our relationships with others through talk and action. Communication scholars advocate examining relationships as a *process* that evolves over time based on the communication between or among the participants.[3]

In organizations the process of relational development is central to the information to which you have access. Who you know and talk to is a vital part of what you know about the organization and its members, as well as an important part of your understanding of how to do your job.[4] Clearly, the relationships you develop at work will be important. How you choose to enter into relationships, their development over time, and their effects on you and your job performance will be shaped by your communication in and about them.

Communication is also important in relationships you develop with present and emerging technologies. Usually technological innovation is something you "hear of," develop an attitude toward, and talk about long before it becomes a reality in your office space. What you hear and how you choose to discuss it will affect the attitude you develop toward the technology, and may even determine your ability to make productive use of it. For example, many organizations are rapidly becoming more computerized. The computer, like the telephone or typewriter before it, is a form of technology with which you interact (e.g., by using the terminal, talking into a voice-activated sensor, etc.). You develop an attitude toward it and a relationship with it. It affects your personal and organizational identity.[5] The computer itself has no inherent meaning, no direct ability to influence you; however, how you think and talk about it, and how you learn to act toward it, will influence your ability to use it as well as the meanings you ultimately attach to it. Again, as in human relationships, what you understand about the computer will change with time as your process of communicating with and through it develops and your relationship with it stabilizes.

Thus, communication is a process that creates and constitutes human and technological relationships. The process develops or evolves over time, and how we talk and act in and about the relationships essentially defines them and our identities in them. But there is a third component in our understanding of the term communication as an evolutionary, culturally dependent system of assigning meanings to symbols.

Communication: Evolution and Culture

Communication is not a "thing." It is not a static entity. Nor is it arbitrary. Many words and actions do have predetermined meanings that we learn but that we can alter or change to fit the needs of our environment. When we think of communication, we should include in our definition a sense of its permanence and change, an appreciation of its belonging to a particular time and place.

Communication is evolutionary because all human technological relationships have identifiable beginnings, developments, and endings. We meet our boss, interact with him or her over time, and suddenly find we have been transferred to another location half a world away. Our relationship with this person has changed, and even if we stay in touch, it will continue to change as long as we communicate. As relationships between or among people emerge, the individuals learn to share common meanings for past experiences, something the ancient Greeks called *commonplaces.* In organizations commonplaces such as "my first day on the job," "our first argument with the competition," or "the day the old goat got fired" reference experiences shared by those who communicate about them. Merely mentioning a few words can call up a host of old memories, images, faces, and words. They are a kind of verbal shorthand we use to communicate more effectively with those with whom we have shared the experiences. They couldn't exist unless our relationships evolved over time.

We also believe communication is *culturally dependent.* When referring to the term *culture* in this book, we mean both the general cultural milieu of our time (e.g., American culture, Indian culture, Italian culture, etc.) and the culture of the specific organization (e.g., how we do things here). By "culturally dependent" we mean:

1. *Our understanding of relationships, and communication in them, is derived from our culture.* Every culture develops its own standards for behavior. In any organization these standards govern relationships between and among persons of varying status and power and between the sexes. These standards also influence when, where, and how communication proceeds, what issues may be discussed, and how disagreements are adjudicated. "The ropes" you learn in one organization may differ from "the ropes" you must learn if you change jobs.

2. *Our understanding of appropriateness and inappropriateness are derived from cultural standards.* It is important to know the rules. In some cultures, such as the federal government, telling jokes may be a sign of a character flaw because it shows you are not a serious person, whereas in other cultures, such as Toastmasters International, Inc., joketelling is a vital skill for success. Because all rules for etiquette and appropriateness are communication rules, you need to see communication as a culturally dependent system for assigning meanings to symbols.

You may behave intentionally and understand that communication is a process that creates relationships, but if your understanding is not tempered with an appreciation of the culture's values, rituals, and mores, your communication may be evaluated negatively. As the communication theorist I. A. Richards once put it: "Communication doesn't have meaning, people do." And people are always members of particular and general cultures.

These three perspectives on the term *communication* point out why and how it is a complex concept. They also show you what we mean when we use the term *communication* in this book. The term *communication* references (1) intentional behaviors (including the irony of assigning intention to spontaneous behaviors), (2) a process that creates and constitutes human and technological relationships, and (3) an evolutionary, culturally dependent system for assigning meaning to symbols.

Now that you understand our way of defining communication, let's examine its functional components.

THE FUNCTIONAL COMPONENTS OF THE COMMUNICATION PROCESS

Our definition provides three interrelated perspectives on the communication process. In this section we explain how these perspectives cna be used to describe the functional components of any communicative performance. By functional components we mean (1) the source(s) of a message; (2) the channel(s) conveying the communication; (3) the receiver(s) of the message; (4) the message itself, including any noise or distortion of it; (5) the feedback, or responses made to the message by the receiver; (6) the physical and cultural environment; and (7) the effects of the communication, or the *meanings* assigned to the episode and relationship.

The Source(s)

When using the term *source,* we are referring to the *initiator* of any communication. For example, if an auditor enters the office of a local manufacturing firm and asks to see the books, the auditor is the source of the communication. If a woman turns on her computer one morning and finds a message left by her counterpart in another location, her counterpart is the source.

In other words, by using the term *source,* we are referring to a momentary, static description of any communication. When the manager of the local manufacturing firm responds to the auditor, he is becoming the source and the auditor becomes the receiver. When the woman answers the message on her screen, she becomes the source and her counterpart becomes the receiver.

For many years the source of communication was the focus of research and theorizing. From Aristotle's *The Rhetoric* (fourth century B.C.) down to contemporary times, researchers have isolated key factors in understanding the *appeals* of a speaker. Scholars have focused on this aspect of source because of its pervasive impact on the receiver of the communication. Aristotle, for example, believed the goal of any communication was the enhancement of *ethos,* or the credibility of the speaker. More recently, researchers have identified the two central features of a source's credibility: (1) *competence,* or how receivers evaluate what the speaker knows about the subject and his or her general intelligence and (2) *character,* or how receivers judge the trustworthiness, sincerity, and concern for them displayed by the speaker.[6] Furthermore, a source's credibility can and does change as receivers are exposed to messages over time. For this reason, we speak of three kinds of credibility in any communication episode:

1. *Initial credibility*—what receivers think about sources prior to communicating with them.
2. *Derived credibility*—what receivers are induced to see and believe about the source's competence and character during the communication episode.
3. *Terminal credibility*—what receivers believe about the source's character and competence after the communication episode.

As you can see, the credibility of the source of any message is important. If one of America's leading management theorists, such as George Odiorne or Peter Drucker, was scheduled to present a talk at your university or college tonight, your interest in attending it would be influenced by your perception of the speaker's credibility. If you elected to attend the event, your estimate of the speaker's credibility would influence how you perceived the message. If the speaker's message violated your beliefs, his credibility, from your point of view, might decrease; if the speaker spoke directly to your interests, his credibility might be enhanced. By the end of the evening you would have a revised estimate of the speaker's credibility based on your experience communicating with him.

To say that an individual is the source in a communication simplifies what is actually more complex. Usually people are both sources and receivers of communication simultaneously. As soon as any communication episode begins, the give-and-take of conversation, the flurry of actions, and the interplay of meanings coalesce to blur the easy distinction provided by the terms *source* and *receiver.*

In fact, there are few communication situations characterized by the presence of a single, identifiable source. When a leader of a problem-solving group provides directives or a supervisor explains a new policy or an executive gives a public presentation about the strategic financial planning of a company, we can identify a source, at least temporarily. However, when a group member, employee, or audience member asks a question our source changes.

Regardless of whether the source gives a speech, leads a group, or initiates a conversation, her or his *credibility* is a key component of the source. In a practical sense it will be productive for you to consider yourself, and your messages, in relation to your credibility. In any organizational setting the meanings attributed to messages are at least partially dependent on the perceived credibility of the source(s) sending them. What others think about you, your character, your reliability, your honesty, your depth of understanding will influence the meanings they give to what you say and do. Messages do not have meanings, people do, and most of the time most people use their perceptions of your credibility to evaluate your messages.

The Channel(s)

A *channel* is what a message passes through between source(s) and receiver(s). Traditional communication makes use of two primary channels: airwaves and light waves. Sound is carried by airwaves, images are conveyed by light waves.

In contemporary mediated communication, many messages are carried by electronic impulses, minor changes in the current.

In 1948 an engineer, Claude Shannon, and a mathematician, Warren Weaver, developed a model of the telephone communication process. They were interested in measuring the static interferences in the channel with the aim of reducing them. Their model demonstrated how much interference (known as *noise*) existed in a telephone system and how communication effectiveness could be improved by reducing it. Their interest in the channel for communication sparked new research into sources of distortion and noise that typically interrupt or decrease the effectiveness of communication.

The Shannon/Weaver model demonstrates one way to conceptualize noise —as a direct interference in the channel for telephonic communication (see Figure 1.1). By analogy, we use this insight to see how the channel can become a problem for any communication:

1. *The channel can be physically or electronically distorted.* The noise you see on a television screen during a bad program transmission is an example of how your ability to receive communication can be distorted by electronic noise in a channel designed to convey a mediated communication. Physical noise can also be understood by remembering the last time you were engaged in a conversation when a loud noise occurred. Didn't the noise disrupt your reception of the message? The channel can be physically or electronically distorted and the result is an interference in the communication episode.

2. *The channel can be manipulated.* Political communication theorists point out that one negative influence of television is the systematic control of information by well-financed candidates and causes. Literally, the channels for public access to information can be controlled or manipulated. Similar charges have been made about televised news broadcasts or commercial advertising. Because the channel is the road for any communication, and because the road can be blocked, altered, or manipulated, the channel is an important ingredient in the relationship between communication and power.

3. *The channel can be overloaded.* Since humans can only process a limited amount of incoming information at any time, we have all experienced "information overload." The Nobel prize-winning economic/management theorist Herbert Simon, in 1982, advocated giving up reading newspapers (the print channel)

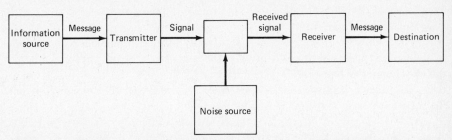

Figure 1.1   The Shannon-Weaver model of communication. (*Source:* Data from Claude Shannon and Warren Weaver, *The Mathematical Theory of Communication.* Urbana: University of Illinois Press, 1949. Reprinted by permission of the University of Illinois Press.)

as an alternative to lessen information overload. In our technological information age there is more available information than our channels can readily handle. Simon was not entirely serious, of course, but his point should serve to remind us of how vital the channel of communication is to our understanding of anything.

One additional way to think about the importance of channels for communication is to remember the psychological principle of *selective perception.* We tend to filter out information in a channel that does not appeal to us, or that seems uninteresting, and focus on information to which we can relate or with which we can identify. For example, many theorists have described our culture as dependent on images of physical attractiveness, or beauty. Researchers have consistently demonstrated that we often "mistake the beautiful for the true" in our evaluations of credibility.[7]

The visual appeal of a person's physical appearance can distort our perception and understanding of his or her message—an interference in the channel of communication. Depending on the values of the receiver, this distortion can result in *improperly labeling* what we are actually responding to. In studies of organizational communication our "culture of beauty" tends to work against the efforts of women who are encouraged to become both physically attractive and professionally competent. The paradox is expressed by many women who feel they are treated more as objects of desire than as professional colleagues, and who complain about how males spend more time looking at them than listening to them.[8] As our culture evolves toward enlightened understandings between women and men, these organizational communication problems deserve special attention. Truly, the channel must be made freer from distortions.

The Message

Our third functional component in the communication process is the *message.* The message is "the thing itself," the object of most analyses of communication in organizations and the target of scholars in a variety of disciplines.

The term *message* refers to three coactive parts of any communication:

1. *The verbal message,* or the words spoken, or symbols transmitted, by the participants. However, as you undoubtedly realize, words are subject to *semantic* distortions. Dictionary definitions are not the only meanings assigned to these symbols. Some words connote emotionally charged experiences (e.g., sexual, racial, and ethnic slurs); some have no apparent meaning outside a limited group of users (e.g., in-house jargon and highly technical language); and some, when spoken, mean the opposite of what they say (e.g., "Thank you very much" uttered upon the late receipt of a report). When using the term *verbal message* we are referring to *what* is said, *how* it is said, and the *intended meaning* of what is said and how it is said.

2. *The nonverbal message,* or the acting out of behavior. This term refers to facial expressions, body movement, gestures used while speaking or responding, eye contact, use of space, and any other visual clues that contribute to perceived meanings. Scholars confidently point out that nonverbal messages co-

contribute to the meaning of any communication, adding at least as much meaning to the episode as verbal communication does.[9] Here again, we find possible distortions of messages. For example, *hierarchical noise* refers to how differences in status affect the perceived meaning of messages. Consider how you felt the last time you were led into your department chairperson's office and asked to sit down. The nonverbal power of the office space and furnishings indicated your hierarchical inferiority in the situation. Or, consider how the fashionable dress of a higher paid employee influences your responses to her or him. As clear as these examples may appear, you need to be cautious about the *meaning* of any nonverbal cue. There are at least as many opportunities to misread nonverbal cues as to misread verbal cues.

3. *The metaverbal message,* or what is implied or suggested by the words spoken and the actions performed. You could think of the metaverbal message as "a message about a message," such as when a supervisor approaches a subordinate with the statement "You probably already know about this, and I don't want to upset you, but the performance appraisals have been moved up one month." Which message should the subordinate respond to—that she or he should not be upset, he or she should already know about the decision to move the appraisal reviews, or the appraisal reviews have been moved up? As you can see, metaverbal messages tend to create situations in which communication between people is made more complex by the fact that several messages, each with differing interpretations, are made available to the participants simultaneously. Opportunities for distortions are at least as available as are opportunities for accurate readings of the message.

Thus, the message is a complex part of the communication process. It attains little meaning apart from the perceived credibility of the source and receiver, the opportunities for noise or distortion in the message and in the channel, the environment in which it occurs, and the time of its occurrence. All functional components in the communication process reveal aspects of the message's meaning.

The Receiver(s)

What you have read concerning the source is also true of the receiver of any communication. By definition, a *receiver* is the target or audience for a message. In reality, however, we are usually both sources and receivers simultaneously. The term *receiver* is only a descriptor used to identify a position in the beginning of any communication episode.

The receiver(s) is an important area for communication researchers. Ever since Aristotle identified three specific audiences for public rhetoric in ancient Greece (i.e., forensic, or audiences in law courts; deliberative, or audiences for legislative decisions; and epideictic, or audiences for public celebrations or ceremonies), communication scholars have labored to identify and describe the characteristics of audiences that influence their responses to messages and sources. For example, let's consider the various types of audiences for presentations commonly encountered by persons in organizations: in-house technical audiences, who might be attracted to the technical dimensions of the presentation; in-house managerial audiences, who might be interested in how the presentation will affect their decision making and planning schedules; external market audiences, who might contract with the organization if the presentation meets their needs and expectations; and a general public audience, who might respond to how the presentation will influence the economic development of the community. In each case the type of audience, or receiver, for the message helps define the meaning of the situation to which the message should respond in order to be effective.

In our own time both organizational behavior and communication theorists have attained consensus on a view of the communication process favoring *systematic adaptation of the message to the needs and expectations of the receivers.* [10] This tenet is both essential to your understanding of effective communication and central to this text.

Feedback/Responses to Messages

Communication is a *circular* activity. By *circular* we mean a message usually is given by a source, through a channel, to a receiver who in turn responds to it. Let's consider the model of communication in Figure 1.2.

The responses, or *feedback,* given to communication are messages provided by the receiver to the source. They provide the source with information about how the receiver heard, interpreted, and responded to the original message. Feedback is an essential component in the communication process because it reveals how meanings are assigned by both participants and are negotiated through interaction.

There are three important conceptual frameworks for understanding how feedback affects the communication process:

1. *The multilateral effect* [11] emphasizes the reciprocal nature of assigning meanings to communication. By *reciprocal* we mean the give-and-take of ordinary interaction that emphasizes the *dual* nature of meanings assigned to symbols. Feed*back* describes how receivers reference the messages just encountered with their own past experiences to create meanings. Feed*forward* describes how receivers use present messages to construct relational understandings and predictions in the future. Let's take an instance in which a manager defers making an important decision while conversing with a subordinate. The subordinate may use this instance of communication to predict how the manager will behave in other similar situations in the future.

2. *The amplifying and goal-changing effect* [12] refers to the ability of feedback

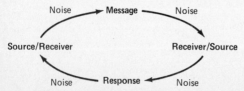

Figure 1.2 Communication is a circular activity.

to *regulate* communication between or among persons. By *regulate* we mean that talk about one subject tends to confine responses to that subject or to provide opportunities to change the subject. For example, during a briefing members of an organizational group tend to confine their responses to the subject of the briefing. When someone gets "off the track," it is reasonable for another group member to remind him or her of the purpose of the meeting. Furthermore, this effect can aid in assessing how interested your listener is in what you are saying, and thus you are able to change your communication goals by monitoring the responses given.

3. *The self-corrective effect* refers to how feedback allows for negotiations of meanings assigned to symbols. By asking questions, a receiver can clarify information or reference commonplaces. By watching for changes in facial expressions during conversation, a source can see how his or her communication is affecting the listener. In fact, one common complaint made by executives about communicating on the telephone concerns their inability to see how their verbal message is being received.

Feedback is a powerful tool of communication. However, feedback is also affected by internal and external sources of *noise*. External noise, such as people talking loudly in the hall while a meeting is being conducted, interferes with our ability to hear and interpret communication. Internal noise, such as personal concerns that direct our attention away from present communication or hierarchical differences between our supervisor and ourself, can distort feedback processes by bringing additional meanings beyond the scope of the present communication to the exchange. In subsequent chapters we will describe how to improve our communication skill by learning productive uses of feedback.

The Physical and Cultural Environment

Communication is always *situational*. It occurs within specific physical and cultural contexts, and its meaning is always informed by the physical and cultural setting.

The physical environment includes consideration of the time, space, and physical properties of the place. Research into these variables consistently demonstrates how important the physical environment is to perceived meaning. For example, the arrangement of a conference table often dictates who will talk to whom; the arrangement of chairs during an interview usually influences the interviewee's perception of interest, formality, and friendliness in the interviewer.

The cultural environment includes consideration of specific values, standards, and rituals governing the communication process and assigned meanings. In subsequent chapters we will discuss how cultural factors influence communication overtly and subtly.

The Effects of Communication

One productive way to consider any communication is as an *episode*. An *episode* is a segment of a communication having an identifiable beginning, development, and ending. It can be recognized by the presence of (1) a limited purpose, (2) a focused exchange of talk on a particular subject, and (3) a limited time for the communication. The result of the episode is the *effect of the communication on assigned meanings.*

This concern for the effects of any communication episode is a natural part of your understanding of how communication functions to create meaning and bond relationships. You may refer to it as "what happened when I talked to John," or "the bottom line of the conversation," but any way you look at it, every communication encounter leaves you with a sense of what took place—its assigned meaning.

As you can see from these brief, introductory descriptions of the functional components of the communication process, there is a special language of communication study that you need to learn. These seven terms are important keys to that language. They describe how communication happens in organizations, and, as you will see in later chapters, they help to identify problems you must overcome in order to become a more effective, responsible communicator.

DEFINING ORGANIZATION AND ORGANIZATIONS

As already discussed, there are several different ways to define the term *organization.* In this section we present four major sources of definition: (1) a basic definition, (2) a general systems theory definition, (3) a managerial definition, and (d) a cultural performance definition. Then we summarize what can be learned by defining organizations from these perspectives.

A Basic Definition

As Gerald M. Phillips puts it, "organization is the opposite of confusion."[13] The concept of organization is based on the idea of order. And order, as we know, is what humans are supposed to bring out of chaos. Phillips's definition, which represents the essential character of any organization's meaning, can be used to describe how many philosophers, such as Plato and Aristotle, thought about organizations while describing political, social, and moral features of them. An organization is, at its roots, a cooperative attempt to overcome confusion, chaos, anarchy, and personal feelings of boredom, meaninglessness, and ineffectuality. Therefore, an organization is what gives meaning and purpose to working life.

General Systems Theory Definitions

Modern organization theory posits a more complex definition. William Scott, for example, defines organization as "a system of coordinated activities of a group of people working cooperatively toward a common goal under authority and leadership."[14] Stephen Robbins, another organizational theorist, defines an organization as "the planned coordination of the collective activities of two or more people who, functioning on a relatively continuous hierarchy of authority, seek to achieve a common goal or set of goals . . . organizations are made up of parts or subsystems within larger systems."[15]

These definitions, which describe a *formal* organization, can be used to explain how most organizational communication scholars have viewed organizations. The *nouns* in these definitions (e.g., system, activities, group, people, goal, authority, leadership) reveal the major features of organizational study, from Max Weber's idea of bureaucracy through Gerald Goldhaber's integration of organizational and systems theories.[16] Thus, organization is synonymous with *human work,* and it is difficult to conceive of any human work that is not conducted within an organization (e.g., the family, the business, the educational institution, etc.).

Modern organization theory evolved from a tradition of examining formal organizations from a bureaucratic model to examining them from a general systems theory perspective during the late 1960s and throughout the 1970s. Perhaps the elegant integration was performed by Richard Farace, Peter Monge, and Hamish Russell, who, in 1977, provided the following descriptions of the idea of organization.[17] Two or more individuals:

1. who recognize that some of their goals can be more readily achieved through interdependent (cooperative) actions, even though disagreement (conflict) may be present;
2. who take in materials, energy, and information from the environment in which they exist;
3. who develop coordinative and control relationships to capitalize on their interdependence while operating on these inputs;
4. who return the modified inputs to the environment in an attempt to accomplish the goals that interdependence was meant to make possible.

For shorthand labels, these five elements in organization will be termed *size, interdependence, input, throughput,* and *output.*

As you can see from Farace, Monge, and Russell's definition, *organization* is an environment in which humans channel their energies toward the accomplishment of goals. That is, an organization is a system amenable to systems theory, a place to be talked about, a theoretical continuum. It is important to remember that although a general systems theory provides ways with which academicians communicate about organizations and students learn essential words in the language of organizations, this perspective has produced very little empirical research. It is, unfortunately, a paradigm in search of reality.[18]

The failures of systems theories to describe organizations adequately led to two different paths, each one a "rediscovery" of older traditions, and each one ripe with meaning for our study of the term organization. Perhaps the most important contribution of both of these academic camps is their shared belief that organization should be understood *from the perspective of the actor,* or employee, in the organization under study. These two approaches may be called the (1) *managerial definition* and the (2) *cultural performance definition.*

A Managerial Definition

Henry Mintzberg is one of the most highly regarded experts on what managers do and how best to train them to do it. For this reason, we believe it is instructive to examine his definition of organization. He writes, "the term *organization* describes that unit of work directly under the manager's formal authority."[19] From Mintzberg's definition, we see that the manager views an organization from a more *personal* perspective.

Mintzberg continues, "the words manager and his organization can mean a president and his company, a supervisor and his branch, or a foreman and his shop. The manager's organization may in fact be a subunit of a larger organization (a division of a company, for example), and outsiders may in fact be other members of the larger organization who are not in a direct line relationship with the manager in question."[20] This definition focuses on Mintzberg's concern for *doing* managerial work, including three kinds of *roles* managers assume to plan, coordinate, carry out, and evaluate work (e.g., interpersonal, informational, and decisional roles); on contingency variations in how those roles can be conducted and controlled; and on ways in which technology and science can inform a manager's selection and use of roles.

Mintzberg's approach to organization is also found in how instructors educate students in the *basic skills* of doing managerial work and in how professional trainers and consultants provide instruction and advisories about improving managerial performance and organizational efficiency. The goal of this perspective is to help persons who plan organizational careers to understand what is expected of them and to learn how to perform their jobs using those understandings. From this approach, *an organization is a managerial situation, or a place, in which communication episodes must be planned for, coordinated, and controlled.*

The Cultural Performance Definition

An emerging and powerful focus for organizational communication research is becoming known as the *organizational cultures* perspective.[21] From this perspective scholars begin with the assumption that every organization has a "unique sense of the place," a particular and sometimes peculiar "way of doing what it does and its own way of talking about what it is doing."[22]

The goal of research, then, is to *understand* and *appreciate* how organizations create, modify, and destroy things, thoughts, actions, and words. Put simply, *an organization is an organic, active, changing human and technological environment.* That is, an organization is a place where lives are lived as well as where work is done.

This organizational cultures approach to understanding organization provides what we believe to be a rich and detailed method for examining how persons make their lives interesting and their work important in unique, individual ways. Through appreciation of the *culture* of an organization, including its rituals, stories, jokes, language, and fantasies, a person can learn not only *about* an organization, but perhaps, more importantly, can also learn how to *perform* his or her roles more efficiently and productively.

Summary of Definitions

In this section we provided four ways to look at the term *organization*. The question you should now be asking is, "What do all these definitions add up to?" What should you know?

First, you should know that there are *competing* definitions of organization. Each definition reveals a particular perspective on what an organization is and how you should think and talk about them. Although this competition is academically healthy and is a natural part of your learning process, it can be confusing. We advise you to investigate each definition carefully, compare its advantages and disadvantages to those of other competing definitions, and learn why and how productive distinctions can be made among them. The purpose is not to choose one definition and abandon the rest, rather, it is to become educated in the rich diversity of perspectives. As you will see later in this book, the more educated you become, the more likely you will learn how to analyze critically other people's points of view accurately. As a result, your performance on the job will improve.

Second, these definitions reveal the *complexity* of organizational thought. Nothing that is ultimately valuable is ever very simple or easy. Because these four definitional camps encourage particular points of view, to understand any organization adequately will require a more complete, integrated, and complex effort than any one of them provides. Hence, there is no one definition that can provide all of what you need to know about organization. You must have some of the insights each perspective encourages, that is, you need to acquire the *language competencies* each definitional camp offers. How you learn to communicate with others about organizations will be a fundamental part of your overall organizational performance.

Third, these definitions should spark your interest and induce you to *read about these points of view* in greater detail. If you are serious about becoming a productive, vital member of any organization, you will need more substance than this introductory chapter can provide. In Chapter 3 we provide a tour of organizational theories, complete with suggested readings. We hope you will make use of them.

Finally, these definitions allow us to argue for viewing the term organization and organizations as *manageable communication environments.* By this definition we imply:

1. The primary purpose of any organization is the successful accomplishment of its objectives.

2. Communication is the means by which any organizational objectives are accomplished.

3. A practical view of managing the organizational environment is required to improve how objectives are accomplished through communication. Specifically, persons must learn how to manage (1) themselves, (2) their social and professional images with others, (3) their ability to perform assigned duties and tasks, and (4) the human, material, financial, and technological resources available within the environment. Furthermore, no organizational environment exists in a vacuum. Organizations, and the persons within them, must learn to be responsive to the needs and expectations of the larger communities in which they reside and to the societies that sponsor them.

Now that we have defined both communication and organization, let's integrate the two terms.

COMMUNICATION IN ORGANIZATIONS

Our definitions of communication and organization should guide your understanding of what the terms reference when we use them and should suggest ways to integrate them. In this section we combine the terms by showing why organizational communication is *an evolutionary, culturally dependent process of sharing information and creating relationships in environments designed for manageable, cooperative, goal-oriented behavior.* First, we discuss the organization as a productive communication environment. Second, we explain how communication is an evolutionary, culturally dependent process. Third, we show why we believe organizational communication understandings and skills can be learned.

The Organization as a Productive Communication Environment

We focus our definition on the *process of communication* in environments designed for manageable, cooperative, goal-oriented behavior. In this sense communication *produces* the organization.[23]

Communication creates the relationships between and among persons and with technologies; communication is how the work is planned, coordinated, controlled, assigned, evaluated, and made into the collective memory of those who have experienced it. Communication is not merely the *means* of doing organizational work, it is also the *process* by which the organization is brought into existence and given personal, social, and professional meanings.

This idea may strike you as both new and unusual. Most persons are reared to think of communication as just another tool, or technique, in the human repertoire. To be asked to conceive of communication as the process through which, and by which, an organization attains purpose and meaning is not only surprising, it might also seem unrealistic.

Now consider the following notion: The American philosopher Richard McKeon says the world and all that is in it can be discussed by using four basic categories:

1. things
2. thoughts
3. actions
4. words

Of these four categories, *only words* can bring the other three into existence.[24] *Things* are conceived of in symbols, discussed in words and numbers, and constructed using instructions that are written, spoken, or mediated by communications technology. *Thoughts* are made known in the symbols used to represent them. Although thought processes are chemical and electrical in nature, we only know what we think when forming words to describe it.[25] *Actions* are nonverbal sources of communication. We only know what others think, feel, and believe when they tell us, or show us through facial expression, eye movement, gestures, and use of space—all of these realms make sense only in terms of the words we use to make them attain meaning. So, at least in a philosophic sense, you can see how words, or symbols, create the possibilities and understandings in every aspect of your lives.

Communication is, as McKeon points out, the *architectonic, productive* process. By *architectonic,* he means communication is the structure of our understanding because it structures our interpretations of symbols. There is not a subject that does not depend on communication to attain meaning. By *productive,* McKeon means communication is goal-oriented, informed by purposes, given meaning in relation to what it can do. As you will see, we believe communication is both architectonic and productive in every aspect of organizational life.

Communication is the organizational environment.

Communication Is Evolutionary and Culturally Dependent

In our definitions of communication and organization we stressed the influences of evolution and culture. Communication attains meaning and purpose in reference to specific cultures over time; organization is best understood in relation to its own, unique cultural history. For these reasons, we believe communication is evolutionary and culturally dependent.

This is a practical claim. In one organization the following sentence is easily understood: "The AFOLDS-MIMICS peripherals are ready for processing, but config is a little behind, so gear up for VIMS now and BLIPS if you get a chance." Do you understand the meaning of that sentence? Probably not. You are not a member of the organization's culture. Your past experiences have not taught you the meaning of symbols such as AFOLDS, MIMICS, VIMS, or BLIPS, much less config. These words sound foreign to you, as if spoken by a visitor from another planet rather than from an otherwise ordinary American citizen who works for a computer software company.

Every organization has a culture. The culture, like the organization itself, is created in the symbols exchanged between and among its employees and how the employees feel and act toward those symbols.[26] As you evolve an understanding of the organization's culture, you will become a part of it and influence it through your own presence, talk, and actions. And when you leave the organization, your memories of it will be shaped by your understanding of its culture. This is why you can tell somebody a story about what happened at work and get nothing more than a polite, but blank stare. Your response? "Well, I guess you had to *be there.*"

Learning Organizational Communication

Communication is both an object of understanding and a learned skill. The definition points out three areas of understanding: (1) the process of communication that allows you to share information and create relationships, (2) the need to approach organizations as unique, evolutionary cultures, and (3) the need to see organizations as manageable communication environments. These are intellectual understandings that should help you comprehend those features of human behavior, technology, and decision making that prepare you for an organizational career.

However, communication should also be approached as a learned skill. No matter how deeply you investigate the intellectual bases of organizational communication, your study is incomplete unless it is coupled with systematic improvement of your communication ability. Intellectually, you can understand the process of communication as what happens when a source gives a message to a receiver and receives feedback. But you will also be required to *be* a source, who must *produce* messages *adapted* to the needs and expectations of listeners, and who must *interpret* feedback. Your understanding of communication must be linked with improved performance.

This book cannot make you a better organizational communicator. It can, however, provide you with the intellectual resources, provide applications of the concepts and theories, explain how to improve your communicative performances, and encourage you to use them. But, as with anything worthwhile, you must put forth the effort. Your desire to understand organizational communication and improve organizational performances must be matched with a willingness to work hard toward individual improvement.

It will not be easy. But look how far you have already come. Perhaps you began this chapter confused by the terms *communication* and *organization,* and now, three sections later, you have worked through an important definition and its rationale. You understand what we mean when we write: Organizational communication is an evolutionary, culturally dependent process of sharing information and creating relationships in environments designed for manageable, cooperative, goal-oriented behavior. From this beginning, your progress begins.

SUMMARY

This chapter is designed to overcome confusion about the terms organization and communication. Toward this goal, we offered a rationale and definition of organizational communication.

First, we examined the intellectual bases for understanding human communication. We demonstrated why it is helpful to think of communication as (1) intentional behaviors, (2) a process of creating human and technological relationships, and (3) an evolutionary, culturally dependent system of assigning meanings to symbols. The result of communicating is organizational *identity,* and your identity is based on the judgments others arrive at based on your organizational *performances.* The rule is "the more intentional your behavior is, the more control you exert over its outcomes."

Second, we explained the seven functional components of the communication process: (1) the source(s), or the initiator of communication whose identity is shaped by *credibility;* (2) the channel(s), or what the message passes through, which can be manipulated or controlled; (3) the message, which includes verbal, nonverbal, and metaverbal elements; (4) the receiver(s), or target for communication, who must be adapted to for communication to be understood and accepted; (5) feedback, or responses given to a message, which can construct relational understandings, regulate the talk, or correct misunderstandings; (6) the physical and cultural environment, or the *situations* that call forth the need to communicate and help shape its intentions and meanings; and (7) the effects of communication, or what you think about communicating following a specific episode.

Third, we defined organization and organizations. We showed how our understanding of these terms was influenced by research and theory-building. Our basic definition revealed the centrality of order in any concept of organization. This basic definition was then influenced by the development of general systems theory, which provided a grander framework and language for describing communication processes. However, the systems definition lacked the power to understand communication and organization from the perspective of the actor. Hence, research into managerial behavior underscored the importance of seeing the organization from the manager's point of view; and research in the cultural performance tradition underscored the importance of appreciating the evolving, changing, unique features of any organization. Although these definitions compete with one another and add to the complexity of understanding organizations and communication, they lead to appreciation of organizations as *manageable communication environments.*

Finally, we combine the terms organization and communication to reveal how our definition can help you intellectually comprehend organizational communication and guide improvement of your performances. From our perspective, organizational communication means an evolutionary, culturally dependent process of sharing information and creating relationships in environments designed for manageable, cooperative, goal-oriented behavior.

ENDNOTES

1. See George Herbert Mead, *Mind, Self, and Society* (Chicago: University of Chicago Press, 1934); see also Gerald M. Phillips and Julia T. Wood, *Communication and Human Relationships* (New York: Macmillan, 1983), especially Chapters 1, 2.
2. Michael E. Pacanowsky and Nick O'Donnell-Trujillo, "Organizational Communication as Cultural Performance," *Communication Monographs* 50 (1983): 126–147.
3. Gerald R. Miller and Mark Steinberg, *Between People: A New Analysis of Interpersonal Communication* (Chicago: Science Research Associates, 1975); see also Julia T. Wood, "Communication and Relational Culture: Bases for the Study of Human Relationships," *Communication Quarterly* 30 (1982); 75–83.

4. See Noel M. Tichy, Michael L. Tushman, and Charles Fombrun, "Social Network Analysis for Organizations." *Academy of Management Review* 4 (1979): 507–519; Peter Monge, Jane Edwards, and Kenneth Kirste, "The Determinants of Communication and Communication Structure in Large Organizations: A Review of the Research," in *Communication Yearbook 2,* ed. Brent D. Rubin (New Brunswick, NJ: Transaction Books, 1978), pp. 311–334.

5. Robert D. Gratz and Phillip J. Salem, "Technology and the Crisis of Self," *Communication Quarterly* 32 (1984): 98–103.

6. James C. McCroskey and Thomas J. Young, "Ethos and Credibility: The Construct and Its Measurement After Three Decades," *Central States Speech Journal* 32 (1981): 24–34; see also Stephen E. Lucas, *The Art of Public Speaking* (New York: Random House, 1983), pp. 297–300.

7. Elaine Walster and Ellen Bersheid, *Interpersonal Attraction,* 2d. ed. (Reading, MA: Addison-Wesley, 1979).

8. See especially Julia T. Wood and Charles Conrad, "Paradox in the Experiences of Professional Women," *Western Journal of Speech Communication* 47 (1983): 305–322; see also Tricia S. Jones, "Sexual Harassment in the Organization," in *Women in Organizations,* ed. Joseph Pilotta (Prospect Heights, IL: Waveland Press, 1983), pp. 23–39; and Susan Brownmiller, *Femininity* (New York: Linden Press/Simon & Schuster, 1984).

9. See Don Stacks and Mark Hickson III, *Nonverbal Communication* (Dubuque, IA: Brown, 1985); and see also the classic work by Mark L. Knapp, *Nonverbal Communication in Human Interaction,* 2d. ed. (New York: Holt, Rinehart and Winston, 1978).

10. H. Lloyd Goodall, Jr., "The Status of Communication Studies in Organizational Contexts," *Communication Quarterly* 32 (1984): 133–147; see also H. Waylon Cummings, et al., *Managing Communication in Organizations* (Dubuque, IA: Gorsuch Scarsbruck, 1983), especially Chapters 1–3.

11. Brent D. Rubin, "General Systems Theory," in *Approaches to Human Communication,* ed. Richard Budd and Brent D. Rubin (New York: Spartan Books, 1972), pp. 130–134.

12. D. J. Crowley, *Understanding Communication: The Signifying Web* (New York: Gordon & Breach, 1983), pp. 9–10.

13. Gerald M. Phillips, *Communicating in Organizations* (New York: Macmillan, 1983), p. 3.

14. William G. Scott, *Organizational Theory* (Homewood, IL: Irwin, 1967).

15. From Stephen P. Robbins, *Organizational Theory* (Englewood Cliffs, NJ: Prentice-Hall, 1983), pp. 5–9.

16. See Gerald M. Goldhaber, *Organizational Communication,* 3d. ed. (Dubuque, IA: Brown, 1983).

17. Richard V. Farce, Peter R. Monge, and Hamish M. Russell, *Communicating and Organizing* (Reading, MA: Addison-Wesley, 1977), pp. 15–19.

18. See Michael E. Pacanowsky and Nick O'Donnell-Trujillo, "Communication and Organizational Cultures," *Western Journal of Speech Communication* 46 (1982): 115–130; and Charles W. Redding, "Organizational Communication Theory and Ideology: A Review," in *Communication Yearbook 3,* ed. Dan Nimmo (New Brunswick, NJ: Transaction Books, 1979), pp. 309–341, for exhaustive critiques of the failures of general systems theory to produce viable research findings.

19. Henry Mintzberg, *The Nature of Managerial Work* (New York: Harper & Row, 1973), p. 29.

20. Ibid. p. 29.

21. Linda Putnam and Michael Pacanowsky, *Communication and Organizations: An Interpretive Approach* (Beverly Hills, CA: Sage, 1983); see also Andrew Pettigrew, "On Studying Organizational Cultures," *Administrative Science Quarterly* 24 (1979): 570–581.

22. Quotations taken from Pacanowsky and O'Donnell-Trujillo, "Communication," p. 128.

23. See Leonard C. Hawes, "Social Collectivities as Communication: Perspectives on Organizational Behavior," *Quarterly Journal of Speech* 60 (1974): 497–502.

24. Richard McKeon, "Rhetoric as an Architectonic, Productive Art," in *The Prospective of Rhetoric,* ed. Lloyd F. Bitzer and Edwin Black (Englewood Cliffs, NJ: Prentice-Hall, 1971).

25. See Michael C. Corballis and Ivan L. Beals, *The Ambivalent Mind: The Neuropsychology of Left and Right* (Chicago: Nelson Hall, 1983); see also Richard B. Gregg, *Symbolic Inducement and Knowing* (Columbia, SC: University of South Carolina Press, 1984).

26. The need to examine feelings and actions in relation to symbols is underscored in Clifford Geertz, *The Interpretation of Cultures* (New York: Basic Books, 1973).

chapter 2

Understanding Human Behavior in Organizations

PERSPECTIVES ON HOW AND WHY HUMANS BEHAVE

The Classical School
Frederick Taylor / Henri Fayol / Max Weber

The Human Relations School
Elton Mayo / Other Human Relations Theorists

The Systems School / The Technological School

THE ASSESSMENT OF HUMAN ACTIONS

The Traits Approach / The Situational Approach / The Contingency Approach / The Behavioral Approach / The Relational Approach

ORGANIZATIONAL GOALS AND ASSESSMENTS OF HUMAN PERFORMANCE

Efficiency, Productivity, and Profitability / Accounting for Individual Versus Group Performance

When casually observing human behavior in any organizational setting, you will see two types of behavior. Some people will be acting as you would act and what they do will seem natural and reasonable. The rest of what you see may appear unreasonable, purposeless, and a waste of time. The behavior of others may seem totally individual. You may even be mystified by the differences between people. But you can think beyond your individual perspective by applying appropriate concepts from organizational theory.

The purpose of this chapter is to discuss the major theoretical options available to help you understand organizational behavior. Internalizing these perspectives on organizational behavior can offer you rational, systematic explanations for any behavior you encounter. Perhaps you may still favor your own point of view and style, but understanding other concepts will enhance your ability to coordinate your actions and goals with the organizational situation.

This chapter provides a wide variety of analytical concepts and principles with which to compare your own intuitive judgments. First, we present research and theory from four perspectives on how and why humans act in organizations: the *classical, human relations, systems,* and *technological* schools of organizational behavior. Second, we focus on the individual within the organizational setting. We examine five ways to diagnose human actions like organizational communication, taking an approach centered on traits, the situation, contingencies, behavioral responses, and/or relational options.

Third, we extend these theoretical perspectives by shifting from analysis of organizational behavior in the past to setting practical goals for assessing future performance. By setting goals for efficiency, productivity, and profitability in ways that account for performance at the individual and group levels, we can anticipate the impact of communicative behavior on organizational effectiveness.

Fourth, we address four issues in planning for organizational communication assessment: the importance of choice, the need to identify productive behavior, the importance of managing relationships, and the benefits of negotiating goals. Although this chapter cannot include every option for understanding human behavior in organizations, we have selected these fundamental principles to give you a balanced theory base.

PERSPECTIVES ON HOW AND WHY HUMANS BEHAVE

Various schools of thought have emerged from organizational research. Organizational theories from the classical school, the human relations school, the systems school, and the technological school are the dominant perspectives; each school of thought accounts for a specific type of organization and presents a profile of preferred organizational behavior and appropriate communication style. We describe the salient features of each perspective and discuss research supporting these theoretical assumptions.

The Classical School

Frederick Taylor   The classical school focuses on the principles of scientific management as introduced by Frederick Taylor.[1] Imagine yourself in Taylor's situation, faced by an industrial expansion that still seemed novel. New factories for new products and a continual demand for cheap goods promised success to somebody who could harness labor efficiently to industrial tasks. Taylor was a mechanical engineer who was influenced by a paper delivered in 1886 to the American Society of Mechanical Engineers by Henry Towne. The paper suggested that engineers should begin to set forth ideas about management and science. Taylor believed that work activity, especially blue-collar work, could be improved by scientific investigation. By observing how the most productive work-men performed their jobs, science would help the manager discover the "one best way" to do organizational tasks.

There are three key terms in Taylor's contribution to the classical school: structure, economic motivation, and organizational efficiency. If the *structure* of the organization can be optimized for maximum efficiency through the division of labor in organizational operations, then human behavior is also assumed to be optimally organized. *Economic motivation* reinforces the fundamental structural efficiency of the organization by providing incentives for individual effort in production, exemplified by tying wages to units of production. *Organizational efficiency* is monitored by time-and-motion studies of production techniques, coupled with analysis of the flow of resources through the organizational struc-ture. Thus, human behavior under scientific management becomes an extension of organizational structure, with little recognition of social needs to blur scientific prescriptions for efficient production. Even the workers are scientifically selected so that their abilities and temperaments match their tasks.

The task orientation of the classical school emphasizes job-related and downward communication *within the channels* of the organization's formal com-munication network. Managers do all the planning, preparing, and inspecting. Workers do the *work,* with all decisions preplanned for them. There is little need for upward communication. Since this formal network is predefined according to rules for maximum efficiency, informal communication outside these channels is not encouraged. Formal communication in this type of organization flows from the top of the organizational hierarchy down through the chain of command, the formality of this one-way channel further emphasized by reliance on documents made part of the organization's formal records.

Henri Fayol   A French industrialist of the 1920s, Henri Fayol started with the concept that organizational operations could be systematized. He applied this principle to management, extending Taylor's production-oriented analysis to identify a manager's functions.[2] These functions are: planning, organizing, com-manding, coordinating, and controlling. Together, they call for communication focused on the fundamental goals of maximizing profit for the organization and wages for the employee. *Planning* analyzes the organizational environment to discover the best possible use for organizational resources to reach economic goals. *Organizing* gathers these resources so that *commanding* can give instruc-tions and directions to set the organization moving toward its goals. *Coor-dinating* tunes the organization to increase efficiency, whereas *controlling* en-forces the plan according to prior commands and organizational goals.

The manager can most effectively carry out these functions by applying Fayol's principles of scientific management. He suggested that these principles should be applied flexibly, but stressed that they are tested and proven by experi-ence. The principle of *authority* separates each member of the organizational hierarchy by establishing formal job relationships. The principle of *unity* connects each member of the organization to the authority giving that member commands.

The principle of *definition* makes public distinctions between each member's duties and responsibilities. The principle of *correspondence* ensures that authority is contingent upon appropriate responsibility. And the principle of the *span of control* specifies the manager's responsibility by limiting the number of people reporting to each authority (9 to 15).

Fayol extended the systematic nature of organizational structure by separating purely managerial elements of middle management from other specialized functions. For example, an accountant with a specialized financial expertise would not be asked to manage an office of clerks. That task would be more effectively performed by an office manager with no other duties. These managerial functions are coordinated in turn with five other middle management functions of the organization: responsibilities in technical, commercial, financial, security, and accounting operations. Although we do not know if Fayol ever heard of Taylor, Taylor's concept of a chain of command appears in Fayol's plan; line positions of authority remained throughout the organization in specialized operations from technical to accounting departments. Each specialized function required the organization to employ personnel as staff, agents reporting to functional or line authorities. Thus, the specialized nature of organizational structure in Fayol's theory produced a formal communication system between line and functional positions, each also communicating with its own staff. Such a complete treatment of the structural options for management has made the classical perspective appealing as the most scientifically structured, formal type of organization. For example, military operations have long been organized and carried out according to many of these principles.

Max Weber   Max Weber added to the structural appeal of scientific management by explicating the concept of *authority.* Distinguishing between the authority a leader derives from charisma and the authority a leader derives from tradition, Weber didn't place the source of authority within the modern organization with either of these two. Instead, he took the position that the organization itself is the source of legitimate authority. For Weber, bureaucratic authority thereby became the form of authority most legitimized by both the rules of the organization and the laws of the land. It was seen as controlling the emotional, irrational potential of charismatic authority. In his advocacy of bureaucracy as the most rational form of organizationn, Weber extended Taylor's assumption that an optimally efficient organizational structure could be scientifically calculated.[3] He set the goals for beaucratic structure in terms of communication efficiency, seeking optimum reaction time in processing information and responding to the external environment. By separating administrative functions into segments clearly dividing work responsibilities with calculable communication requirements, Weber organized the formal communication network to maximize work efficiency. This emphasis minimized informal contributions to organizational communication, and thus fell in line with the rules of scientific management.

Weber's perspective also required control of the influence of informal communication on the organization's structure and efficiency. When organizational communication efficiently focused on task-related issues, on impersonal application of rules, it could not accommodate personal concerns and social relationships outside formally calculated channels. Weber supported this dictum by citing the success of the rational specialist in previous Roman and medieval bureaucracies.[4] But the realistic outcome of limiting communication to formal channels was failure to account for the impact of informal communication on the efficiency of the organization's structure. Weber recognized that scientific management was limited by individuals' capacity for rational judgment and used the limits of science to control the informal potential of organizational communication that lay outside the scientific system.[5]

The Human Relations School

The significance of informal authority and its communication network was confirmed by a series of studies conducted in Chicago at the Hawthorne plant of the Western Electric Company. These studies began with an attempt to determine scientifically the effect of working conditions on productivity.[6] Workers were found to ignore both handicaps created by manipulation of lighting and incentives to production in favor of the social forces of the work group, status as the subjects of management's attention, and opportunities for improved communication with management. Thus, factors beyond scientific management's one best way accounted for increased productivity. Social forces and the informal communication network operating in this well-planned bureaucracy exerted powerful influences on workers' motivation to produce.

In response to the incompleteness of scientific management theories, theorists such as Elton Mayo[7] and Chester Barnard[8] directed their attention to the social aspects of human behavior in organizations. Rather than viewing employees as mechanical elements in production or as governed entirely by formal authority, these theorists concentrated on informal communication networks produced by the interpersonal relationships within organizations.[9]

Elton Mayo   Elton Mayo, an industrial psychologist of the Harvard School of Business, was a principal investigator in the Hawthorne studies. His experience led him to offer an alternative to scientific management. Rejecting Taylor's principles of motivation through economic self-interest as a "rabble hypothesis," Mayo postulated that informal organization existed because of spontaneous cooperation and other natural social forces. His theory of optimum human relations called for this cooperative instinct to be utilized as a source of motivation in every organization.

A close, cooperative relationship between different individuals and groups within the organization depended on the awareness of needs, problems, and interests, all coordinated to support organizational goals. Thus, the traditional formal communication pattern from management down through the hierarchy needed to be balanced by communication up from the production level. By including more members of the organization in formally planned communication networks on more levels, Mayo intended to take advantage of the fundamentally cooperative nature of human beings while improving the effectiveness of organizational communication. By taking the human relations potential of every employee into account when planning communication channels, the organization could tackle the organic, social structure of every human community. Organizational planners now had good reason to believe that the potential for human social relationships didn't necessarily interfere with efficient organizational behavior.

Let's consider the role of authority from the perspective of the human relations school. The role of authority in a human relations-oriented organization is not compromised by extending the formal communication network to include otherwise informal channels. Mayo honors Chester Barnard's principle that formal authority exists only with the consent of those governed.[10] Thus, mutual cooperation in socially significant relationships within the organization should increase the power of authority by increasing the extent of employees' consent.

Barnard had also indicated that *systematically* developing and maintaining all types of communication is the primary function of the executive.[11] Therefore, social relationships are clearly targeted areas of responsibility for the human relations-oriented manager. And when cultivated appropriately, they should enhance authority and communication. The power of social relationships in the workplace makes sense. Let's take this typical five-person work group in an insurance company, four claims adjusters and a secretary. One of the new agents is assigned to work with the most senior member of the group. When she asks her mentor how long it takes to get the paperwork done on each case, he tells her to let him give her files to the secretary the first time, to make sure the secretary doesn't give her a hard time. Offering this type of help extends the social structure of the work group to include the new employee. Recognition of his assistance reinforces the authority of the senior claims adjuster while promoting open communication with the new employee. Thus, social relationships might not be proscribed in a job description, but they do facilitate an efficient work climate.

Other Human Relations Theorists   Other human relations theorists have presented critical profiles of scientific management assumptions about human behavior, offering socially sensitive alternatives. Chris Agyris pointed out that an organization adhering to scientific management principles does not help its employees become self-actualized.[12] He suggested that the organizational setting has a natural potential for growth in interpersonal competence and personal maturation of its members where the organization has a concern for self-actualization. If employees can reach their personal goals through their work, the organization could benefit from increased involvement with work as a rewarding and fulfilling activity. Work itself can become a motivation equal to more traditional incentives such as money or power. Agyris claimed that the organizational climate produced through scientific management was unnatural, constraining personal development and the potential of every employee. By focusing on the employees' needs rather than on working behavior, Agyris identified new areas of concern for managers. From a human relations' perspective, effective organizational communication must provide ways for employees to reveal their needs so that the organization can discover how to help them become self-actualized.

Douglas McGregor presented his Theory Y as an alternative to Theory X, his label for formal bureaucratic management through authority and coercion.[13] McGregor assumes that under Theory Y employees have the potential to seek out responsibility and pursue organizational goals in a climate where those goals have personal meaning. Given this opportunity, employees will rise to their greatest potential for performance and productivity if they have any interest in the organization's goals. Thus, Theory Y focuses on the relationship between the organization and the individual employee. Theory Y managers must identify the personal implications of organizational goals for their employees so that all are aware of the opportunities for personal growth. Putting Theory Y into effect produces an organizational climate whereby all employees are more closely identified with organizational goals because the organization's objectives also have potential for personal gratification.

Rensis Likert discovered the relationship between productivity and effective human relations.[14] In his studies of management style he defined two kinds of relationships, job-centered and employee-centered. Although *job-centered* management invoking the principles of scientific management claimed more efficient work behavior, *employee-centered* management achieved greater efficiency by increasing job satisfaction and avoiding work-related problems like material waste and high turnover in trained employees.

To account for varying degrees of job-centered and employee-centered management, Likert described four management systems: System 1, exploitative authoritative, worked through fear and one-way communication down the hierarchy. In system 1 a manager would communicate direct orders backed up with threats of dismissal if anyone questioned or disobeyed. Workers in system 1 were to be exploited without reward for productivity; there was simply the absence of punishment. System 2, benevolent authoritative, also conformed to the principles of scientific management but motivated through rewards as well as through punishments. In this system productivity was rewarded to satisfy economic need, but workers were still treated as an extension of the production mechanism. System 3, consultative, combined the authority of top-down management with rewards for low-level contributions to decision making. For example, system 3 contributions to decision making could come through a suggestion box to which management could choose to respond. System 4, participative, called for communication among all members of the organization through all channels, rewarding employees for participation in decision making by offering opportunities for self-actualization through sharing in organizational processes and goals. For example, system 4 communication would bring managers, supervisors, and production workers together in regular meetings to discuss production problems. Such regular meetings would be supplemented by open-door policies offering access to management for workers' complaints or opinions. As a result of using this theory, increased efficiency in human relations should reduce labor/management conflict as an organization moves toward system 4 operations, increasing productivity along with employee satisfaction.

Job satisfaction and its effect on organizational efficiency has continued to attract human relations theorists, more recently in terms of Japanese management styles. William Ouchi contends that transcendent self-actualization has made Japanese employees achieve high efficiency, high productivity, and high job satisfaction.[15] In Theory Z transcendent self-actualization permits employees to optimize their relationships with the organization by identifying personal goals in terms of organizational objectives. Participative management techniques like quality circles (where employees on the production level discuss production problems and corporate goals with supervisors and managers) and Ringyi on the management level (where expression of personal reactions to plans for corporate policies is encouraged) permit transcendent self-actualization throughout the organization. The manager must promote human relations on both levels to facilitate free and open communication about organizational philosophies and procedures. Thus, human relations are clearly part of any complete appraisal of efficient and productive organizational behavior, the social dimension of work.

The Systems School

Social dimensions of work combine with task-related behaviors to produce complex organizational systems. The systems school examines organizational behavior as a set of relationships in an interdependent structure.[16] Although the system may be so complex as to seem random, systems theory assumes that the relationships between elements in the system are maintained long enough to be worth discovering. The cause-and-effect relationships between parts in a system may shift as the organization develops, but the forces at work in the system can still be understood.

The elements of one system may also participate in other systems, linking operations within an organization as a set of subsystems within the organization. This theoretical perspective looks at social and task-oriented behaviors as parts of an integrated system of events and environments. Systems analysis based on the principles of Von Bertalanfy can reconstruct the functions and operations of an organization as subsystems, calculating structural design, information flow, and the probable uncertainties of human factors.[17]

General system theory as stated by Von Bertalanfy also evaluates the degree of interdependence between a system and the external environment. A *closed* system is isolated from its environment and reaches a state of entropy or maximum probable disorder, coming to equilibrium over time. An *open* system is in constant interaction with its environment and develops an equilibrium with environmental forces known as a *steady state*. The principle of *equifinality* recognizes that outputs of the system develop from inputs into the system according to probability and the interdependence of elements of the system. Thus, an organization can be conceptualized as a set of open and closed systems, each operating within the organizational hierarchy and interacting through the organization's formal and informal communication channels.

The relationships between subsystems within the organization can be studied to coordinate known elements of the organizational structure and its contents. But uncertain human response combines with employee-generated informal communication networks to limit the science of systems analysis. When a given system is *closed* and its parameters and factors are clearly identified, relationships between factors can be planned within reasonable probability for error. The more *open* a system is to interaction with other systems or environments beyond its parameters, the less likely analysts can identify enough factors for accurate projection of probable events. System analysis is most effective in controlled environments with known and clearly delineated characteristics.

Systems analysis of organizational networks can accommodate factors that are probable because of the relatively permanent nature of the organization's structure. Individual differences that produce the social subsystem of informal communication are not part of the modeling capability of projections such as computer simulations, unless conditions for a given case are factored into the analysis to evaluate system response to that contingency. Interest in systems analysis has led to the concept of contigency planning, trying to anticipate how parts of a system will interact under certain conditions so that we can plan our range of responses to various likely situations.

The principles of contingency planning developed by Paul Lawrence and Jay Lorsch can be adapted to general systems analysis.[19] Lawrence and Lorsch include the probable impact of people on the system by factoring the personnel in each situation into the organization's structural and functional systems. Choosing the appropriate communication style is determined by the degree of task orientation.[20] Here is a systems analysis problem that must also consider human factors such as past performance in work situations and communication networks available to a given group.

Formal and informal groups within every organization can also be understood as systems in which *inputs* of personnel and resources are processed (e.g., *throughputs*) according to characteristic group interactions to produce *outputs* like decisions and job satisfaction.[21] This perspective on groups as systems treats the task and social dimensions of smaller organizational units as if they were relatively closed systems. The relatively larger-scale organizational system becomes the environment external to the group, and the environment external to the organization becomes a cultural force operating on the group at a distance. Thus, interpersonal communication structures on the group level can, theoretically, become part of organizational systems analysis. To date, no research has actually been done by using any systems model. Systems theory has been most productive for engineers and scientists in mathematical control modeling of systems with minimal human involvement.

The Technological School

Technology influences organizational communication in two distinct ways. The primary influence of technology on an organization could be through the *routinized use of technology* for enhanced communication *via* devices like computers. But some organizations also communicate *about technology*, operating in terms of specialized high technologies and corresponding technical vocabularies in areas like the electronics and aerospace industries.

Communicating about the technology supplies the means for conceptualizing the product of the future, sustaining the basic technology's usefulness, and giving the technology a futuristic image. Technologically oriented organizations use communication to produce new ideas, an outcome that is as valuable as the physical product of the moment. For example, as specialiats in aerospace technology, engineers working for NASA communicate to produce two outcomes: a physical product and a cultural product. The physical product is as ordinary as any other industrial artifact; a fabrication like a nose cone could be as commonplace in another era as a washing machine. The cultural product of this communication is an aerospace terminology based on a technologically informed language and ways of thinking.

Behaviors produced by organizational communication can also be studied as an information-processing system in which human behavior interfaces with computer hardware and software.[22] The technology of this situation differentiates computer-oriented information flow from information processed and mediated by humans. The traditional functions of the executive can't be completely executed by computers, but a technologically sophisticated information-handling network can move data more quickly and accurately throughout an organization. The mediating function of a middle manager in this situation focuses on human relations issues like motivating job performance, stimulating feedback about problems, and assessing job satisfaction. Organizational communication becomes a question of appropriate use of hardware in a formal communications network, limiting the formal communication of the organization to computer programs' capabilities. For example, using the organization's computer to distribute and store supervisors' weekly status reports on current projects would require careful thought about how the reports could be formatted and careful planning about who would have access to this information. Should every supervisor be provided with a terminal and required to use it with a secure password on every report? Should branch offices be wired into the mainframe in the head office, or should they be on separate systems? Should a report be filed in the archives after a project is finished? These and other questions must be answered to control the computer's role in the formal and informal organizational communication networks.

The technological school views technology as an opportunity for enhanced communication, whereas a more objective systems analyst would see technology as a network for communication or a way of expressing ideas within an existing system. Regardless of perspective, technology has joined human relations as an integral element in theories of understanding human behavior in organizations.

Now that we have examined some alternative organizational communication theory bases, let's consider some fundamental assumptions about interpersonal communication and the assessment of human actions within the organization. The purpose of this section will be to connect theoretical and practical concerns.

THE ASSESSMENT OF HUMAN ACTIONS

Individual human actions within the organization can be connected to models of managerial communication by assessing each behavior in terms of leadership and relational objectives. This section describes three ways to evaluate leadership objectives and opportunities for fulfilling management functions. We discuss the traits approach, the situational approach, and the contingency approach to leadership planning. To assess human actions in terms of private and public relational objectives, we examine interpersonal communication from two perspectives, taking a behavioral and then a relational approach. These social forces combine to create an organizational culture that gives each organization a unique social identity. Organizational communication networks make the organizational culture possible while also regulating the culture's maintenance and development as a social entity.

The Traits Approach

Scientific management theory suggests that a manager could discover and apply Taylor's principles of efficiency and Weber's theories of authority in order to become an efficient leader. But the trait approach, which emerged in the same time period, assumed that effective leaders were naturally endowed with their ability to lead. By observing successful leaders and cataloging their physical traits, organizations could effectively select future leaders. By 1940, desirable leadership traits numbered at least seventy-nine in a composite profile of the perfect leader.[23] Finding one person who possessed all of these characteristics would be impractical.

Growing recognition of the social influence of human relations on organizational efficiency prompted research into psychological traits expressed as a style of leadership. Kurt Lewin's 1939 study of autocratic, democratic, and lasissez-faire leadership styles focused on leadership and social climate.[24] The relatively random anarchy of laissez-faire climates is not competitive with the structured operations of other climates. The apparent operational efficiency of autocratic leadership was surpassed by the quality and satisfaction of democratic leadership. Aside from the obvious political need in 1939 to demonstrate the superiority of democracy, Lewin's work extended leadership trait research into the social domain. If the manager exercises leadership in a style conducive to job satisfaction as well as to high quality decisions, then sacrifices in quantitatively assessed efficiency could be accepted. The traits of a democratic leadership style transfer directly from the democratic political model, applying proven social principles to the organization in addition to the nation.

Leadership traits like encouraging participation have since been found to aid in setting up a democratic climate.[25] More recent studies have identified psychological traits that are part of a leadership style; these are usually expressed as *personality*.[26] This research has maintained Lewin's autocratic/democratic continuum but has not clearly detailed the characteristics of an authoritarian or democratic personality.

The functional approach also focuses on leadership traits, but without regard for individual physical traits or personality. Consistent with Barnard's description of the functions of the executive, the functional approach to leadership describes what a leader should do to act and be perceived as a leader.[27] For example, in decision-making meetings a leader should serve the group by setting an agenda for discussion, summarizing and testing consensus on each topic, and directing the group toward the next topic. Such task-oriented leadership behavior will lead the group to regonize the leader clearly. Benne and Sheats identified task and social maintenance functions of group leadership that would lead to effective group performance.[28] The most important finding in this research was that a leader needs to display social leadership as well as task-oriented leadership. For example, by encouraging participation and mediating conflict between members, a leader can also function as a social facilitator for the group. This research assumed that effective leadership would always require the same types of behavior in different situations.

The Situational Approach

The focus in leadership research hasn't always been on generalized optimum leadership behavior profiles. Ralph Stogdill's research represents the assumption that leadership requirements are defined by the situation.[29] Leadership potential may be derived from physical, psychological, or functional characteristics, but the situation determines which behaviors are most desirable and effective. The significance of meeting a group's expectations with appropriate leaderlike behavior is so strong in the situational approach that research shows only that each case calls for a leader whose style is compatible with the group and the norms for the situation.[30]

In a situation such as a construction site where physical strength and agility are highly valued characteristics in the work crew, the foreman must be able to display these traits. The foreman's superiority can't be based on strength and agility alone, since some younger worker is likely to be champion in these areas. The foreman who maintains leadership in this situation must develop brute strength into a style with psychological force. An apparent lack of fear might impress some workers but threaten safety on the job site. A more effective style might be one built around strength, agility, and an absolute insistence that everything be built to the construction code. By refusing to tolerate shoddy workmanship, the foreman displays a high standard for performance that could acquire the force of a moral code.

In an office setting, social maintenance might require the supervisor to organize social events like lunch-time card games or social events after work. But every situation where the supervisor is included in such office social activities is matched by a situation where the social expectations of an office are such that the supervisor will not interfere with the workers' fun. If the supervisor does show up at a card game, work relationships may be modified to permit the supervisor to join the group. The important point about the situation approach to leadership is that the situation dictates the norms for the leader's behavior to the degree that is permitted by the organizational culture. The leader can only change the situation as much as the identity of the organization permits, and only with some struggle against prevailing conditions.

The situational approach suggests leadership requirements are defined by what is occurring at the time.

The Contingency Approach

Anticipating logical or reasonable chains of events in a particular situation permits a leader to plan a range of responses to likely developments. The people influencing the events at hand are the source of variation and a principal subject of the contingency approach. But the situation itself must also be considered. The situation is clearly one of the forces determining *what* leadership is most effective.[31] Fred Fiedler[32] examined the differences between task-motivated and relationship-motivated leaders. Their behaviors showed a response to group members' expectations for either task-motivated or relationship-motivated behavior. The most effective leader responded to participants in the situation in terms of how the situation was organized. The more structured the situation was, the more task-motivated leadership behavior became, whereas less structured situations called for relationship-motivated leadership. The leader was motivated to act according to the demands of the situation, and the leader's analysis of the situation depended on contingencies produced out of the basis situation by the members. Thus, the task-motivated leader could become relationship-motivated once the task was accomplished or under control.[33]

For example, once the contract is signed or the project delivered, a manager might organize a picnic for the office whereby all expenses are paid by the company. The picnic is more than a reward, which could have been a cash bonus. The picnic is a relationship-motivated commitment by the manager to increase the friendliness of the office once the job is done. The holiday atmosphere could easily vanish once a new project started, but the camaraderie of good times together would be pleasantly remembered and looked forward to at the end of every task.

Fiedler assumes that motivation for the leader to take a task or relationship orientation comes from assessing the conditions of the situation in terms of a combination of three factors: (1) the quality of leader/member relations, (2) the amount of structure in the task, and (3) the position power of the leader. Together they indicate the most productive style for the situation. Directive or permissive styles are both possible as task-motivated and/or relationship-oriented styles of leadership. By choosing a directive or permissive style according to the situation and the responses of the participants, a leader can respond to the contingencies of each situation. The position power in the situation comes from legitimate and referential power sources attached to the leader's position. This position power combines with the quality of the relations between the leader and the members to make a leadership style that is contingent upon the degree of structure in the situation. The leader can either select an appropriate style or change factors in the situation such as position power, leader/member relations, and task structure subject to modification. Thus, leadership based on contingency theory is not a passive response to the situation; rather, it is an effort by the leader to find the most effective leadership style according to the observable conditions of the situation.

This view is supported by the work of Julia T. Wood. She found that effective leaders displayed this flexibility, even within a single group meeting. As conditions changed, leadership style changed.[34]

Now that we have examined some leadership-oriented perspectives on organizational behavior, let's consider behavioral and relational views of interpersonal communication within organizational environments.

The Behavioral Approach

The behavioral approach centers around the assumption that every decision must ultimately be expressed as a behavior. The key to motivating or controlling behavior thereby requires appealing to the individual's reasoning process leading up to the decision to act.[35] B. F. Skinner set aside the role of reason and focused on controlling behavior directly.[36] The individual is controlled by structuring the environment so that choices preferred by the controller also seem appropriate to the individual. Operant conditioning or behavior modification motivates response through behavior rather than through feelings by concentrating on the actions of the subject. Thus, behavior modification must identify behaviors as targets for modification and modify the consequences of the target behavior until the desired behavior is achieved.

For example, a manager may want every report to be prepared in the same format. After circulating a description of the preferred format, the manager evaluates every report in terms of how closely it follows the format. Even if a report is adequate, any deviation from the format is criticized, first privately and then publicly at weekly meetings. Those who follow the format are praised privately and publicly until the report format is clearly identified as a significant accomplishment that is important to the manager and those making reports. Internal emotional processes in the subject are not an issue, but are assumed to respond to rewards and punishments until the desired behavior is understood and produced.

Various consequences can help ensure desired behavior if the individual is cooperative and there are sufficient opportunities for conditioning. For example, positive reinforcement (e.g., raises in pay, increased power) can be offered as stimuli to increase the probability of a desired response to induce that behavior. The probability of desired behavior can also be increased by offering an individual an opportunity to avoid an unpleasant experience through avoidance or escape. Once a behavior has been learned, reinforcement need be less frequent, but withdrawal of stimuli leads to extinction of the desired behavior as the learned response, being unreinforced, is forgotten. If, in the last example, a new manager comes into the office and abandons the report format, employees will still continue to use the old format until the conditioning fades from memory. Those who deviate from the old format will not be punished, and individual reporting styles will proliferate. Removing a reward can also be perceived as punishment, which is equivalent to presenting an unpleasant consequence that is contingent upon a behavior. Those who remember the format but are not rewarded for using it will perceive this fact and may believe that they have made some small mistake. Since punishment also controls undesired behavior and can be combined with rewards for desired behavior, those making reports may experiment to see what format pleases the new boss. Using the old format elicits a loss of reward, so some other behavior might produce a reward of some kind.

The Skinnerian approach to human behavior ignores internal motivation. Human motivation becomes subject to mechanistic stimulus/response manipulation. More concerned about internal motivation for social interaction, relational theories of human behavior offer an emotionally sensitive alternative.

The Relational Approach

The relational approach to human behavior offers an explanation of both internal and external causes for action. Abraham Maslow's hierarchy of needs includes a wide range of motivators, which are expressed in terms of increasing potential for individual satisfaction.[37] Once lower-level needs, like physiological needs for food, or the need for safety or physical security, are satisfied, we act to satisfy higher-level needs. Higher-level needs motivate social interaction through social needs—the need for esteem and the need for self-actualization. As people move toward self-actualization, they learn how to satisfy their needs through relationships with others. Thus, Maslow's hierarchy of needs accounts for organizational behavior in which the individual member seeks satisfaction in the social relationships offered by other members of the organization.

As a personal goal, self-actualization also satisfies organizational objectives in two ways. If one or more of the organization's objectives coincides with the member's personal goals, then that individual can reach full potential as an individual while also acting on behalf of the organizational objectives. For example, a salesperson may perceive that growth in her territory also enhances her personal prestige in the home office. She will be self-actualized by being responsible for a growing territory, part of a need-fulfilling experience that also benefits the organization. The need to self-actualize in these terms is personal, that is, individualized according to each employee's personal goals.

But self-actualization permits a closer integration of individual goals with organizational objectives. Transcendent self-actualization allows the employee to identify organizational objectives as personal goals, achieving a level of harmony between member and organization that was previously blocked by separate personal goals. For example, being part of an organization that dominates its market may coincide with a computer software designer's need to work on the most powerful, most current software. By joining the dominant organization's software development team, this designer is able to do exactly what seems best as a personal goal, and by doing it for the organization, she enhances the desirability of the job. The better the designer's work is, the more dominant the organization becomes and the more the designer wants to work for that company. Thus, the social implications of Maslow's hierarchy of needs explain how social relationships can be coordinated with organizational goals to maximize job satisfaction and productivity.

We have discussed how human actions can be assessed to understand leadership and the relationships that leadership facilitates. The next section looks at organizational goals and the assessment of performance according to different theories of organizational behavior.

ORGANIZATIONAL GOALS AND ASSESSMENT OF HUMAN PERFORMANCE

Every theory of organizational behavior sets up models of ideal behavior meeting the theoretical requirements for perfection. By comparing actual behavior to these ideals, analysts create organizational objectives for increased efficiency, productivity, and profitability. But assessing actual performance requires that current efficiency, productivity, and profitability be measured accurately enough to distinguish different levels of performance. Thus, performance assessment is a process that starts with identification and definition of key performance elements, which become the subject of later evaluation.

Efficiency, Productivity, and Profitability

Scientific management's goal of organizational efficiency is still a primary objective for any realistic model of organizational behavior. Organizations exist to accomplish their stated objectives. But, in addition to classic studies of production efficiency, any definition of organizational performance must also account for the effectiveness of human relations. The organization that has integrated individual goals with organizational objectives makes the most efficient use of human resources by motivating through identification. As discussed by Tompkins and Cheney, identification of the individual with the organization simplifies decision making when it works (1) to select problems and possible solutions for decision making and (2) to direct the individual toward alternatives that are appropriate for both the individual and the organization.[38]

For example, when faced with a subordinate who is late three times a week after missing two days without a good excuse, a supervisor knows that the rules of the organization define this behavior as absenteeism, a problem for which the solution is a written warning. Identification with the organization and its rules simplifies decision making for the supervisor by telling him or her how to label the problem and solution. Identification also helps the supervisor choose among appropriate alternatives. Choosing to issue a written warning benefits the supervisor by keeping a record of the action while benefiting the organization by maintaining formal communication channels.

Burke and Schmidt's concept of organizational development identified this level of integration of the individual with the organization as part of the process of carrying out the organization's mission.[39] Relational efficiency and the subsequent effects on job satisfaction have consequences for productivity and profitability in all functions of every operation. This is true because social forces are part of any systematic assessment of organizational structure and function, and because the organizational value structure identified by Bennis reflects relational goals as well as organizational objectives.[40] Thus, traditional measures of organizational effectiveness must include assessment of the quality of the relationships offered to members in addition to the quantitative indicators of efficiency, productivity, and profit.

Accounting for Individual Versus Group Performance

The issue of analyzing individual or group performance evolves out of the importance of relationships between and among members and between the organization as a whole and individual members. If individual performances can't be assessed separately, it shouldn't be rewarded or punished as if the individual acted autonomously. Performance within a system's model of organizational behavior evaluates the individual as a factor in the system, a part of the formal and informal communications networks. If every member of a system performs as anticipated, the system could still fail to perform as a whole because of weakness in the system design. The effective organizational system may show how informal networks have been created to enhance the efficiency or productivity of the original formal design. Thus, an individual member's deviation from planned performance could be assessed negatively on the individual level if the benefit to the organization was visible only in performance at the system level.

In Chapter 10 we will address issues of organizational communication diagnosis and repair. That chapter will apply the relational and cultural approaches to organizational behavior to assess communication performance on the individual and organizational levels.

Marge Johnson represents a potential problem for her manager. She says of her job, "It's hard to get excited about the kind of work I do. I sit at a computer terminal and type dictation into it. Most of the time it is the same old stuff. How can I say, 'Gee, I can't wait to get back to work tomorrow!' "

Since there is not much her manager, Philip Wilson, can do to change her job, what is he to do? Phil's problem is not an unusual one. He does have some options for developing her as an employee—a human resource. He also has a number of options for motivating her to perform. It is a serious problem and provides the purpose for the material in this chapter—to develop organizational members through motivation.

Phil may not be successful in his effort to motivate Marge even if he understands his options and has a clear understanding of human motivation. Phil must also understand the communication issues involved in this attempt to motivate Marge. Communication is a central part of the process, too.

We begin with several theoretical ideas you will need to know before a discussion of communication issues can be meaningful to you. First, we present the underlying assumptions of those who view people as human resources, which provide a basis for the problem for managers in organizations. Second, we examine content theories of motivation that seek to answer the question, "What causes behavior to be initiated or terminated?" Third, we address process theories of motivation that answer the question, "How does behavior come into existence and how is it carried out?" Finally, we discuss communication issues that must be considered if a manager is to be successful in motivating people.

UNDERLYING ASSUMPTIONS OF HUMAN RESOURCE DEVELOPMENT

A number of theorists have drawn their ideas about human development from basic assumptions about human beings. Among these theorists are those who see people as a resource to be motivated, to be developed. These theorists fall within a group whose approach can be described as *human resource development.* Their underlying assumptions about people were aptly described in a classic essay written by Raymond Miles.[1] These general assumptions fall under three broad categories: attitudes toward work, the role of the manager, and expected outcomes.

Attitudes Toward Work

There are two assumptions these theorists make about attitudes toward work. First, they believe that most people in our culture want to make a genuine contribution in their work—to be doing something worthwhile. This desire goes hand in hand with their need to belong and to be respected. You can imagine that if a person feels a need to belong to a particular organization, that person also wants to be doing something worthwhile for that group and for his or her effort to be recognized and valued.

A second assumption is that people in the work force are far more capable of showing initiative, taking on more responsibility and engaging in more creativity than is required by their jobs. In other words, many people in the workplace are underutilized. Let's consider the person who is on the production line. She may be spending her time watching a line of bottles move through a filling and capping machine. She also must shut down the line in an instant if she detects a problem. Of course, her contribution is important to manufacturing the product. Yet, given encouragement, she might make additional contributions, for example, suggesting improvements in the canning process. Perhaps she can become part of a quality circle that could provide input about work group problems. She is a human resource with potential.

The Role of the Manager

The goal of the human resources-oriented manager is to increase the areas over which her subordinates exercise self-direction and self-control. This might be accomplished by giving subordinates the opportunity to participate in decisions. This is especially important when workers have experienced the problem and the decision is likely to have an effect on their work. These managers believe that tapping these resources allows a decision to be made with maximum available input.

The manager who views her work force as a human resource will attempt to take a variety of actions, such as trying to create a general work atmosphere where subordinates will feel their contributions are noticed and appreciated and encouraging them to try new ideas so that they can discover the full range of their talents.

The Expected Outcomes

The overall quality of the effort within the manager's unit will improve. This expectation is based on the belief that when the members of the organization contribute the full range of their experience, insights, and creative ability, better quality output will result. But beyond this, the subordinate will realize that he or she is being given *responsibility* for self-direction and will work hard to fulfill that trust. The manager believes this to be especially true when the area of involvement is not trivial. Here again, the worker is expected to realize the importance of his or her involvement and to strive to fulfill the boss's expectations.

The ultimate outcome of this improved performance and increased involvement should be increased job satisfaction. Put simply, workers' opportunities to become involved in decisions and to be productive makes the workers feel good about themselves and the work situation. For the manager to develop fully the resources found in his or her people, the manager must understand how to motivate those people. We begin this discussion of motivation by suggesting what motivation means and how it is related to productivity.

MOTIVATION

What Is Motivation?

The term *motivation* is derived from the Latin word *movere*, which means to move. But when the term motivation is used in an organizational context, it encompasses more than movement. Motivation is the inducement of a person's thoughts and actions through appeals to that person's particular needs and personality to work toward organizational goals. The expectation is that the person will be able to see that he or she can achieve personal goals through achieving the organization's goals. The key ideas and their definitions are:

1. *Inducement* is a reward that stimulates a person to think and act.
2. *Appeal* would be any behavior or argument the person who is trying to motivate might make.
3. *Needs* and *personality* are the loci of internal stimulation toward which the motivator might direct appeals.

The Problem of Motivation

We can safely say that there isn't an effective manager of people who hasn't worried about motivation. The productivity and reputation of the manager's department depends on it. And few people would deny that motivation and communication are connected. *It is through the communication* process that the effective manager motivates his or her subordinates to a level of productivity that allows achievement of the unit's goals.

From our own personal experience we know that motivation can be a problem. Think of your current work group situation, such as a classroom group to which you belong, or a club or organizational group. More likely, you can point to at least one or more members of each of these groups whom you would describe as an underproducer. Rarely is a group formed that doesn't experience motivation problems.

Motivation problems are difficult to address. The individuality of a person's need structure is partly responsible for this problem. For example, let's take the matter of salary. If you are a young person looking for your first professional job, salary may be very important to you. You might have been rather poor as a student and are looking forward to having more money. Salary might be an important *motivator* for you during the first several years on the job. But consider a different perspective your colleague, Joe, might have in midcareer. His children have grown and he doesn't feel the need for large increases in salary. His home is nearly paid for and he earns enough to meet his financial needs. For Joe, challenge in the job has become increasingly important. He has been doing the routine aspects of his job for several years, knows how to do them well, and does them well. For him, the ability to take on a new and exciting challenge in his work is motivating. Susan, on the other hand, is nearing retirement. She knows her pension is related to the 5 highest salary years within her last 10 years of employment. She is back to being motivated by salary and wants to be sure her boss notices and rewards her for her excellent performance. As you can see, the need to be compensated for work varies from person to person. By adding to this situation the many other needs a person may experience, and then considering the effect of the individual personality, you begin to understand the complexity of a person's need structure.

Furthermore, there are many ways a person might fulfill a need. Steve Johnson, a sales representative for a local real estate firm, is a good example of a person who is difficult to motivate for exactly this reason. Steve has been with the firm for 25 years. For the past several years his work has been only minimally successful. He sells enough real estate to make enough money to feed and clothe his family adequately. He is unlikely to be fired, even though he doesn't seem to take much pride in his work. One way to motivate him would be to find an outstanding job he did with a customer and then praise him for it—you would be appealing to his need for esteem. Let's assume you, in fact, find such an occasion and do praise him. But you notice the praise seems to have little effect. Why not? To answer this, you need to dig deeper into Steve's life.

Recently, Steve has been unable to fulfill his esteem needs through his work. Instead, he has become involved in a local self-help group as a lay counselor, receiving several plaques and certificates for his work with this group which he proudly displays in his office. In addition, Steve is very involved with his church; currently serving as chairperson of an important committee. The pastor of his church reinforces him by telling him how valuable he is to the church. Steve is meeting his esteem needs outside the workplace and has given up caring what his boss thinks about him. He gets his "strokes" elsewhere.

The motivation process is further complicated by the factor of ability. Leon Megginson and his colleagues have illustrated the effect of ability and motivation on performance (see Figure 3.1). They speculate that if motivation weren't a factor in performance, then we might expect a performance curve similar to curve 1 in Figure 3.1. Curve 1 represents some level of inborn ability and learning over time to some level of productivity. Curve 2, showing a faster rate of gain in level of performance, is an increasing ability to do the job (learning) being induced by strong, positive motivational appeals. In theory, curves 1 and 2 would intersect at the point where maximum learning had taken place in the curve 1 situation —the person is at his limit of inborn ability.

But most of us know that in the work situation, we seldom work up to full ability, or even some high percentage of our ability, unless we are motivated by some purpose or goal. Thus, our learning—the ability to do the job in this case—increases at a faster rate when we are motivated to learn. Not only might learning increase faster, but ability might reach a higher level than under the condition of unmotivated learning. Striving toward a goal can induce a higher motivation to learn. On the other hand, curve 3 indicates what lack of motivation, coupled with ability, does to performance. Here motivation is not being provided to induce the employee to learn. The consequence is a lower level of performance.

Thus, as J. P. Campbell and R. D. Pritchard[2] suggest, *the employee's per-*

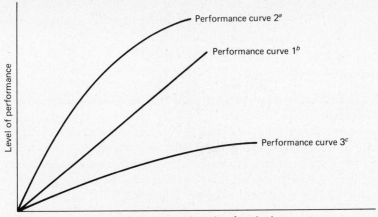

a Result of increasing ability and strong positive motivation.
b Level of performance expected with a given increase in ability but disregarding motivation.
c Result of increasing ability but with a strong negative or weak positive motivation.

Figure 3.1   How ability and motivation affect performance. (*Source:* Leon C. Megginson, Donald C. Mosley, and Paul H. Pietri, Jr., *Management: Concepts and Applications.* New York: Harper & Row Publishers, 1983, p. 351.)

formance is a function of that person's ability times the motivation to perform. This often is represented by the equation

$$P = f(A \times M)$$

where P is the level of performance, f is the function, A is the ability, and M is the motivation.

This equation does not suggest, however, the *complexity* of the motivation. Nor does it point to where a manager might turn to discover how to motivate a subordinate. Thus, we turn to a discussion of motivational theories and their implications.

THEORIES OF MOTIVATION

It is important to understand that motivational theories generally fall into one of two classes—either content theories or process theories. The importance of this classification is that theories falling into one class provide one kind of information about motivation while others yield a different kind of information. The kind of information available from a particular class is best understood by suggesting the underlying question each seeks to answer.

Content theories try to answer the question, "What causes behavior to be initiated or terminated?" The usual answer to this question is satisfaction of needs. Two of the most prominent need theories are Abraham Maslow's needs hierarchy and Frederick Herzberg's two-factor theory. *Process theories* seek to answer a different question. They suggest the answer to the question, "How does the behavior come into existence and how is the work carried out?" Two theories fall into this category—the goal-setting theory and the expectancy/valence theory.

Content Theories

Maslow   Abraham Maslow is undoubtedly one of the most famous motivational theorists. His framework for understanding human needs was explained in his book, *Motivation and Personality,*[3] published in 1954. He constructed a hierarchy of needs based on two fundamental assumptions. First, the needs a person has are arranged in a hierarchy of importance from lower-level needs to higher-order needs. Second, once a need is satisfied, it will no longer motivate the person, and some other need, usually considered to be the next higher need in the ranking, will provide the motivation until it, too, is fulfilled. According to Maslow, the human need structure can be divided into five levels of need. First, we discuss the concept of hierarchy; then we turn our attention to each of the needs. Figure 3.2 illustrates this hierarchy of needs.

In 1968 Maslow[4] argued that these needs in his hierarchy should be grouped into two classes—deficiency needs and growth needs. *Deficiency needs* are those that must be satisfied if the individual is to be healthy and secure. "Needs for safety, the feeling of belonging, love and respect (from others) are all clearly deficits."[5] It is necessary for an individual to meet these in order for healthy personality development to take place. *Growth needs* go beyond the healthy personality. They are the needs a person has with respect to developing and achieving his or her potential. Maslow suggests that a wide variety of needs fall into this area, making it a more difficult concept to grasp. "Growth, individuation, autonomy, self-actualization, self-development, productiveness, self-realization, are all crudely synonymous, designating a vaguely perceived area rather than a sharply defined concept."[6] We might think of this concept as taking in what Maslow calls the esteem and self-actualization needs. Let's examine each one of these need levels.

Physiological needs.   Maslow located the physiological needs at the bottom of the pyramid. This is because these needs are supposed to be the strongest. The strength of those needs is found in their biological origin, because biological equilibrium is an important factor in the life of any organism. If one or more of

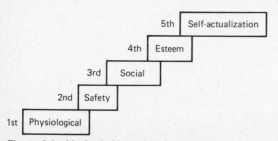

Figure 3.2   Maslow's hierarchy of needs.

these biological needs is unsatisfied, our system pursues it to regain its equilibrium. Humans operate on the *homeostatic principle*. The need activates a person's behavior in response to disequilibrium and ceases the behavior when equilibrium is achieved.

Presumably a starving person would not care much about esteem and would even risk his or her own security to meet the need for food, water, shelter, and the like. Taylor and the Scientific Management movement relied heavily on this need—the employee will work hard for money which will satisfy her or his basic needs for food and shelter.

Employees satisfy these needs in the work situation through pay, vacations, and holidays. They also are given rest periods, lunch breaks, restroom facilities, safe and comparatively pure air to breathe, and water to drink. Since most of the physiological needs are reasonably satisfied in the modern world of work, they don't often serve as powerful motivators.

Safety and security needs.   Safety and security needs become important if the physiological needs are satisfied. Basically, these needs are related to a person's self-preservation—both present and future protection from bodily harm. Safety needs require that a worker be free from accidents, fire, and assaults. Security needs seem to be related to possible dangerous conditions. Examples of areas of security concern are losing one's job, not being able to pay medical bills, not having enough money to live in retirement, being overtaken by technology, being replaced by a machine, and being treated unfairly by management. Employees satisfy these needs through demanding safe working conditions, seniority plans, unions, saving plans, pension vesting, insurance plans, and grievance systems.

Social and belonging needs.   There are two distinct sets of needs in this area: (1) the need to accept, associate with, and be accepted by others and (2) the need to belong to or feel like you are part of a group. The first is a more intense socialization need than is the second. You want to exchange signs of love, affection, and/or friendship here. This need is satisfied through appropriate interpersonal relationships within your work group. The quest for this kind of relationship finds its outlet in informal work groups within the organization.

The second of these needs, association with and acceptance by others, is primarily an affiliation need. Members of work groups want to say and believe that they are one of them. We often don't want to feel alone, set apart from our work group. Research suggests that total isolation is nearly intolerable, even if a person's physiological needs are satisfied.[7] In fact, this tendency to seek out others may be related to overcoming the stress and anxiety brought on by facing uncertainty alone.[8] Employees may have these needs satisfied through formal and informal work group memberships and company-sponsored clubs and activities.

Esteem needs.   This fourth level of needs consists of esteem or ego needs —being recognized and rewarded for what you have accomplished. Fulfillment of this need comes from respect and recognition from your colleagues, as well as

A manager might develop her employees through involvement in decision making.

from respect and recognition from your superiors—appropriate advancement, position, and power in the organization. This is an area where the rewards may be more important than increased monetary compensation. Thus, organizations may motivate their employees by giving them power, titles, status symbols, recognition, praise, awards, and promotions.

Self-actualization needs. At the top of Maslow's hierarchy is the need for self-fulfillment, for achieving our potential, for our continued self-development, for creativity. According to Maslow, this is the "desire to become more and more what one is, to become everything one is capable of becoming."[9]

As you can imagine, this is a difficult need for many people to satisfy in the workplace. Let's consider the line worker who does some sort of routine job. Jennifer, a stamping machine operator, spends her day inserting an 8" by 11" piece of metal into her machine and engaging a lever with her foot that causes the machine to cut an image through the metal. Her work provides only limited opportunity for self-fulfillment.

Beyond these needs, Maslow recognized two additional needs that seem to transcend his notion of hierarchy—cognitive needs and aesthetic needs. *Cognitive needs* are those that drive a person to try to understand his or her world. These include the desire to satisfy a person's curiosity and to learn what the person doesn't know. *Aesthetic needs* include the desire to experience harmony and beauty in a person's environment. Although it may certainly be important to recognize this need in some organizational settings, often it is not so relevant as cognitive needs.

The cognitive need, on the other hand, explains the employee's desire to understand the task he or she is performing and to know how what he or she is doing fits within the overall picture. This represents a need to be master over his or her environment. This need appears in part to be the basis for the emphasis in redesigning jobs so that they become more challenging and meaningful. By appealing to this need, the organization hopes that job redesign will create a job having more challenge to its mastery, thereby satisfying the cognitive and competence needs of the employee.

Research Findings on Needs Hierarchy   Maslow's work included very little research in support of the theory and no research that tested the whole model. Regardless, there has been wide presentation and acceptance of the model without solid evidence of its validity. This acceptance might be attributed to a widely circulated paper by Douglas McGregor,[10] who gave the impression that the model could be accepted without reservation and that a manager would find it rather easy to apply.

Maslow, himself, recognized the need for testing his model and therefore expressed the tentativeness of his theory:

> My work on motivations came from the clinic, from a study of neurotic people. The carryover of this theory to the industrial situation has some support from industrial studies, but certainly I would like to see a lot more studies of this kind before feeling finally convinced that this carryover from the study of neurosis to the study of labor in factories is legitimate. The same thing is true of my studies of self-actualizing people—there is only this one study of mine available. There were many things wrong with the sampling, so many in fact that it must be considered to be, in the calssical sense anyway, a bad or poor or inadequate experiment. I am quite willing to concede this—as a matter of fact, I am eager to concede it—because I'm a little worried about this stuff which I consider to be tentative being swallowed whole by all sorts of enthusiastic people, who really should be a little more tentative in the way that I am.[11]

Maslow's theory has prompted considerable research into its usefulness in organizational settings. However, *it has not been possible to establish the validity of the* need hierarchy itself. One of the best known investigations attempting to substantiate empirical support for the three main propositions of the theory was conducted by Wahba and Bridwell.[12] They investigated the support of three aspects of Maslow's model: (1) the validity of the principle of hierarchy, (2) the idea that being deprived of a particular need yields a domination of that person's need structure by that need, and (3) the notion that the gratification of a particular need leads to an actuation of the next higher need.

The validity of this approach was examined by reviewing seventeen studies that investigated needs. These studies employed either a factor analytic approach or a ranking approach to test this idea. Their conclusion after examining this literature was that:

> Taken together, the results of the factor analytic studies and the ranking studies provide no consistent support for Maslow's need classification as a whole. There is no clear evidence that human needs are classified in five distinct

categories, or that these categories are structured in a special hierarchy. There is some evidence for the existence of possibly two types of needs, deficiency and growth needs, although this categorization is not always operative.[13]

Wahba and Bridwell examined the second proposition of Maslow—deprivation leads to domination of the person by that need. Maslow assumes that the greater the deficiency is in meeting the need, the greater is the drive for gratification. Wahba and Bridwell found no consistent support for this proposition. Some studies provided support, whereas others failed to uphold it.

The third proposition these researchers investigated was support for the gratification/activation of the next level of need. Maslow assumes that once a need is gratified, it diminishes as a motivator. Then the next higher-order need is activated as a motivator. Here again, Wahba and Bridwell found that the proposition was not supported by the evidence. They say that these patterns suggested by the research "are not in agreement with those proposed by Maslow as far as the progression of satisfaction."[14] An engineer, for example, may be motivated to design the perfect machine to the extent that she sacrifices her family life and much that is at the basic level of her needs in order to achieve self-actualization.

What might we conclude about Maslow's theory based on the research? First, clearly, an individual's need structure is more complex than Maslow would suggest, there being possibly additional needs that motivate a person. One prominent needs theorists, H. A. Murray,[15] posits that a person might be motivated by any one of thirteen needs—achievement, affiliation, aggression, autonomy, endurance, exhibition, harm avoidance, impulsivity, nurturance, order, power, succor, and understanding. Beyond this, evidence points to the fact that the hierarchy doesn't hold for all people. A person might be motivated by a higher-order need, even when a lower-order need is not fulfilled.

Second, research supports the idea that there are probably two general levels of needs—deficiency needs and growth needs. People appear to try to satisfy their deficiency needs before being concerned about growth needs. Understanding this fact might allow a practicing manager to know the general level of needs that might be salient to a particular person.

Finally, we can reasonably acknowledge that Maslow's need categories give the practicing manager a starting place to look at an employee's motivation. When considering what organizations do to motivate workers, we find that much of their actions do appeal to the needs that Maslow presented. In other words, it is helpful to know that these are *some* of the needs that motivate people.

Herzberg   Fredrick Herzberg's two-factor *motivator-hygiene theory* is probably the most familiar motivational scheme among the members of the business community.

Herzberg's theory evolved from a study he and his colleagues reported in 1959.[16] Two hundred engineers and accountants in nine companies were interviewed to discover job experiences that they believed to be "exceptionally good" or "exceptionally bad." For each of these situations, they were asked to indicate the *degree* to which the experiences had influenced their positive and negative feelings.

This group of scholars then took the statements and broke them down into what they termed "thought units." For example, a thought unit might be "I feel fresh and eager, ready to come to work," or "I like to know there is a reason for doing the job." This process resulted in 5,000 statements which they classified into sixteen categories. These categories included factors such as achievement, recognition, and work itself. All sixteen categories are displayed in Figure 3.3. Notice also that the Herzberg researchers tabulated how frequently the factors led to either dissatisfaction or satisfaction.

Some of the factors seemed to be remembered by the subjects as satisfying, whereas others seemed to be remembered as dissatisfying. Herzberg saw them as falling into two classes which he called *motivators* and *hygienes.* Motivators are the factors that, when present, will lead the person to strive. Although they lead to satisfaction and striving, they don't lead to dissatisfaction if absent. They lead only to poor motivation. Hygiene factors relate to making the workplace tolerable. They aren't the opposites of motivators, however, since they don't lead to satisfaction. Here the opposite of dissatisfaction, what is claimed if these needs are met, is *not satisfaction.* Thus, you might hear a person, who is fulfilled with

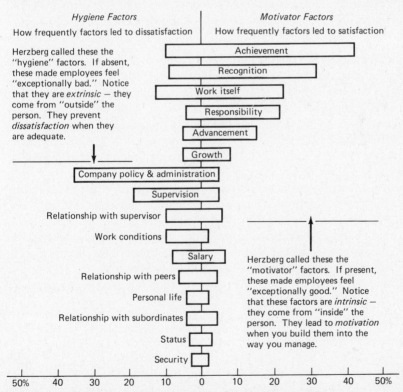

Figure 3.3 Herzberg's motivator-hygiene theory findings. (*Source:* Adapted from Frederick Herzberg, "One More Time: How Do You Motivate Employees?" *Harvard Business Review* (January–February 1968), 53–62.

respect to hygiene needs, say, "This is a good place to work." This means that the company's policy, administration, working conditions, pay schedule, interpersonal situation, and benefits leading to security are "OK"—the person isn't dissatisfied in the job. On the other hand, if the individual says that he or she believes his or her job provides opportunity for personal growth, advancement, responsibility, recognition, and/or achievement, and perhaps the work itself is interesting, then the person may be motivated to achieve. These factors, according to Herzberg and his colleagues, lead an individual to strive. Figure 3.4 shows how this theoretical concept would be illustrated visually.

Herzberg is fond of illustrating his theory with an analogy. He says sanitary conditions at home will not make a sick person well. They may help the well person from becoming sick though. The absence of sanitary conditions may very likely make a person sick. Similarly, the presence of hygiene factors at work will not make an unproductive worker productive. They will not even make the average worker more productive. But take them way and the average worker may become unproductive.

There is some similarity between the way Herzberg and Maslow viewed needs. Both describe motivators and growth factors (esteem and self-actualization) in the same terms. The hygiene factors of Herzberg seem to fall at the lower end of Maslow's hierarchy. Thus, physiological, security, and belonging needs are largely hygiene factors. Davis[17] has suggested the comparison presented in Table 3.1.

Research Findings on Herzberg's Two-factor Theory   The two-factor theory has generated considerable interest and a corresponding body of research. Like the research on Maslow's needs hierarchy, studies have both supported and been critical of Herzberg's idea. One study carried out at Texas Instruments by M. Scott Myers[18] supported the two factors. The method used to collect data was similar to that used by Herzberg, including the interview of 282 employees. There is also limited evidence that this theory holds cross-culturally. Donald Mosley[19] found support for the theory among workers in New Zealand.

Just how widespread is support for Herzberg's theory? H. M. Soliman[20] reviewed the research literature to answer this question. He found that only three of twenty studies using the Herzberg technique to gather data failed to support the theory. The results were generally supportive of Herzberg, but pointed to the likelihood that some occupational groupings might be more motivated by hygiene factors (like pay) than by motivator factors (like recognition).

Critics claim that Herzberg's theory is method bound. They suggest that

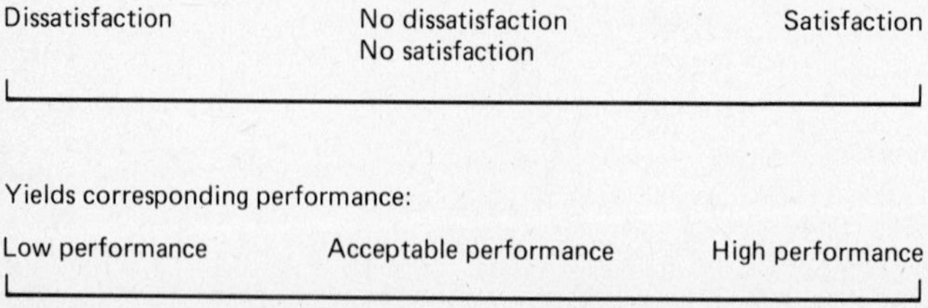

Dissatisfaction   No dissatisfaction   Satisfaction
                         No satisfaction

Yields corresponding performance:

Low performance   Acceptable performance   High performance

Figure 3.4   Correspondence between satisfaction/dissatisfaction and performance.

Table 3.1 COMPARISON OF MASLOW'S AND HERZBERG'S NEED CATEGORIES

Maslow		Herzberg
Self-realization and fulfillment	Maintence factors	The work itself Achievement Possibility of growth Responsibility
Esteem and status		Advancement Recognition

Belonging and social activity	Motivational factors	Status
		Interpersonal relations
		  Supervision
		  Peers
		  Subordinates

Safety and Security		Supervision—technical Company policy and administration Job security
Physiological needs		Working conditions Salary Personal life

Source: Keith Davis, *Human Relations at Work: The Dynamics of Organizational Behavior* (New York: McGraw-Hill, 1967), p. 37.

Herzberg asks questions in a way that might bias the response by restricting the employees' "opportunity to register negative reactions to motivators and positive reactions to hygienes."[21] In other words, an employee is more likely to mention something that she or he did when asked to recall a satisfying experience, but is more likely to mention something she or he couldn't control when asked to recall a dissatisfying work experience.[22]

Robert J. House and Lawrence J. Wigdor[23] have produced an exhaustive review of the evidence for and against the theory. One compilation of data suggests that individual differences may play an important role in whether a factor is viewed as a satisfier or dissatisfier. They compiled the actual frequencies reported by 1,200 people in six of Herzberg's studies for each factor. Their results are displayed in Table 3.2.

This ranking can be explained in part by understanding that every factor didn't appear in all of the studies reported by Herzberg. But this is tempered by the evidence that all factors presumably had an equal chance of occurring yet didn't because of the respondents failure to mention the factor. Consider, though, that 122 people considered achievement to be a dissatisfier and 110 saw recognition as a dissatisfier. These data put achievement and recognition third and fourth on a list of dissatisfiers, with only company policy and administration and supervision being named more frequently. We must conclude that the motivational factors are more individualized than Herzberg suggests.

This debate is likely to go on. Although it is clear that the theory may not apply equally to all classes of people, it may be applicable to those groups who have provided the supporting data—engineers—for instance.

Table 3.2   FREQUENCY REPORTS FOR SATISFIERS AND DISSATISFIERS

Frequency of Reports for Satisfiers and Dissatisfiers out of Total Number of 1220 People in Six Studies Reported by Herzberg (1966)

Factor	Reported as Satisfier	Reported as Dissatisfier
Achievement	440	122
Recognition	309	110
Advancement	126	48
Responsibility	168	35
Work itself	175	75
Policy and administration	55	337
Supervision	22	182
Work conditions	20	108
Relations with superior	15	59
Relations with peers	9	57

Source: Robert J. House and Lawrence J. Wigdor, "Herzberg's Dual Factor Theory of Job Satisfaction and Motivation: A Review of the Evidence and a Criticism," *Personnel Psychology*, Vol. 20, No. 4 (1967), p. 375.

Process Theories

Goal-setting Theory   Edwin Locke[24] suggested that conscious goals, incentives, and intentions are related to job performance. More specifically, goals and the goal-setting process are seen as antecedents to motivated behavior. The basic premise of Locke's model is that *people set goals concerning* their future behavior and these goals influence the actual behaviors they perform.

Research support for this basic premise is strong.[25] But to understand goal-setting fully, let's examine some of the generalizations with respect to goal-setting per se. The process is influenced by six task/goal dimensions: goal specificity, goal difficulty, participation in goal-setting, feedback on goal-directed behavior, peer competition, and goal acceptance.

Goal specificity.   You shouldn't be surprised by the fact that employees perform better when the goal is specific. Locke found that employees who were given specific goals consistently performed at higher levels than when instructed to "do their best" or weren't given instructions at all. In fact, the more specific the goals were, the higher was their performance.[26] Goal specificity reduced the ambiguity of the task, thus limiting the amount of nonspecific goal behavior.

Goal difficulty.   Another facet of goal-setting theory has to do with the difficulty of the goal. The manager might ask, "Just how difficult should I make the task so that it will serve as a motivator?" The argument behind setting goals at the proper level of difficulty is that a challenge can be perceived as something to be taken on and achieved. There is a certain satisfaction in attaining a somewhat difficult goal that might not be present in achieving a not so difficult goal.

The research literature has supported this view. Increased goal difficulty, as long as the goal is attainable, and if the attainment is properly reinforced, can be perceived as a challenge.[27] Yet it is important to note that if not reinforced properly (the boss doesn't notice the effort), or if the goal is only rarely achieved, employees are likely to stop trying. The result is reduced effort. So, with these conditions in mind, we can say that *increased goal difficulty does motivate the employee.*

Participation in goal-setting. The effectiveness of participative decision making as a strategy for increasing worker involvement, employee job satisfaction, and organizational effectiveness has long been recognized.[28] Yet the reports of the effect of participative goal-setting on actual improvement of performance are mixed. R. M. Steers and L. W. Porter,[29] after tracing these mixed reviews about participation and performance, suggest it isn't the participation per se that increases performance. The specificity with which goals are set during the participative goal-setting process and the fact that a low level of threat is present— the proper climate—are the factors increasing performance.[30]

Feedback on goal-directed behavior. A manager might suppose that the extent of feedback on goal-directed behavior should affect a person's effort toward reaching a goal. The assumption is that feedback will serve two functions. First, the feedback ought to point the person in the right direction, serving to direct his or her activities. It should keep the person's behavior within acceptable limits as he or she moves toward the target goal. Second, the feedback ought to be an incentive. Receiving the feedback should signal that the person is progressing toward the goal. This might be a source of pride for the employee, spurring the person to greater effort.

Steers and Porter,[31] after reviewing the goal-setting literature, conclude that feedback is important in stimulating performance. But they go on to say that *individual differences* are often mitigating variables. In other words, some individuals may want close observation of their work and to know how the boss thinks they are doing. Others may have a need for independence; wanting their employer to give them an assignment and then leave them alone until it is completed. Thus, the effective manager of people will draw a conclusion for each individual as to the type of feedback that will be most motivating.

Competition and goal attainment. We have all heard the statement, "A little competition is a good thing." This is a widely accepted societal attitude. Many managers believe there is a positive connection between performance and competition with a person's peers. Thus, we might see production graphs, contests for bonuses, "employee-of-the-month" contests, and the like. But before installing some sort of peer competition program in a unit you're supervising, you ought to understand that this relationship is not so simple as most people might think.

There are three factors that should be analyzed when considering competition as a motivator. First, people strive for the measurable outcome. Often the quantitative aspect of somebody's performance is more easily measured than is the qualitative part of the job. For instance, take the production graph posted on the departmental bulletin board. You can imagine a graph indicating the number of units produced. Can you also imagine a graph demonstrating the quality of the product. Although constructing such a graph might be possible, it is inevitably more difficult. Our point is that *it is easier to measure and reward people for the quantity of their output.* Thus, we conclude that competition is generally a positive influence on productivity when quality of output isn't a problem.

Second, it is probably more difficult to generate a spirit of competition in a highly mechanized industry or business than it might be in other less mechanical circumstances. When a task is divided into a number of parts, as is often the case in a highly mechanized industry, and each step is dependent on the other, the motivational task is to generate enthusiasm among all the members who are involved in the task. Each member's performance is essential for the group to compete successfully. On the other hand, if the completion of a task is discrete, the person's completion of the particular goal is independent of others, then use of competition is likely to be more successful.

Finally, striving to compete for a reward for achievement is likely related to the nature of the reward structure itself. Imagine the reward system being what is known as a *zero-sum* situation. (A *zero-sum* game is one in which there is only one winner.) Perhaps the reward for selling the most cars in a particular dealership is an all expense paid vacation to the Bahama Islands. If you were a salesperson, you might be highly motivated to sell under these circumstances. Now suppose instead that the company took the money they expected to spend and divided it among the top salespersons—a nonzero-sum outcome. The reward is now a $300 bonus. You do reasonably well salary wise, so now you ponder whether the $300 is really worth what it will take to be among the top of the group. Perhaps you decide to make an effort as long as you don't have to put in too much extra time. The reward system has made a difference in your resolve to compete.

Goal acceptance. The congruence between the externally assigned goal— the goal of the organization with respect to a task and the internally assigned goal —the individual's goal with respect to a task, has a significant effect on that individual's motivation.[32] This statement probably needs little explanation, but when you look to your own experience, you might find evidence that managers you have worked for believe it. They seem to pass on organizational goals with a faith that you, the employee, will accept them. Rarely do managers make the effort to gain the employee's goal acceptance. The manager might move in this direction if he or she explained the importance of the goal to the organization and work unit and suggested the benefits that the employee might receive by attaining the goal.

Research Findings on Goal-setting Theory We discussed the research related to goal-setting as we presented these ideas because of the number of elements involved. Here we will summarize those conclusions.

Research supports the idea that goal-setting serves as a motivator. Goals will be most motivating if those set are specific, the level of difficulty is moderate and attainable, and feedback on the progress is given by the supervisor.

Research supports the idea that participation in goal-setting contributes to overall satisfaction. On the other hand, support has been mixed between participation and increased performance. If participation enhances goal acceptance, then it may contribute to performance. Research shows that acceptance of the goal is very important to the motivational process. Finally, data suggests that competition may enhance performance when the outcome is measureable, when the task is individual, and when the reward system can single out a winner.

With these conclusions in mind, let's examine the expectancy/valence approach to the motivational process.

Expectancy/Valence Theory   Interest in expectancy theory dates back to the work of Kurt Lewin and Edward Tolman during the 1930s and 1940s. Lewin and Tolman rejected other theories in favor of an explanation that takes into account *characteristics of the individual. They* believed that values, attitudes, needs, and personality traits, as well as the particular environment, play an important part in motivation. This basic idea was then applied by Basil S. Georgopoulos and his associates[33] which they called the goal-path theory. (The expectancy/valence theory has been called the goal-path theory, instrumentality theory, and valence-instrumentality-expectancy theory.) This work was followed by Victor Vroom's classic book, *Work and Motivation,* in 1963,[34] which was the first systematic and comprehensive presentation of the theory. What followed were extensions and refinements of the work.[35] We will draw a general model from this work rather than presenting any one of these particular formulations because no one presentation includes all the pertinent details.

Expectancy theory is based on the fundamental assumption that an employee can *expect* that a particular behavior, perhaps working hard, will lead to a specific outcome, perhaps a higher salary. This notion breaks down into three components. Employees will perform well when they believe:

1. There is a high probability that their efforts will lead to intended behavior or performance level (E → P).
2. There is a high probability that the intended behavior or performance level will lead to certain outcomes (P → O).
3. These outcomes are on the whole valued positively by the employees.

Motivation is a function of expectancies and valences. An *expectancy* is the belief that a particular behavior will lead to a specific outcome. There are two components that make up expectancy: effort and instrumentality. The first, *effort,* is the E → P relationship. You may, for example, believe that your effort expended in writing a good report will yield a well-written report. This is the confidence dimension of motivation. If you don't believe that you can produce a well-written report, you may not try to do so. The second component, *instrumentality,* is the P → O relationship. It would be represented by a statement like, "The boss appreciates a well-written report and will reward me for producing one." Expectancy is quantified by using 0 to signify the situation in which the person sees no likelihood that the behavior will lead to the outcome and 1.0 where the person sees the outcome as absolutely certain if the behavior is performed.

A *valence* is the positive or negative value a person associates with a particular outcome of behavior. In expectancy theory terms this can range from $+1$, a high positive value (maybe a promotion), to -1, a high negative value (maybe losing one's job). Perhaps you value highly a well-written report. These components fit together in the following equation:

$$(E \rightarrow P) \times (P \rightarrow O) \times \text{valence} = \text{motivational force}$$

Edward E. Lawler[36] suggests how a manager may figure out how to fit this equation to the case of a particular employee. He contends there are three factors that help to determine the value of the $E \rightarrow P$ expectancy. These are: (1) the level of the person's self-esteem, (2) the past experience the person has in similar situations, and (3) the perception of the particular situation. Of course, the manager has a better opportunity of estimating these if she or he knows the employee well.

For the $P \rightarrow O$ expectancy Lawler suggests that there are five factors: (1) past experience in similar situations, (2) general attractiveness of the outcomes, (3) the degree of the person's internal locus of control and that person's belief in an ability to control the environment, (4) the $E \rightarrow$ value, and (5) the person's perception of the actual situation.

A simple illustration will show you how this model works. Suppose you took a part-time selling job in a stereo sound system shop. You have a strong belief that effort will lead to higher sales. Suppose you think that eight out of ten times your hard work will produce a sale (i.e., 0.8). Now assume you also believe that the increased sales would be recognized by the boss and would yield a bonus at the end of the month. You believe this to be true with high confidence because the boss has paid off in the past. So, the value that represents your expectancy is again 0.8. Now, you aren't feeling so well and want very much to have time off and the bonus at the end of the month. Knowing that you are going to have a few days off and that the extra money will allow you to have an extended weekend holiday, you perhaps place a value of 0.9 on receiving this bonus. You compute the motivational force as follows: $0.8 \times 0.8 \times 0.9 = 0.58$. But suppose instead that you had all the money you needed and didn't expect to have any time off anyway. The equation might look like this: $0.8 \times 0.8 \times 0.1 = 0.06$. As you can see, a low value for any factor in the equation has a sizable influence on the motivational force.

Research Findings on Expectancy/Valence Theory   Much of the research conducted on this model seems to support its usefulness. Over forty studies have been conducted using this theory and are reported in detail in two excellent reviews of the literature.[37] Campbell and Pritchard conclude that *each of the components is moderately and independently related to* effort and performance. The relationship is especially strong with respect to the $P \rightarrow O$ expectancy. This is particularly the case when the $P \rightarrow O$ relationship is structured since there is a *clear relationship* between performance and reward for performance (e.g., pay incentive systems that work).

There is also support for the idea that *all three elements must be at a relatively high level to support a high motivational force.* Campbell and Pritchard[38] compared studies, adding the elements with those multiplying the elements (translated into the previous examples, this is the difference in adding $0.8 + 0.8 + 0.1 = 0.17$ and multiplying $0.8 \times 0.8 \times 0.1 = 0.06$). Adding suggests that a particular element being high can compensate for a low element, that is, it will compensate for the lower number. This doesn't make much sense when you look at an actual case. We know that even though we strongly believe that our effort will lead to particular behavior, and that our behavior will be noticed and rewarded, when we don't value the outcome much we are unlikely to put forth much effort. So, the fact that the equation is $0.10 + 0.10 + 0.0 = 0.20$ doesn't mean that we are motivated. Adding produces inaccurate figures; multiplying is needed here. The research shows that this is the case. Multiplying the factors turns out to be a better predictor of motivational force.

COMMUNICATION ISSUES

Thus far we discussed two general theoretical perspectives on motivation. The content theories suggest needs an individual might have that could be used to motivate the person to action. The process theories explain how these needs might fit together to produce a motivational force. This section shows how to apply these as a communicator within an organization. We suggest the communication issues that must be addressed in order to motivate members of any organization.

Issue Number 1: Individual Differences in Motivation

Porter and Lawler[39] argue that there are two primary kinds of rewards an organizational member might receive for his or her performance. The person might be rewarded by the organization, that is, by fellow workers, the boss, or some higher superior. The reward comes from outside the person and is therefore called *extrinsic.* Another kind of reward comes from within the person and is therefore called *intrinsic.* An individual gets a sense of self-satisfaction from knowing that he or she did an outstanding job.

The content theorists presented earlier in this chapter base their models on the assumption that both external (extrinsic) and internal (intrinsic) motivators cause behavior. Maslow, of course, doesn't elaborate on the specifics of the sources for satisfying as Herzberg does. Herzberg says the extrinsic factors are supervision, interpersonal relations, company policy and administration, job security, working conditions, and salary. The intrinsic factors are the realization of potential from the work, achievement, possibility for growth, advancement, recognition, and status.

Porter and Lawler believe that a person's behavior at one point affects his or her future behavior. Once an individual behaves and receives a reward, he or she is motivated by the reward to future behavior. Porter and Lawler call this reward—the response the behavior receives—a *motivational stimulus.*

Lewis, Cummings, and Long[40] have taken these motivational patterns, extrinsic and intrinsic, and found a strong correlational link between the person's communication activity and the person's motivational pattern. They posit the four ideal categories of motivational patterns pictured in Figure 3.5. An organizational member will move from pattern to pattern depending on the situation. Thus, you might be influenced by intrinsic motivation in one case and then by both intrinsic and extrinsic motivation in another. Intrinsic motivators are those that relate to achieving personal needs—security, satisfaction, esteem, and value. On the other hand, extrinsic motivators such as compensation, promotion, recognition, and other symbols of achievement tend to result from doing work.

Lewis and his associates believe that satisfying these needs is related to a particular style of managing people. They illustrate this by creating two stereotypical managerial types: the *highly professional manager* and the *highly personal manager.* They see these styles as meeting the organizational member's extrinsic or intrinsic needs. The highly professional manager's style is considered to be externally focused. This manager will focus on the employee's professional life rather than on the person's personal life. He or she will consider the organization's needs over the person's needs. On the other hand, the highly personal manager's style is believed to be internally focused. This manager is interested in understanding the employee's personal interests, which are believed to be tied to the person's productivity. Worker satisfaction is an important issue for this type of manager. Let's turn to examples of how these managers might approach the same communication situation.

As you can imagine, these two types of managers are likely to approach communication activities quite differently. Cummings and his associates suggest the following overview of these manager's communication tendencies:[41]

The Professional Manager	The Personal Manager
Managing Information	
Attempts to be highly objective in passing information on. Also tries to control the amount of information passed on to workers.	Tends to exchange large amounts of information with workers. Wants workers to know most of what the manager knows. Also tends to pass on personal opinions about the information he or she receives from upper management.
Problem and Solution Identification	
Tends to identify problems and solutions in view of the major goals of the organization. This manager tightly controls the problem and solution identification process.	Tends to identify problems and solutions that are more people oriented. Keeps the problem and solution identification process more open, more participative.
Conflict Management	
Manages conflicts mostly by using power strategies (win-lose).	Manages conflicts mostly by using win-win and/or lose-lose strategies.
Behavior Regulation	
Relies on compliance strategies to regulate the behavior of others.	Tends to use mostly internalization strategies for strategies for regulating behavior.

High in intrinsic motivation; low in extrinsic motivation	High in intrinsic motivation; high in extrinsic motivation
Low in intrinsic motivation; low in extrinsic motivation	Low in intrinsic motivation; high in extrinsic motivation

Figure 3.5 Ideal categories of motivational patterns. (*Source:* H. Wayland Cummings, Larry W. Long, and Michael L. Lewis, *Managing Communication in Organizations.* Dubuque, IA: Gorsuch Scarisbrick Publishers, 1983, p. 251.)

Now consider what might happen if a professionally oriented manager were pursuing this style with a highly personally oriented employee. The manager is objective in transmitting information, trys to limit the amount of information she will pass on, and rarely inquires about the employee's personal opinions. The employee concludes that the boss doesn't care. On the other hand, suppose the opposite—the manager spends a good deal of time talking to the highly professional worker. Since the manager is highly personal in her style, she inquires frequently into how the employee is doing, is concerned about the person's opinions, how the person is personally experiencing work, and is open about decision making. Now the employee may think that the boss is nosey and unable to make hard decisions.

There are rigid people in this world, some of whom undoubtedly are managers of people. We may suspect that such a manager will not be particularly successful. The rigid professional manager is apt to be less successful with personally oriented members, whereas the opposite is true of the rigid personal manager. The manager who recognizes the type of person he or she is dealing with and responds accordingly is likely to be successful. Leaders can be, and in fact *are* flexible in their style.[42] Long and his associates called this type of manager the *versatile manager.* This manager would observe a person and respond in a style that seems appropriate to the individual's needs.

Indicators of Motivational Patterns　The obvious question that this discussion yields is, "How does a supervisor assess a particular organizational member's style?" Cummings, Lewis, and Long[43] suggest those indicators that may be present in the person's talk.

Intrinsic indicators of motivation

1. People blame themselves when their work interest is down: "I just don't know what is wrong with me; the work just isn't challenging any more."
2. People talk often about their relationships with others: "Isn't it great that we have a sense of teamwork around the shop?"
3. People talk often about their relationships with others: "The work I'm doing is going to benefit a large number of people."

4. People are present- and/or past-oriented in their conversation about the job: "This has always been a good place to work."
5. People talk often about conditions outside the organization: "My family and I went to the movies last night. . . ."
6. People talk about their need to be understood: "It's important to me that the vice-president understands what he's asking us to sacrifice."

Extrinsic indicators of motivation

1. People talk about promoting: "Explain to me again how I can become a supervisor around here."
2. People take great care in using proper titles: "Mr., Mrs., Ms., Dr., President. . . ."
3. People's conversations reflects competitiveness between workers: "Those dummies in the production department are not in our league."
4. People talk most of the time about the task: "Now that we're on break, I'll have a chance to ask George if there's a better way to do this job."
5. People's conversations suggest outside relationships are separate from work: "Frank and I had a fight this morning, but I'll worry about it when I get home tonight."
6. People blame the organization when their work interest is down: "This company needs to provide me with more incentive."
7. People are future oriented in their conversations about the job: "I'll be glad when we get our new drill so we can get the work done."

A skilled manager must realize there are individual differences in motivation and respond to them. One way to do so is by adapting communication style to the individual's needs. Remember, however, the motivational style needed may *change* from situation to situation. You, as manager, may need to adjust your style even though you are working with the same organizational member.

Issue Number 2: The Effort → Performance Element

A manager may address the problem of motivation further by attempting to enhance the perception of the organizational member to show that effort will yield the desired performance. In other words, the member must believe he or she can do the job at some reasonable level of performance. Without this confidence, the person is unlikely to strive. There are three possibilities for intervention: training, coaching, and task selection.

When a person's performance is low, the first question to ask is why the employee is failing to perform. Is it that the organizational member *can't* do the job or *won't* do the job? If the person can't do the job, then you have a training issue. If the person won't do the job, you have a problem with the P → O relationship or the valence portion of the expectancy/valence equation.

Whether training will be helpful is related to ability. What kind of ability is lacking? If it is intelligence or manual dexterity, there isn't much chance of producing a change. Here the solution is job change. Otherwise, training is in order. A specific training program would include identification of the skills needed, teaching those skills, practice, and evaluation. We address the issue of communication and training in Chapter 10.

You can assuage a person's fear of failure by adopting a coaching behavior toward the less confident organizational member. This kind of fear seems to be particularly prevalent in new employees. We believe that in order for coaching to be successful, several guidelines must be followed. First, let the person know that you expect a new employee might have questions when doing a task for the first time and that it is only a sign of the novelty of the situation. Second, let new employees tell you how much coaching they need and what kind of coaching it should be. Ask, "Would you like me to watch you go through this once? Or, would you like me to let you try it and check back?" "I am more than willing to answer any questions that might come up. Be sure to ask what you don't know so that you will feel OK about this new job." Also, be sure to decrease the coaching as the person's skill progresses. Confidence requires that the person know that he or she is doing the job. Continual coaching beyond what is necessary is likely to be viewed as meddling.

Finally, confidence is enhanced if the supervisor selects a task that is moderately difficult but clearly attainable. Goal theory suggests an important element of motivation is to structure a task so that it has some difficulty. The research also shows that if the task is too difficult an employee may become discouraged.

Issue Number 3: The Performance → Outcome Relationship

The manager can enhance this relationship by being careful to communicate organizational goals and the benefits associated with meeting them. This means the manager should begin with a careful orientation for the new organizational member. In this meeting the manager should be careful to state the expectations in terms of behavior and the rewards connected with that behavior. Beyond this meeting, an ongoing program for keeping the workers informed is important; utilizing multiple communication channels—that is, monthly meetings, bulletin boards, memoranda, performance appraisal interviews, and informal talks. Of course, once standards are set for performance, the manager must follow through on the promised outcome. The follow through here is crucial in reinforcing the member's confidence.

Another area of reward is promotion. In organizations where promotion is one of the outcomes of performance, the manager can cultivate the perception of a relationship between performance and outcome. Members of the organization are more likely to strive—assuming they value promotion—if the path to that promotion is clear. As you can easily imagine, employees who can't tell what they need to do to advance may not even try. Conversely, when employees know what is involved in being recognized for advancement, they are more likely to make the effort. This advice clearly coincides with the research we reviewed with respect to goal theory. When the goal path to a valued goal is made clear, it becomes a source of motivation.

SUMMARY

This chapter focused on developing organizational members through motivation. The purpose of the chapter was to provide an understanding of the assumptions underlying human resource development, motivation, and the communication implications of these issues.

We began by suggesting that human resource development indicates specific beliefs about people in the work force. These beliefs fall into three broad categories: attitudes toward work, the role of the manager, and expected outcomes. Two particular attitudes about people in the workplace are: (1) most people in our culture want to make a genuine contribution in their work and (2) people in the work force are far more capable of showing initiative than their jobs require. The manager's role is to discover ways to develop employees so that they increase the areas over which they exercise self-direction and self-control. The expected outcome of this effort is that the overall quality of the work effort will improve.

Second, we addressed the issue of motivation. One of the most important communication situations for any manager is where he or she is motivating organizational members to perform. Motivation is inducing a person through appeals to that person's particular needs and personality to work toward the organization's goals. Hopefully the person can see that he or she will be able to achieve personal goals through achieving the organization's goals. Motivation becomes a particular problem because of individual differences in needs and multiple methods of filling these needs. The matter is further complicated by the fact that a person's ability also affects motivation.

Third, we examined content and process theories of motivation. Abraham Maslow suggests a hierarachy of needs: physiological needs, safety and security needs, social and belonging needs, esteem needs, and self-actualization needs. Two additional needs transcending the notion of hierarchy are cognitive needs and aesthetic needs. The manager may look to these as a catalog of needs, but research suggests that the hierarachy may not hold for some people.

Fredrick Herzberg offers a two-factor motivator-hygiene theory of motivation. This theory posits *motivators*—achievement, responsibility, recognition, advancement, creative and challenging work, and possibility of growth—and *hygienes*—company policies and administration, quality of technical supervision, interpersonal relationships, salary, job security, working conditions, employee benefits, job status, and personal life. The motivators, sometimes called satisfiers, lead to motivation and striving. The hygienes make the workplace tolerable, thereby keeping the employee happy (not dissatisfied). Herzberg's research has been criticized as being method bound. When his procedures are used the research yields supporting results. But when other methods are used the theory may not be supported.

Goal-setting is one of the process theories of motivation. Edwin Locke suggests that conscious goals, incentives, and intentions are related to motivation of job performance. This central idea has strong research support. Goals must be specific, have a moderate level of difficulty, but be attainable. Acceptance of the goal by the member as well as feedback by the supervisor on the person's progress are important. Beyond this the organizational member's participation in the goal-setting process will contribute to overall satisfaction.

Expectancy/valence theory explains the components of the motivational process. These are: effort, instrumentality, and valence. The elements lead to this equation which suggests the relationship:

$$(E \rightarrow P) \times (P \rightarrow O) \times valence = motivational force$$

The $E \rightarrow P$ relationship is the expectancy of the person that his or her effort will lead to the desired performance. Although the $P \rightarrow O$ relationship is the expectancy that the performance will lead to the desired outcome, the outcome being some reward, the final element is valence. This is the degree of positive or negative valuing of the reward. A low value for any one of these components will mean low motivation. Over forty studies have supported this model. Research reveals that it is especially important for the employee to see that effort will result in the desired reward.

The final topic discussed was communication issues related to motivation. First, the implications of individual differences was developed. The manager of people must assess an individual's source of motivation—extrinsic, intrinsic, or mixed (extrinsic/intrinsic). This will allow the manager to adapt his or her style to that of the employee. Second, the manager should attempt to enhance the effort $\rightarrow$ performance element of motivation. This involves a decision such as whether training would increase confidence. The manager may also adopt a coaching relationship with the member and pick a goal that is easily attainable. Finally, the manager may be careful to indicate clearly the organization's goals and rewards connected with them. These should be communicated frequently and through multiple communication channels—that is, monthly meetings, bulletin boards, memoranda, informal talks, performance appraisal interviews. The manager may also be explicit about the path to promotion for those individuals who want to be promoted.

ENDNOTES

1. Raymond Miles, "Keeping Informed—Human Relations or Human Resources?" *Harvard Business Review* 43 (July–August 1965): 148–163.
2. John P. Campbell and R. D. Pritchard, "Motivation Theory in Industrial and Organizational Psychology," in *Handbook of Industrial and Organizational Psychology,* M. D. Dunnette, ed. (Chicago: Rand McNally, 1976).
3. Abraham H. Maslow, *Motivation and Personality* (New York: Harper & Row, 1954).
4. Abraham H. Maslow, *Toward a Psychology of Being,* 2d ed. (New York: Van Nostrand, 1968).
5. Maslow, *Toward a Psychology of Being,* p. 10.
6. Ibid., p. 24.
7. Bernard Berelson and Gary A. Steiner, *Human Behavior* (New York: Harcourt Brace Jovanovich, 1964), p. 252.

8. Stanley Schacter, *The Psychology of Affiliation* (Stanford, CA: Stanford University Press, 1959), pp. 6–8.

9. Maslow, *Motivation and Personality,* p. 82.

10. Douglas McGregor, "Adventure in Thought and Action," Proceedings of Fifth Anniversary Convocation of the School of Industrial Management, Massachusetts Institute of Technology (Cambridge, MA: MIT, 1957), pp. 23–30.

11. Abraham H. Maslow, *Eupsychian Management* (Homewood, IL: Dorsey, 1965), pp. 55–56.

12. M. A. Wahba and Lawrence G. Bridwell, "Maslow Reconsidered: A Review of Research on the Need Hierarchy Theory," *Organizational Behavior and Human Performance* 15 (1976): 212–240.

13. Ibid., p. 224.

14. Ibid., p. 227.

15. H. A. Murray, *Explorations in Personality* (New York: Oxford University Press, 1938).

16. F. Herzberg, B. Mausner, and D. B. Snyderman, *The Motivation to Work* (New York: Wiley, 1959).

17. Keith Davis, *Human Relations at Work The Dynamics of Organizational Behavior* (New York: McGraw-Hill, 1967), p. 37.

18. M. Scott Myers, "Who Are Your Motivated Workers?" *Harvard Business Review* 42 (January–February 1964): 73–88.

19. Donald Mosley, "What Motivates New Zealanders?" *Management* (New Zealand Institute of Management, October 1969): 53–62.

20. H. M. Soliman, "Motivator-Hygiene Theory of Job Attitudes," *Journal of Applied Psychology* 54 (1979): 452–461.

21. Michael E. Gordon and Norman M. Pryor, "An Examination of Scaling Bias in Herzberg's Theory of Job Satisfaction," *Organizational Behavior and Human Performance* 11 (1974): 106–121.

22. Victor H. Vroom was one of the first to point this out, a contention that is supported by D. A. Ondrack's research. See D. A. Ondrack, "Defense Mechanisms and the Herzberg Theory: An Alternate Test," *Academy of Management Journal* 17 (March 1974): 78–89.

23. Robert J. House and Lawrence A. Wigdon, "Herzberg's Dual-factor Theory of Job Satisfaction and Motivation: A Review of the Evidence and a Criticism," *Personnel Psychology* 20 (1967): 369–389.

24. Edwin A. Locke, "Toward a Theory of Task Motivation and Incentives," *Organizational Behavior and Human Performance* 3 (1968): 157–189.

25. Ibid., 157–189.

26. Edwin A. Locke, "The Motivational Effects of Knowledge of Results: Knowledge or Goal-setting?" *Journal of Applied Psychology* 51 (1967): 324–329.

27. R. B. Zajonc and J. J. Taylor, "The Effects of Two Methods of Varying Group Task Difficulty on Individual and Group Performance," *Human Relations* 16 (1963): 359–368.

28. Victor H. Vroom, *Work and Motivation* (New York: Wiley, 1964).

29. R. M. Steers and L. W. Porter, "The Roll of Task-goal Attributes in Employee Performance," *Psychological Bulletin* 81 (1974): 434–451.

30. L. C. Lawrence and P. C. Smith, "Group Decision and Employers Participation," *Journal of Applied Psychology* 39 (1955): 334–337.

31. Steers and Porter, "Roll of Task-goal," pp. 434–451.

32. Locke, "Toward a Theory," pp. 157–189.

33. Basil S. Georgopoulos, G. M. Mahoney, and N. Jones, "A Path-goal Approach to Productivity," *Journal of Applied Psychology* 41 (1957): 345–353.
34. Vroom, *Work and Motivation.*
35. J. Galbraith and L. L. Cummings, "An Empirical Investigation of the Motivational Determinants of Task Performance: Interactive Effects Between Valence-instrumentality and Motivation-ability," *Organizational Behavior and Human Performance* 2 (1967): 237–258; L. W. Porter and E. E. Lawler, *Managerial Attitudes and Performance* (Homewood, IL: Irwin, 1968); G. Graen, "Instrumentality Theory of Work Motivation: Some Experimental Results and Suggested Modifications," *Journal of Applied Psychology* 53 (1969): 2, part 2; J. P. Campbell, M. D. Dunnette, E. E. Lawler, and K. E. Weick, *Managerial Behavior Performance and Effectiveness* (New York: McGraw-Hill, 1970).
36. Edward E. Lawler, *Motivation in Work Organizations* (Monterey, CA: Brooks/Cole, 1973).
37. T. R. Mitchell, "Expectancy Models of Job Satisfaction, Occupational Preference and Effort: A Theoretical, Methodological and Empirical Appraisal, *Psychological Bulletin* 81 (1974): 1096–1112; J. P. Campbell and R. D. Pritchard, "Motivation Theory in Industrial and Organizational Psychology," in *Handbook of Industrial and Organizational Psychology,* M. D. Dunnette, ed. (Chicago: Rand McNally, 1976), pp. 63–130.
38. Campbell and Pritchard, "Motivation Theory," pp. 63–130.
39. Porter and Lawler, *Managerial Attitudes.*
40. M. L. Lewis, H. W. Cummings, and L. W. Long, "Communication in Roles as Indicators of Management Preferences: An Integrative Approach to the Study of Communication in Organizations." A paper presented at the annual meeting of the International Communication Association, Acapulco, 1980.
41. H. Wayland Cummings, Michael L. Lewis, and Larry W. Long, *Managing Communication in Organizations* (Dubuque, IA: Gorsuch Scarisbrick, 1983), p. 253.
42. Julia T. Wood, "Leading in Purposive Discussions: A Study of Adaptive Behavior," *Communication Monographs* 44 (1977): 152–165.
43. Cummings, Long, and Lewis, *Managing Communication,* pp. 253–254.

two

CREATING AND COMMUNICATING ORGANIZATIONAL MESSAGES

chapter 4

The Process of Communicating in Organizations

THE BASES OF COMMUNICATION EXCHANGE

Communication as a Commodity and Investment / Communication and Equity

ANALYZING LEVELS OF COMMUNICATION MEANINGS

Digital and Analogic Levels of Communication Analysis / Analyzing the Goal of Communication Exchanges

FUNCTIONS OF MESSAGES IN ORGANIZATIONS

Task Functions / Integration and Differentiation / Maintenance

COMMUNICATION PROBLEMS IN ORGANIZATIONS

Serial Distortion / Perceptual Distortion / Semantic Distortion / Overload and Underload

COMMUNICATION NETWORKS

Network Functions / Network Composition and Roles / Formal Networks
Decision-making Networks / Decision-implementing Networks / Telemediated Networks

Informal Networks
Gossip and Rumors / Informal Networks and Social Control

RITUALS: LEARNING THE ROPES

Rituals of Arrival / Rituals of Full Participation / Rituals of Belonging and Exclusion

In his book, *High Output Management,* Andrew S. Grove, president of Intel, one of America's premier high technology organizations, explains how his company prospers in the highly competitive microchip and microprocessor industry. He describes Intel's unique approach to strategic planning, the manufacturing process, and use of human and technological resources. Not surprisingly, the book reveals the centrality of communication processes within Intel, underscoring the importance of effective, timely interactions among managers and subordinates. What may surprise you is Grove's pronouncement: "The information most useful to me, and I suspect most useful to all managers, comes from quick, often casual verbal exchanges. This usually reaches a manager much faster than anything written down. And usually the more timely the information, the more valuable it is."[1]

Most contemporary books about effective management include consideration of communication in formal and informal settings. Unfortunately, as Sandra O'Connell points out, they do so by confusing management *processes* with management *functions.*[2] According to O'Connell, communication is a management *process* that allows management *functions* to be carried out.

For example, strategic planning is a management function. To do strategic planning, however, requires verbal exchanges, analysis of verbal and written reports, and often small group problem-solving or decision-making sessions. Therefore, communication is how strategic planning is accomplished. Fortunately, Andrew S. Grove and Intel recognize this fact. Unfortunately, many individuals, groups, and organizations do not.

This chapter is about communication processes in organizations. Specifically, its purpose is to indicate the complex influences of verbal and nonverbal communication on the operation of any company. First, we define the nature of information exchange, exploring the pragmatic bases of analyses directed toward the objective of understanding how communication processes attain meaning. Second, we investigate the various *functions* of messages in organizations and develop a way of looking at communication processes at micro- and macrolevels of analysis. Third, we discuss *message transmission and reception problems* that interfere with communication in organizations. Fourth, we examine *communication networks,* from the loose collections of individual communicators forming links between levels of authority within an organization to more formal groups of persons carrying out specific political, social, or professional strategies and tasks outside the organization. Finally, we end the chapter with a probing examination of *communication rituals,* in which various communication processes within organizations are revealed.

THE BASES OF COMMUNICATION EXCHANGE

For most persons, talk is natural. We grow up using it to accomplish tasks; create, maintain, modify, and end relationships with others; engage in discussions; or make presentations. We accomplish goals with talk, seldom giving talk much thought unless it causes a problem or fails us.

For those who are interested in the study of communication, however, talk is much more complicated. Although we use it from childhood naturally, our abilities to make talk efficient and creative differ as widely as the anxiety or enthusiasm we feel when asked to speak. Furthermore, we characteristically define our relationships with others based on *the frequency and quality of talk we exchange* and on the responses we receive to our talk from friends, family, peers, and colleagues.

To begin our examination of information exchange processes, we investigate why and how human beings view communication as a commodity, or an investment. Second, we examine two distinct levels of analysis used by scholars to explain how meanings are exchanged and the value persons give those meanings in working relationships. Finally, we explore the relationship between communication and goals that provide a valuable source of information about the meaning of talk. Explaining these three keys to understanding communication processes in organizations will help you improve your ability to make sense out of the talk of others. Increased understanding of others should also improve your own strategic communication skills.

Communication as a Commodity and Investment

How many times have you heard someone say, "It just isn't worth my time to continue that relationship," or "What's the point of continuing this conversation, you won't give me what I want anyway?"

Consider what is actually being said. In both cases the persons making the complaints are referencing the *inequities of exchange* governing the particular relationship or message under scrutiny. In the first instance the *time spent* developing or maintaining the quality of the relationship is said not to be *gaining the desired outcomes;* hence, an inequity in the relationship exists because the time spent in it doesn't justify the investment. In the second case the complaint is based on a perceived unwillingness to "give me what I want," which the complaint maker believes is a *commodity that can be exchanged during the conversation.* Furthermore, we must assume that exchanges of this commodity are *fair* (given the nature of the relationship).

Every communication between or among people contains *information exchange.* The information contained in the discussion can be thought of as its *commodity value,* much like the present cash worth of stock or the present market value of a product or service. The exchange value of the communication, however, refers to the *relationship* and its *meanings* for the participants, similar to the attitudes, feelings, and motives you and a stockbroker might attribute to each other while developing a portfolio of investments.

Think about it this way. Let's suppose that you are dealing with two stockbrokers on a regular basis. Let's further suppose that you enjoy being with Broker B more so than with Broker A. Both give you the same investment advice. Which broker do you retain to handle your investments? Chances are you will chose broker B because the exchange value of your relationship weighs heavily in your decision. In other words, *both the information content and the exchange value of the relationship figure into your evaluation of any communication.*

Communication and Equity

The economic metaphor is important to comprehending communication processes within organizations. To help you see its importance, we now introduce four principles of social exchange theory derived from the early work of George Caspar Homans, Peter Blau, and Elaine Walster, G. William Walster, and Ellen Bersheid.[3]

1. *Individuals will try to maximize their outcomes* (where outcomes = anticipated reward − perceived costs). No information comes free, nor is there such a thing as a free relationship. Every person will try to get the most valuable return for his or her investment, which translates, using the economic metaphor, to maximizing outcomes. Therefore, every message includes a perception of *anticipated cost and/or perceived reward.*

2. *Groups within organizations will collectively evolve accepted systems for apportioning resources among members so that each individual can attempt to maximize outcomes equitably. Furthermore, groups will generally reward individuals who treat others equitably and punish (increase the costs for) members who treat others inequitably.* Within any organization or group, informal and formal rules, rituals, and guidelines for equitable treatment will evolve, and organizations will reward those individuals/groups adhering to them. In addition, individuals develop, or bring with them to the job, a sense of fairness and equity governing treatment of others and expected returns on investments.

3. *When individuals find themselves participating in inequitable relationships, they will feel distress. The more inequitable the relationship is, the more distress individuals feel.* In organizations, rules, rituals, and senses of fairness are sometimes violated. When this happens, the persons who feel they have been treated badly become aware of their animosity, envy, greed, jealousy, or fear of failure.

4. *Individuals who discover they are in inequitable relationships will attempt to eliminate their distress by restoring equity.* After the perception of inequity occurs, persons tend to act on it, to "get even" with the offender, to find some rationalization for the act of unfairness, or to seek a formal apology. The degree of unfairness displayed in the relationship will determine the degree of restitution or retaliation sought. If no equitable solution can be found, the person may choose to leave the organization or seek a transfer to another work group.

You can see how prevalent the economic metaphor is to any complete understanding of equity theory, and why it is important to see the commodity and exchange values of any communication. It's as if most persons most of the time carry a "mental balance sheet" on which they record rewards and costs. This analysis also holds true for groups within departments, for departments within organizations, and for organizations with other organizations within the general economic community. Let's consider the following testimony from Kara:

KARA M: When I worked for _____ I tried to do my job without interfering with anyone else's life. The problem was, they kept interfering with mine. I made one major mistake which labeled me as a loser, and no matter what I did to try to overcome it, nothing worked out. I tried and tried and tried, until the pressure almost drove me crazy.

Fortunately, I was able to find another job with another company in town. There I was treated well from the start, and I have worked hard to maintain my image. I see everything differently because of it. What I mean is that every statement that is made concerning my work becomes important. I don't take anyone or anything for granted anymore, and I try to be fair with others because I have learned that is the best way to get them to treat me fairly. Now, however, the scandal isn't personal, it's divisional. Our division constantly fights with another one in the company, and it's odd, but I can see how what happened to me at my last job, and what is going on now between these divisions is essentially the same thing—something happened that could not be repaired, and nobody is willing to give in because that would mean the original error didn't count. Everything counts. Nobody forgives and forgets.

The assumption governing the equity theory is that humans are basically *selfish*—otherwise, why would everyone try to maximize their outcomes? But the principle governing your understanding of how the equity theory applies to human communication is *reciprocity of exchange*. No matter how selfish you may be, or may want to be, you can't be totally selfish if you expect others to help you obtain your outcomes. Furthermore, because everyone is essentially selfish, you need to work out ways of cooperating with others.

Here is where the principle of reciprocity of exchange comes in. You have to "give a little to get a little." Perhaps, more importantly, you must demonstrate to others that you are willing to help them if, in return, they will help you. If this sounds a bit idealistic, we admit that it is. After all, if everyone lived by the golden rule (e.g., "Do unto others as you would have them do unto you"), there would be no need for understanding the basis of the equity theory. The fact is, however, most people don't obey the golden rule, nor do they unconditionally aid you in obtaining your rewards. To receive cooperation means that you must first demonstrate your cooperativeness with someone or some group whose support or aid you need and value. Then they will feel some degree of *inequity* and be motivated to restore equity by cooperating with you.

One final word about equity and reciprocities of exchange. The economic metaphor assumes that an ideal balance can exist between rewards and costs and that ideal relationships can be created when both parties maintain a 50/50 balance between them. In reality, you may never expect a perfect balance, nor a perfect relationship to exist between rewards and costs. Research indicates that most individuals believe they give just a little bit more than they receive, and furthermore, they report being happier when they do. Why? Because we like to have the economic advantage, or at least perceive that we do.[4]

ANALYZING LEVELS OF COMMUNICATION MEANINGS

The economic metaphor suggests that we keep a mental balance sheet of our communication exchanges. However, we also keep a mental/emotional record of our *experiences* in communicating with others. We pay particular attention to the *meanings* we attribute to others' messages, and reciprocally, the meanings others attribute to what we say and do.

How many times have you found yourself wondering what a friend, lover, or colleague *really meant* by a particular statement, or even by a raised eyebrow? When this occurs, how do you figure it out? Perhaps you scrutinize the actual, observable behavior of the other person for cues to the meaning. Perhaps you think about past experiences with the person, trying to see the statement or look in relation to past shared meanings. Or, perhaps you consider the statement singularly, as a discrete unit of analysis, as something you couldn't have predicted, and therefore as something that caught you by surprise. You might even compare the person's actions to other people's actions to see if any correlations might suggest the real meaning. Chances are you have done exactly this sort of thinking when confronted with communication you wanted to understand. In this section we explore a method for understanding the *meanings* of the communication you exchange with others.

Digital and Analogic Levels of Communication Analysis

Let's begin with the assumption that there are at least two interrelated components in any analysis of communication:[5]

1. *Digital component* refers to the factual bases of information contained in the words we speak. By *factual* we mean the raw information content of the message. Digital talk is the substance of exchanges we routinely make with persons with whom we must work but do not know very well. For example, a manager in charge of fifteen individuals probably will not know many employees well, but nevertheless must direct their work. Instructions and evaluations of work will form the basic pattern of communication between them, and in both cases the information contained in messages will demonstrate the limited nature of their relationship.

2. *Analogic component* refers to the various meanings attributed to the message because of the *relationship* between the participants and their ability to reference other message contexts using *shared meanings*. For example, a manager may develop a close personal relationship with another manager over time. When these two individuals communicate, they may use a kind of verbal shorthand that allows them to process a great deal of information and shared meanings that will be unavailable to others present. Simply saying "Yeah, that's like old Saginaw," may call up a whole host of shared meanings (commonplaces) without further discussion; to the uninformed observer, however, this exchange will be as meaningless as it is to you now.

These two interrelated components of verbal communication point out the complex possibilities of any verbal exchange. Not only does talk carry information about a task or a goal or a problem; but it also carries information about relationships, intentions, and meanings among the participants. The digital and analogic possibilities for talk exist in most communication situations.

An individual can choose to read analogic intent into a purely digital message. Conversely, any analogic meaning can be ignored or devalued by someone who doesn't want to participate in the message at that level of analysis.[6] For example, women often report that they can tell when a man is interested in accomplishing something more than in carrying out the assigned task with them, but that one effective strategy they employ is simply ignoring the analogic intent in favor of a simpler reading of the meaning.[7]

Digital and analogic readings of communication are important to your understanding of two things: (1) the *ways* in which communication attains meaning and (2) the *strategies* you can use and choose to respond to when dealing with others. When you combine your appreciation for the possibilities of meaning (via the digital and analogic pathways) with your understanding of the economic value attributed to exchanges of talk (via an analysis of the equity of relationships), you have two methods of understanding the nature of information exchange in any relationship. These two methods provide means of assessing the value of the exchange and its meaning to the participants. But you still need a third cue to complete the analysis—the *goal* of the relationship/information exchange.

Analyzing the Goal of Communication Exchanges

Communication is generally considered to be an intentional, goal-directed activity.[8] People talk to address problems, overcome deficiencies, meet exigences in situations, express themselves, explain themselves, and entertain themselves. But, as you probably already suspect, most of us do not consciously govern our choices of talk in every situation. Only during important situations when we need to find precisely the right word or phrase does conscious control of talk seem real to us. Put simply, most of us, most of the time, don't make productive use of the intentional, goal-directed qualities of talk.

Some research even suggests that the goal of having clear intentional communication is *not* normative in organizations. Eric Eisenberg argues that *strategic ambiguity* is an important characteristic of organizational communication: "People in organizations do not always try to promote this correspondence between intent and interpretation. It is often preferable to omit purposefully contextual clues and to allow for multiple interpretations on the part of receivers. Furthermore, *clarity is only a measure of communication competence if the individual has as his or her goal to be clear.*"[9] *Eisenberg provides three general uses of strategic ambiguity:*

1. *Promotes unified diversity.* As we have pointed out, individuals want to be a part of the organization (a sense of belonging) while maintaining a unique sense of individuality. One way organizations can encourage both the sense of belonging and the sense of individuality among employees is to make abstract, or ambiguous, statements about their goals—such as "IBM puts service first," or "I love New York"—that allow individual interpretations of meaning. This facet of strategic ambiguity encourages more creativity and flexibility among employees who are freer to choose how they will respond to organizational symbols and goals.

2. *Facilitates organizational change.* Organizations change when individuals in them alter the ways they think and behave. If goals are precisely defined, change becomes difficult because new ideas are seen against the backdrop of older, more established ones. When goals are ambiguous, change can be encouraged more easily. As we know, survival is dependent on adaptation—and adaptation for any organization is facilitated by flexibility.

A second way in which strategic ambiguity affects organizational change is through interpersonal relationships. People who share meanings often share relationships, and people who may *think* they share similar meanings may be encouraged to develop relationships with others who hold different views but express them ambiguously. Also, tact in resolving conflict is an obvious characteristic of strategic ambiguity.

3. *Amplifies existing source attributions and preserves privileged positions.* The use of strategic ambiguity allows individuals with high credibility to articulate a variety of positions in abstract language capable of encouraging multiple sources of identifications among listeners. This is particularly useful when *power* in deciding future options is part of a negotiating setting. As you know from strategic arms negotiation talks between the United States and the Soviet Union, there are strategically ambiguous messages provided to the public that often carry important private meanings among the negotiators. In this way strategic ambiguity allows for future denial and face-saving communication because of "misunderstanding" or "misreadings" of the formal, ambiguous statement.

These three uses of strategic ambiguity are important. However, as Eisenberg carefully points out, the goal of his research is not to undermine the importance of goal-setting or of clarity in communication, but rather, to show that clarity itself is one goal of communication and that it is not often the norm in most organizations. This doesn't mean that communication is seldom *strategic;* in fact, the ability to become strategic in your organizational communications is vital to your success.

One purpose of this book is to induce you to become more aware, more strategic, more *goal-directed* in your uses of talk. We assume that the more control you exert over your choices of words and actions, the more likely you are to gain the responses you seek from others. Furthermore, if you do not exert conscious control over your communication, you will probably decrease the likelihood of gaining the responses you seek.

If you have trouble with the concept of consciously controlled, or intentional communication, consider this fact. In thinking about how you assess the communication of others, you know that you spend time attributing motives, causes, and goals to others' talk. When communicating with a goal in mind, you contribute to their ability to make the appropriate attributions of meaning and motive to your talk. When communicating less consciously, or spontaneously, you increase the chances of *inappropriate* attributions, of false or incomplete assignations of meaning and motive. To be a more effective communicator requires more than eloquence to induce the desired effects in your listeners; it also should help them find the meaning you intend.

Goal analysis is an important tool of communication. It not only encourages you to see the relationship between your choices of communication and the outcomes you seek, but it also encourages you to seek out the same relationships in the talk of others that you examine for meaning. To complete our understanding of how and why communication attains meaning among persons, use evidence drawn from talk to establish the goals, motives, and causes of communication. To accomplish this form of analysis, you should ask the following questions:

1. *What are the possible goals suggested by the communication?* Try to think of alternatives rather than of absolutes. Remember, most of the time most people are less conscious than they should be of the goals their communication seeks. The off-handed remark, the accidental analogic meaning of a suggestion, the bad manners displayed during a group meeting, or the flaw in the public presentation may or may not be intentional. Try to avoid the easy assignations of meaning that the other's mistakes allow. Zero in on *the sum total of your experiences* with this person when examining the relationship between a statement or action and its goal.

2. *What evidence do I have of each possible goal?* Remember, you need real evidence to build a convincing case. Focus on specific words and actions performed by the person, not on your assumptions about their motives or your reading of their behavior. First, examine the behavior, then try to read meaning into it.

3. *What are the strategic advantages inherent in linking the behavior I've observed with the goals I have suggested?* What will the person derive from behaving this way? What is the payoff? Why would a rational, intelligent individual choose to communicate the way this person does?

4. *Who benefits from this person's public performance(s)?* Consider that some behavior is directed toward satisfying yourself, whereas other behavior is other-oriented, or directed toward gaining or holding the attention of others. You might have been only *part* of the audience for the performance, when a larger public was really the objective. You might tend to respond personally to others' communication despite the fact that sometimes you are not the sole audience for it.

5. *What future opportunities will I have for observing/evaluating this person's performances?* All analyses of ongoing relationships should be kept *tentative* and *contingent.* People do change over time, and judgments made today may prove to be errors in the long run. If you have performed your analysis of another person's goals carefully, then you should be willing to see if your hypothesis fits future situations. One potential problem of goal analysis is that often it allows rigid evaluations to replace behavioral/situational sensitivity, thus reducing the effectiveness of both the analysis and your communication with the person.

6. *How should I act on this information?* Any analytical experience should pay off in your actions. The reason you bother to do goal analysis is to sharpen

your understanding of others', and your own, communication meaning and effectiveness. Not acting on the knowledge gained from the experience would denigrate it, reducing it to mere mental silliness. To modify the words of a great scientist: There is nothing so practical as a good analysis.

In this section we explored the methodological triangle you should use when analyzing your own and others' communication in organizations. By investigating the economics of the exchange value of talk, the possible digital and analogic levels of intent and meaning, and the relevant goals toward which the communication is directed, you can improve your understanding of the communication of others. You should then be able to improve your ability to respond effectively to their messages.

Now let's examine the functions of verbal messages in organizations.

FUNCTIONS OF MESSAGES IN ORGANIZATIONS

In the last section we described how you can learn to analyze *individuals'* communication in organizations. In this section we explore ways of determining how communication functions *across the organization.* The purpose of this section is to introduce you to four basic functions served by communication processes in organizations: (1) task, (2) integration and differentiation, (3) maintenance, and (4) adaptation.

Task Functions

Organizations exist to accomplish goals directed toward improving their chances for continuation. For manufacturing organizations, this goal means producing a quality product at a marketable price capable of gaining enough buyers to ensure the continued existence of the plant. For service agencies, this goal means providing a quality service to persons, corporations, or other agencies that is valued enough to continue the demand for the service. For research and development firms, this goal means producing ideas, reports, studies, analyses, and recommendations about new products or services that can gain adequate support to guarantee the continued operation of the firm.

Because all organizations operate with precise goals and objectives, one major function of communication processes in any organization is to plan, organize, direct, monitor, and evaluate the accomplishment of the task. These communication processes are designed to facilitate the smooth operation of the organization while it accomplishes its objectives.

If you examine the talk exchanged on a daily basis in almost any organization, you will find that the majority of that talk can be said to carry out the task function. Interviews with prospective employees, appraisals of work, meetings held to solve problems or make decisions, presentations given to in-house or out-of-house audiences, and so forth, are all communication activities facilitating the accomplishment of the organization's task. Once we discover the existence of this category of communication, the next question becomes: "What do we know about the task function of communication in organizations?"

First, we know that task communication accounts for most of the *contact time between and among the levels of hierarchy* in organizations.[10] By *contact time* we mean the time actually spent communicating face-to-face, on the telephone, using the intercom, or during meetings and presentations. Hence, the presence of hierarchical differences marks task communication, informs it, and probably exerts influence on the appropriateness of messages exchanged between levels of command.

The fact of hierarchy during task communication also shapes the mutual understanding of the message. Research strongly supports the idea that the person(s) in the one-down, or subordinate position in the relationship will (1) pay closer attention to the message, (2) attribute greater meaning/importance to it, and (3) ask fewer questions about it than will the person in the one-up, or superior, position.[11] Furthermore, superiors tend to believe they spend more time communicating about the task with subordinates than they actually do, and subordinates believe their attempts to intitiate interactions with superiors are more important and successful than they really are.[12] The results of these mixed, sometimes distorted attributions of meaning and significance not only influence perceptions about the task and each other, but they may also interfere with them.

Second, there are a variety of ways to classify task communication, and each schema tends to depend on the level of hierarchy used to generate it. For example, researchers interested in managerial issues tend to define three types of task communication: (1) communication designed to modify or change the *structure* of work to be done, or being done, (2) discussions aimed at completing understandings of work to be done, (3) communication based on prior policies, understandings, or procedures to keep ongoing work organized and/or on schedule.[13] As you can see, managerially oriented schemes tend to focus on decision-making and implementing communication, to the exclusion of the "softer" kinds of talk exchanged about the task (i.e., jokes, stories, remembrances, etc.). Whether or not the fact of managerial communication in organizations follows these academic models has been seriously challenged in the research literature.[14]

Researchers interested in employee issues favor a schema that defines the kind of communication exchanged during the completion of tasks already assigned. Instead of decision-making and implementing classifications, these schemas provide rich descriptions of directions, jokes, stories, initiation rituals, remembrances of similar past situations, asking and answering questions about friends, families, and co-workers, and exchanges of gossip and rumors that characterize *informal* communication between and among employees.[15] Here again, how closely the real talk of workers follows academic research is problematic.

The point of studying the various schemas for characterizing task communication in organizations is not to favor one over another. Our experience with these models suggests that the best use can be made of them by *combining* their understandings into a more holistic approach to task talk. Both managers and subordinates in most organizations engage in decision-making and implementing talk as well as to more informal communication while the task is at hand. More importantly, both subordinates and managers imbue informal ideas with serious goals, and vice versa. Task communication may focus on the task, but there are as many different ways to talk about it as their are persons doing the talking. The issues become (1) the style chosen and (2) the efficiency of the talk in accomplishing its task objectives.

Research on communication style is relatively recent in the literature.[16] Early efforts, principally by Robert Norton and Barbara Montgomery, focus on *the degree of openness* experienced by the receivers of communication and evaluated by trained, academic observers. Although this research will no doubt provide valuable ways of understanding the influences of communication style on task outcomes, at this time the evidence supports only two broad generalizations about style and task communication: (1) the degree of openness between cooperating parties should be about the same for accurate communication to occur and (2) differences in degrees of openness between or among persons may create distortions of information exchanged between or among them.

The second issue is the efficiency of communication to accomplish the objective. By *efficiency* we mean the ability of the communicators involved in the production and reception of the message to improve the likelihood of mutual understanding. For example, we know that messages become more ambiguous, less accurate, and more prone to misinterpretation when the words used to convey them are *abstract.* Saying "What do you think about the management of this place?" can be a loaded question; the receiver may interpret "the management" to mean his or her boss, the next level of hierarchy in the organization, or the executives who are only rumored to exist. If our respondent says "Well, I think they are great!" the person who initiated the conversation may attribute the meaning of the statement to the respondent's boss, the next level of the management hierarchy, or the rumored executives. Furthermore, what does "great!" mean? The respondent could be referencing the raise or bonus just received, the general operation of the organization, or, if the tone used to convey the message is equally ambiguous, the respondent may actually mean the opposite of what the word typically means. Or, if we assume our respondent is just being coy and doesn't want to draw attention to any negative remarks he or she may make, the word "great!" may mean nothing at all—just a ritualized response to an ambiguous situation designed to mean nothing, and therefore risk nothing.

So, you can see how *abstract words create ambiguity* and how *ambiguous situations create the need for abstract words.* In both instances the efficiency of the communication is questionable because neither party can be sure of the meaning the other party is attributing to the words spoken, or to the actions performed. In organizations a good deal of what passes for *communicating* is actually inefficient and ambiguous ritualized responses to situations and others.[17]

A second aspect of the general problem of communication efficiency is the inability of communicators to *give and/or ask for responses to their messages.* Task communication is severely hampered when instructions are given that are instantly misunderstood but no attempt is made to discover the misunderstanding. For example, a supervisor may ask, "Why don't you spend the remainder of the day getting your crew to install the new insulation on the overhead pipes using a No. 4 grade protectant?" The supervisor may then say to his crew chief, "You guys need to put up new insulation that is four times stronger than what we've got now." The crew chief may say to the crew, "We've got some job ahead of us!

The boss wants new insulation on everything by tomorrow morning. Don't ask me any questions, just do it!"

In each incidence of communication described in the previous paragraph, errors in understanding and interpretation could have easily been avoided if the sender of the message would have asked for responses to the directives. The instruction-giver only has to say, "Look, this is an important job. Why don't you repeat those instructions back to me to make sure we both understand what needs to be done?" As simplistic as it seems, merely asking someone to tell you what they think you communicated to them often improves the efficiency of communication.

Third, the efficiency of task communication in organizations assumes that the *most appropriate and expedient channels for conveying information will be used.* By *channels* we are referring to choices among oral, written, or mediated ways of transmitting/receiving the message. For example, if everyone needs to have a copy of a new policy, a memo with a copy of the attached policy can be issued (written) or the person responsible for implementing the new policy could discuss it personally with work groups (oral) or a computerized memo could be issued to all department heads with the request that they, in turn, discuss the policy with their employees (mediated). The choice should be made based on which channel has the greatest likelihood of gaining the desired goal in the shortest amount of time.

Task communication is as varied as it is complex. Although most persons believe that most, if not all, of communication in any organization should be task-oriented, research indicates that it is not. Let's examine the next aspect of messages in organizations—the integration and differentiation function.

Integration and Differentiation

From a broad organizational perspective, communication and organization are synonymous terms.[18] This means that the organization is the sum total of the communication occurring within it. It also indicates that individual similarities and differences in communication must be accounted for if the organization is to operate effectively. Accomplishing this goal requires an understanding of five related aspects of the integrative and differentiation functions of messages in organizations.[19]

1. *Operating the organization.* Information is the lifeblood of any organization. Knowing what resources are available, what resources are in stock, and what resources need to be acquired to complete a task require communication designed to plan, organize, and direct the activities of employees.

2. *Maintaining proper channels for communication.* Virtually every organization fosters an appreciation for formal lines of authority. Employees are expected to receive information from duly appointed personnel, work within established groups or teams, and report to their superiors. Failure to maintain these formal communication channels can disrupt the work process by creating problems caused by information overload/underload. Although every company recog-

Messages function as facilitators for integrating new members into the organization.

nizes the existence of informal channels for communication, maintenance of formal channels is generally recognized to be how appropriate order and stability can be maintained.

3. *Sorting and cross-referencing information.* Consider every organization as a general accounting system in which all information must be accounted for. The number of persons involved in decisions should be monitored, the flows of information throughout the organization should be known, and the ability of members at one level to know what members at another level are doing, and at what pace and on what schedule, should contribute to an integrated accounting system for the sum total of communication within the company.

4. *Integrating the individual parts into a coherent whole.* For any organization to operate smoothly and efficiently requires integrating the available information across departments. The sales force and the marketing personnel must stay in constant contact if a product is to be sold using the plan researched and developed by the persons responsible for that job. The accounting department must be informed about projected resource allocations and current expenditures if the books are to balance.

5. *Confirmation of individual and organizational identities:* Everyone needs to believe that the work they do is valuable to the organization and to themselves. Everyone wants to feel a sense of "belonging" to the company while, at the same time, they maintain a unique, individual identity. Communication within any organization promotes or denies these essential passions by the ways in which it recognizes and rewards individual ideas and talk and responds to problems affecting morale and leadership. Furthermore, every organization needs to foster an identity that employees can share in and value. Its reputation will be carried into the community through its employees, whose talk will symbolize the meaning the organization has for them.

As you can see, these five components of the integration and differentiation function of messages support the view that communication and organization are synonymous terms. What an organization is, does, and wants to become is created by the communication within it, and how employees communicate about the organization outside it.

Now let's examine the third function of messages in organizations—the maintenance function.

Maintenance

Organizations are collectivities of individuals. Looked at this way, the propensity for an organization to act as independent and discrete units of information is large and somewhat forboding. All persons, after all, value their individuality, believe that the way they look at the company and the task is essentially the correct way to do so, and want to seek their own rewards and goals. Hence, the opportunities for individual personalities to wreak havoc and ultimately destroy the organization are clearly a natural part of any company.

However, individuals form *relationships* with each other, which tend to become important sources of information and entertainment and contribute to a sense of *shared organizational realities.* As a result of these relationships, most organizations more closely resemble a community of concerned neighbors than they resemble a series of discrete information units. *Human relationships are primarily responsible for the maintenance of the organization.*

When using the term *maintenance* in this context, we are referring to the ability of the perception of a meaningful relationship between and among persons who work in the same organization to promote, and to maintain, a spirit of cooperation and competition benefiting the operation of the company. Human relationships come to the forefront of working, as evidenced by the research indicating that the major cause of leaving a job is unsatisfactory relationships with co-workers and superiors.[20] Furthermore, because these relationships matter to us, they tend to influence how well or poorly we carry out assigned tasks.

As any seasoned manager knows, the skill of developing relationships with subordinates and peers is vital to the ability to manage. "Manage your relationships with people, and the people will manage the work" is an appropriate description of how management processes are, or should be, accomplished. Therefore, it is unwise to make dichotomous distinctions between communication designed to accomplish the *task* and communication designed to develop and maintain a *relationship.* The perception of the relationship will influence the perception of the task, and vice versa. This text separates the two functions of messages to describe more easily the complexities involved in both functions; however, on a day-to-day, week-to-week, year-to-year basis, maintenance and task functions are inextricably interwoven and always interrelated.

Having discussed the functions of messages in organizations, we now investigate the problems these messages can create.

COMMUNICATION PROBLEMS IN ORGANIZATIONS

Communication should be considered both a *method* and a *goal*. As a method it exhibits a systematic way of analyzing, organizing, and delivering messages in any situation.[21] So intense, however, is our interest in learning how to communicate effectively and efficiently, we often lose sight of the unavoidable fact that *to have communicated* with someone is also a *goal* of any message. Communication can't be taken for granted, or assumed to have occurred; instead, our efforts in carrying out the method of communication should be consciously directed toward accomplishing the difficult goal of having communicated effectively and efficiently.

To do this requires an appreciation of the problems in message transmission and reception. In this section we examine four basic sources of communication difficulties that impede or distort the meanings attributed to messages in organizations: (1) serial distortion, (2) perceptual distortion, (3) semantic distortion, and (4) overload and underload.

Serial Distortion

Try this experiment.

Repeat the following statement to the person sitting behind you in class:

> I can't believe we are that far behind schedule in our inventory. We have less than 50,000 units of wood, more than twice that amount of glue, and our production schedule calls for delivery by the second of next month. Besides, my secretary, Ms. Easygoing, is on vacation and the computer is down for the day.

Now ask the person behind you to repeat the message to someone else in the class, and ask that person to repeat it to another person. Repeat the message a few more times during the class period. Then, toward the end of class, have the last person who received the message repeat it back to the whole class.

We bet the last message and the first message have little in common. Why?

The answer is the serial distortion problem. *The more often a message is transmitted, the more likely errors in the transmission will occur.* This problem is inherent to organizational communication because most messages must pass through a number of persons before work is accomplished or a task is carried out. It also occurs when a grapevine is used to convey gossip or rumors.

Serial distortion is a problem for most organizations, but it is a problem that can be reduced, if not eliminated, by training employees to monitor the accuracy of their message transmission and reception. By *monitor* we mean ask questions about the message when it is received and ask questions about the accuracy of the received message when it is sent. The key to overcoming serial distortion problems is in the willingness of communicators mutually to check message accuracy. And the best way to accomplish this communication goal is to learn how and when to ask questions about messages.

1. *Recognize that most messages pass through other persons before they get to you.* Creating an awareness of the potential for serial distortion can help you overcome problems associated with it. It may be advisable to ask who initiated the information, or, at least, who told the person telling you about it.

2. *Check out the accuracy of messages prior to acting upon them.* Never *assume* you have received accurate information unless the person giving it to you is responsible for evaluating your work on it. Always ask for clarification of ambiguous words, phrases, or task goals before you begin working.

3. *Keep a record of the accuracy of messages given to you by individuals in the organization.* You will find that some persons are more effective and responsible communicators than are others. Keeping track of less able communicators will alert you to possible serial distortion problems by reminding you that in the past this person has distorted information or repeated distorted information.

Serial distortion usually occurs along with other sources of message distortion in organizations. Let's examine one of the potential causes for serial distortion which is a type of message transmission and reception problem—perceptual distortion.

Perceptual Distortion

Perceptual distortions occur for many reasons, all of them related to *differences* between and among persons. If we were all alike in attitudes, values, beliefs, and behaviors, there would be fewer opportunities for perceptual distortion, but, of course, we aren't all alike. Here are the differences that tend to create distortions in message transmission and reception:

1. *Differences in status.* Research demonstrates that differences in status affect the reception and interpretation of messages. Subordinates typically overestimate the importance of communicating with superiors, and typically believe, as we pointed out earlier, that such encounters are more important than they actually are. Conversely, superiors tend to believe they communicate more effectively and more often than research demonstrates they do.[22]

2. *Differences in race, age, and religion.* Your background is a filter through which all messages pass. Because our backgrounds differ, the meanings we attribute to others' communication may also differ. Differences in race, age, and religion all warrant special filtering because of our evolved sensitivity to them. We typically learn to demonstrate public respect for others while harboring private reservations. These reservations serve as perceptual filters, allowing us to interpret communication based on our past experiences, biases, prejudices, and fears about groups of distinct "others." We may be less aware of perceptual filters concerning age than we are of those concerning race or religion, and that lack of personal awareness contributes to distortion.

3. *Differences concerning gender.* Kenneth Burke, the great literary and social critic, once wrote that men and women treat each other as members of different species, or classes, of society.[23] Recent research demonstrates the truth of his claim. For example, men typically believe that women's communication is more emotional, therefore less rational, than men's speech. However, recent empirical research clearly demonstrates that men and women use about the same amount of emotional words and phrases. Nevertheless, men continue to hold those attitudes.[24] More importantly, those attitudes about the quality of women's speech directly influence men's attitudes about women's ability to perform organizational tasks. Gender differences, real or mythical, do influence our perceptions of women and men, and hence, act as perceptual filters on our attributions of importance and meaning to our communication.

4. *Differences in values.* As people get to know each other in any organization, they also become aware of the values guiding their attitudes and behavior. Values about ideas or controversies outside the organization often influence perceptions of the worth or stability of individual personalities. For example, an employee who articulates political preferences in elections may contribute to hostility felt by others who don't share those preferences. Because our personal values carry over into our professional experiences and perceptions, differences in values influence the meanings attributed to communication.

5. *Differences in style.* This category sums up a variety of perceptual filters capable of contributing to message distortion, including differences in personality, style of dress, style of leadership, style of participation, style of conflict management, and style of communication. Because we seldom doubt the validity or "rightness" of our own styles of thinking, when we find that someone differs from us, we tend to use the perception of difference as a filter. We then interpret all aspects of their work by using it, often unconsciously.

Perceptual distortion occurs subtly. We are usually unaware of the filters influencing our perceptions of others, which, of course, contributes to the degree of difficulty we have in reaching awareness of them, or even of overcoming them.

Now we examine the third aspect of message distortion—semantics.

Semantic Distortion

Earlier in this century two men, Sapir and Whorf, suggested that the words we speak directly affect the ways we think about and act toward objects, persons, and ideas. Known as the Sapir-Whorf hypothesis, this proposal generated a generation of research designed to test the hypothesis. The results of that research confirmed the hypothesis and were chiefly responsible for contributing a level of language appreciation to a style of academic theorizing known as *constructivism.* [25]

Words do shape our perceptions and our understandings of things, thoughts, actions, and other words. The language we speak grows out of our cultural and social backgrounds and is the principal means by which we define and act upon reality. Research demonstrates that our languages are indices of our social class[26] and that differences in available vocabulary and language usage control our abilities to perceive, understand, and create new understandings. So closely linked is our language usage to our understanding, we cannot productively separate the two concepts. You are what your language makes you, and the more variations you use in your language style, the more options your world will appear to have.

Because language is fundamental to communication, and because our language usage and understandings differ, the probability of the same word (e.g., nature, science, technology) meaning the same thing to any two people is slim. We have to agree on the meanings of our words in order to agree on how those words should direct our activities and symbolize our experiences. This is why we say that all meanings are *negotiated* between persons.

Many persons take words for granted, acting as if "any word will do," or worse, "every word has one definition—mine!" (or Mr. Webster's). These individuals' lack of sensitivity to the complexities of communicating and the complexities of language use tend to create what we call *semantic distortions*.

Semantic distortions occur because of misunderstanding, or disagreement between or among people over the meaning of words. Generally, we speak of three typical forms of semantic distortion: (1) *definitional distortions*, or disagreements over how something should be defined or classified, (2) *emotional language distortions*, or distortions based on passionate images conjured up by the use of certain words or phrases (e.g., "nigger," "honkey," "redneck," "illiterate bum," "just a woman," "macho man," "Communist," "Republican," etc.), and (3) *processual distortions*, or problems that occur because active, changing phenomena are described in static, pictorial language (e.g., calling an atom a thing).

Semantic problems often become problems with real significance. Our inability to understand instructions, directives, procedures, processes, or decisions contributes to an organizational inability to perform or implement them correctly. Here is a brief guide to improving your sensitivity to semantic distortions:

1. *Ask questions when abstract language is present in the message.* Words such as *employees, management,* the *personnel,* and so on include all members of a given category, so that you should be careful to make sure that it is the intended meaning. Pay particular attention to *evaluative* terms such as *good, great, bad, poor, best, worst,* and so on. Be certain you find out how the evaluations were made, including what criteria were used to make them.

2. *Try not to use present tense descriptors to talk about changing processes.* General semanticists have long pointed out that our everyday language usage suffers from the tendency of words to stop time or to take pictures of situations that are actually alive and changing. Usually this problem rests with the word *is.* To say something *is* something else (e.g., "This project is suffering from a lack of leadership") equates two changing processes as if they were two fixed objects. Both the project and its lack of perceived leadership have important histories and will inevitably change over time. When making a statement about a process, use words more suited to processes: (e.g., "My perception of this project *today* is that for *several months now* we haven't had proper leadership.") When you hear a message containing inappropriate descriptors, ask for clarification. Remember, how you talk about *it* determines how you will think and act about *it;* so you'd better get *it* right!

3. *Never assume you know what someone else means when you meet him or her for the first time:* We tend to need *to learn* how to interpet the words and actions of others. This requires developing a relationship with them over time that allows us to explore the possibilities of mutual understanding and negotiation. The longer we know each other, the better able we are to use past experiences and information to guide present understandings. But to assume we know what each other means initially is to engage in behavior that virtually necessitates semantic distortion.

As you can see, language sensitivity and flexibility is an important part of your repertoire of communication skills. In the following section we describe a communication problem based on having too much, or too little, information at any one time.

Overload and Underload

Thus far we have described three communication problems commonly based in perceptual and language deficiencies. In this section we explore a communication problem based on a different human limitation—the limitation of needing more, or having too much, information.

There are two sources of information-based communication problems. *Information overload* refers to crowding too much information at one time into one channel. For example, let's suppose that you are managing four projects simultaneously, with a span of control encompassing twenty-eight individuals. Now let's suppose that all twenty-eight persons request a private conference with you on the same afternoon. Even if you could meet with each of them, your ability to remember, or act upon, the information they collectively gave you would be severely limited. You simply would receive too much data to comprehend.

Now assume that five of them request a meeting with you, and you successfully schedule and conduct the meetings. This time, however, you get *conflicting* data from each of the persons, and all of them leave the conferences expecting you to believe them, and to act upon their information. And while you are sorting out the data given to you, your telephone rings. Your superior requests a report tomorrow morning on all the projects. As you hang up the phone, your secretary announces that she is resigning, effective immediately, because of sexual harassment by your best friend. What do you do?

Clearly, the amount of information this harried businessperson must deal with goes beyond not only the call of duty, but beyond the capacities of her or his mind, given the time allowed for responses. This is a case of information overload, and it is a typical source of many communication problems in any organization.

The opposite of information overload is *information underload.* Information underload is characterized by a lack of necessary information needed to do a job, or to complete a process. For an example of information underload, let's return to our businessperson.

Let's say our manager stays in the office after hours to write the report requested by the boss. During this time our manager discovers that the five conferences held this afternoon, each one producing conflicting information, present a new problem: There is no way to describe accurately the progress made on any of the projects for the report because no matter who our manager believes, important information will necessarily be left out. In addition, there is no way for our manager to access information that might complete the report by the time it is due.

Confounding the situation further, let's suppose that the secretary who complained of sexual harassment and resigned this afternoon is seen by our manager returning to the office *with the best friend who was accused of the harassment,* arm-in-arm, smiling, laughing, and apparently enjoying some private joke that, by implication, has to do with our manager. Now, if you were our manager, and this was the situation, what would you think about your *relationship* with your secretary, your best friend, and, of course, about *their* relationship? Here again, information overload is the villain. Because you are constrained by time and available information to make decisions concerning your career, your secretary, your best friend, and your projects, no matter what you do you will miss important facts, omit potentially vital information, and do less of a job than you otherwise could do.

These two scenarios depict information overload and underload and point out how common they are. They also underscore an important fact of organizational life: Most of the time you will need more or less information than you have available. What can you do?

1. *Keep accurate records of all meetings, conferences, and other important communication situations.* You may not be able to overcome information overload or underload using this method, but you will be better able to produce documentation showing what information you did use to make decisions or implement them.

2. *Monitor your use of time carefully.* Try to learn how to budget your time and to make time during crises. If a report is requested and you don't, or can't, have the time to do a good job with it, explain the problem and see if you can negotiate a more amenable schedule.

3. *Stay in contact with your networks.* In the next section we discuss the importance of information networks. It is vital to be in touch with persons who can pass along information to you in addition to what you receive through formal channels. This can help you stay ahead of the competition and prepare for change, as well as understand how relationships between and among your peers, superiors, and subordinates are working out.

As you can see, communication problems are common to any organization. They also are impossible to overcome fully. No matter how carefully you prepare for and monitor situations and others, there will be instances in which your perception, language usage, overload, and/or underload will create problems. Becoming aware of these potential problems is useful because it can help you prevent them or respond to them effectively when they occur.

Next, we examine communication networks.

COMMUNICATION NETWORKS

The term *communication networks* refers to serial transmissions and receptions of messages, as well as to the types of information shared among identifiable groups of persons within organizations. In this section we explore (1) network functions, (2) network compositions and roles, (3) types of formal networks, and (4) types of informal networks. The objectives here are to demonstrate how knowledge, information, and persuasion are manifested among persons and groups in organizations over time and to reveal how personal and social relationships influence the overall operation of any organization.

Network Functions

From the grand view of the overall organization, communication networks function in three ways. First, networks *collect* information from different hierarchical levels within the company. Second, networks *disperse* the information throughout the organization. Third, networks *exchange* information, knowledge, and persuasion concerning whatever is being communicated within the organization at any time. Let's examine a typical example of how these three functions are carried out.

Networks are seldom considered to be networks by the persons maintaining them. Instead, employees working in organizations tend to think in terms of the *relationships* they have with other employees, and in some cases, the *reasons* they have for participating in these relationships. So it is in our example that Will D., a technical writer, finds himself communicating on a daily basis with Gloria S., a software analyst. Will and Gloria like each other and enjoy their conversations, perhaps even look forward to them. They are neither romantically involved nor do they see their relationship contributing to either party's professional success within the company. They are best described as individuals who maintain a friendly relationship simply because they are rewarded by the relationship they maintain.

One day, say, yesterday, although it could have been the day before yesterday, Will overheard his supervisor (Rhonda) explaining to her friend, an engineer (Ron), how much space would be required to hire additional technical writing personnel. Will believes they were talking as if a decision had already been made to expand the technical writing operation. This was news to Will. Because he was thinking about it, and because he happened to pass by Gloria's office on the way to deliver a report on a technical manual, he stopped in, told Gloria what he had just heard (as one of several topics they covered, including how Gloria's child, who had a fever, was doing, and why it was almost impossible to find a butcher who could properly butterfly a leg of lamb), and went about his business.

Later that afternoon, Gloria, during a conversation with another software analyst, mentioned the probable expansion of the technical writing staff. Her friend and fellow analyst, Sam, was pleased to hear about it, because, he supposed, it would mean shorter turnaround time for technical documents.

Sam, early the next morning, on his way to his terminal and much in need of a fourth cup of coffee, mentioned to a small group of people at the coffee machine that he had heard the technical writing staff was going to double in the next few weeks (why he said "double" instead of "expand" is unknown, but maybe he remembered hearing it that way, or perhaps he just assumed that all expansions are doubling efforts). The small group hummed over it for maybe 15 seconds, drank coffee, and went about their business.

One of the coffee drinkers, Paula, a chief engineer and another friendly acquaintance of Rhonda's, who happened to be having lunch with her today, mentioned the doubling of the writing staff while munching a Reuben. Rhonda paused, looked a little confused, and said, "That's the first I've heard of it. I knew we were requesting more office space, but I didn't know we were hiring more people. Come to think of it, perhaps now is the time to request those two junior positions we need. . . ."

As you can see, this small network would probably never have seen itself as a network. Instead, the persons involved in it saw themselves as acquaintances or friends or colleagues, and their serial transmission of a statement (and its subsequent semantic modifications) was just part of the ordinary flow of conversation between and among them. Nothing unusual here. However, from an analytical perspective on organizational communication, this *network* of individuals does exist as a network because it comprises a regular, routine passageway for messages involving different levels within the organizational hierarchy. Furthermore, the messages passed throughout this network reveal how information, knowledge, and persuasion are conducted within a network. By slight changes in the message, verbal modifications of key terms, and suggestions of future changes, organizational networks provide part of the operating dynamic of any company, creating realities.

Scholars examining this phenomenon in organizations have focused on three distinct (but sometimes overlapping) kinds of networks:[27]

1. *Social networks* consist of persons who communicate with each other on a friendly, nonprofessional basis. They are primarily interested in the *relationships* themselves, rather than in what the relationships can do for their careers. You can think of these networks as relationships based on gaining a sense of belonging, affiliation, and respect derived from maintaining your personal identity while you work.

2. *Expertise networks* are collectivities of persons who require professional information from each other to accomplish their tasks. These include managers and subordinates, peers and peers, and consultants and their liaisons within the company. Communication exchanged in these networks serves to aid in the plan, coordinating, implementing, and evaluating task goals and processes. You can think of them as networks based on gaining answers to questions related to tasks.

3. *Authority networks* consist of individuals who see profit in their professional relationships, including newcomers who associate with old-timers, peers who form mutually beneficial alliances, superiors and subordinates who maintain relationships because by coordinating their work efforts both can gain strategic advantages within the organization, and mentorships. These relationships are governed by the need to protect yourself from competition while gaining access to information that can improve your chances of succeeding on the job and within the company or field.

As you can see, there are good reasons to become a member of each one of these networks. In fact, researchers have clearly demonstrated that the more balanced your participation in these types of networks is, the more likely you will be satisfied with your job and with your work in the organization.[28]

Now that we have described the functions accomplished by communication networks, we need to analyze the roles played by individuals within them.

Network Composition and Roles

The term *composition and roles* refers to *how* network relationships are established and to *the communication functions* of individuals within those networks. One theorist, Gerald Goldhaber, defines the possibilities for network compositions using the following schema:

> The *role* that individuals play in a communication system is determined by their structural relationship vis-à-vis other individuals within the system. This relationship is defined by the pattern of interaction connecting the individual to the flow of information in the network. In current network terminology, three or more individuals whose majority of interactions are with each other are termed a *group.* Group members whose interactions are with members of other groups are termed *bridges.* Individuals whose interactions are mainly with members of two or more groups but who are not members of any one group are termed *liaisons.* Individuals who are relatively unconnected to the organization are termed *isolates.*[29]

From this perspective, the composition of networks is defined by the role carried out by individual members and the functions of the network within the organization. Now we examine research findings concerning network composition and organizational communication.

First, most information is typically shared within groups.[30] Persons who work together for the common accomplishment of an assigned task tend to discuss, argue, and negotiate more often, using a more diverse latitude of topics than does any other single composition of networks.

Second, persons cited as valuable sources of information in any organization tend to carry out *liaison* functions between and among groups.[31] These individuals always seem to be "in the know," and promote informal transmissions across networks. These persons also express more satisfaction with their jobs than do other categories of network members, primarily because they have access to information, are able to exchange information for perceived rewards, and enjoy the interpersonal privileges accruing from their status and influence as liaisons.[32]

Third, although liaisons tend to be well integrated into any organization, *isolates,* by definition are not. An *isolate* is a person who is essentially a loner, by either choice or the failure to induce others to respond to his or her desire for relationships. The isolate may be a communication apprehensive, or shy individual, who simply does not possess the social skills or initiative to build productive relationships.[33] The isolate may also be a person who has proven to be unreliable, untrustworthy, or incompetent on the job.[34] Research also indicates that isolates tend to be less mature, to be less decisive, to have a weaker concept of self, and to have a higher need for security than do liaisons or other group participants.[35]

Although liaisons and isolates define the ends of the network composition continuum, the great majority of individuals in organizations who simply do their jobs are described as either *participants* or *nonparticipants* in relation to their integration into functioning networks.

Participants are defined as individuals who are members of groups, who may participate in any or all three types of networks, but who generally do not hold a liaison capacity between groups. You can think of them as the general employee who is known as a team player but perhaps not as a leader or as an achiever.

Nonparticipants are defined as individuals who hold formal membership in the group but never really demonstrate "groupness." These are the persons who complete their assigned tasks but neither seek out nor enjoy social relationships with colleagues. They differ from participants in their level of affiliation with other group members; they differ from isolates in their demonstrated ability to communicate and maintain relationships, but are generally unwilling to do so.

Every organization contains liaisons, isolates, participants, and nonparticipants. In part, these basic descriptions allow us to differentiate among persons working in an organization while at the same time point out how their *communication processes* influence not only various organizational tasks and outcomes, but also their individual and organizational *identities.* Indeed, your identity is defined by what, and with whom, you communicate.

We now investigate types of formal networks.

Formal Networks

Formal networks include those relationships fostered by a mutual need among groups and individuals to accomplish formal tasks. As you will see, however, the organizational design of the given company influences how formal networks can and do function, as well as the roles played by individuals in them. Before we explore these important differences, though, we need to define two types of *knowledge* that characterize formal network communication: (1) absolute and (2) distributed.[36]

Absolute knowledge refers to any and all information or understanding that exists at any given time in an organization. You can think of this level of knowledge as "an organization's perspective" or the sum total of data held by all organizational employees used to generate understanding.

Distributed knowledge refers to how parcels of absolute knowledge are dispersed among organizational employees. You can think of this level of knowledge as "an individual's perspective" or the sum total of data held by any one employee about the general state of affairs within the organization.

It is useful to distinguish these types of knowledge when describing formal organizational networks because all descriptions of formal networks assume that every employee has equal access to information (which is seldom, if ever, true)[37] and that the sum total of any organization's knowledge is a definable, possibly quantifiable, entity (which is highly dubious).

Using these distinctions, we can generate a more realistic portrait of organizational knowledge and formal network structures. Begin with the assumption that all formal networks are "communicative communities" based on shared information derived from *different sources of knowledge distribution.* There is not likely to be "equal" access to knowledge or information in any communicative community. Instead, each network at best operates on *partial* information and knowledge that is shaped by their need for the information, their individual and collective uses of the information, and their personal goals. Put simply, all networks "politicize" data to fit their view of the organization and their perceived importance in the organization.

Given this portrait of knowledge, information, and networks, we can now describe not only the three types of formal networks in organizations, but we can also discuss problems associated with their access to, and use of, information: (1) decision-making networks, (2) decision-implementing networks, and (3) telemediated networks.

Decision-making Networks These are formal networks that include persons throughout the organization who are responsible for providing information and expertise relative to making decisions. These executives, managers, supervisors, and consultants hold positions of legitimate authority within the organization.

There are two distinct ways of viewing decision-making networks. First, tradition has it that persons who have risen to the top of their respective ladders within organizations tend to know and rely on each other to accomplish a wide variety of personal and professional goals. Known originally as the "good old boy" network in the industrial American South, and as the "old school tie" network in the industrial and financial centers comprising the eastern region of the United States, these networks are as intricate as private clubs and membership in them is generally exclusive.

A good example of traditional decision-making networks may be found in new and maturing organizations that grew up in high technology locales, which were established by a small group of professionals who began as friends or business associates from competing firms and are recognized by employees as the "people who started it all." Some younger colleges and universities that have maintained a strict hierarchy of persons with tenure also fit this traditional mold.

The second kind of decision-making network is made up of aspiring professionals in virtually every organization. These are the persons who collectively pool their talents to advance their careers by sharing information and persuasion across hierarchies and across departments. In many stable organizations, these networks vie for power with the more traditional network, and there is little, if any, cooperation between the two.

Both of these formal networks are characterized by active attempts to gain and maintain control by planning, making, and implementing decisions having short- and long-term effects. The primary motivation of the persons who make up the network is career advancement, which often closely resembles power plays, intimidation strategies, and communication rituals that symbolize their motives and their ability to make things happen.

As you might imagine, there are problems with decision-making networks. First, because authority and power is centralized, organizations including decision-making networks tend to be characterized by *downward communication* and a genuine *lack of upward mobility* among the middle managerial ranks. These antecedent conditions tend to produce bottlenecks in information flow, which in turn produce information overload and information underload among the persons who must implement the decisions without knowing enough about how the decisions were made, or, in some cases, even why they were made. It also produces morale problems because of the perceived lack of upward mobility among persons who generally aspire to improve their lot in the organization, which in turn inspires high rates of turnover in the managerial and professional categories.

Second, because decisions are made by a select few of the organization's members, often with little input from other sources, organizations may suffer from *Groupthink,* a condition characterized by high levels of cohesiveness among decision makers who fail to take into account alternative points of view.[38] Decisions may be made solely on the basis of the decision makers' self-perceptions of authority and expertise or on the basis of a previously favorable track record, neither of which may have direct or practical relevance to the decision at hand.

Third, organizations exhibiting tight and limited control over important knowledge and information tend to inspire competitive cliques and subcultures that protect themselves from the decision makers by simply following the rules to the letter. In this case we create minor bureaucracies that resemble medieval fiefdoms, complete with senseless wars fought for little gain beyond the momentary feelings of triumph.

As a result of reading this subsection, you may think that all decision-making networks cause negative outcomes. Clearly some do. However, most organizations are to some degree characterized by the presence of power holders and power seekers who form alliances to control decision making and its effects. These are real issues among organizational employees and must be treated as such in a text claiming to present a realistic portrait of communication in organizations.

Decision-implementing Networks   Decision-implementing networks include all personnel who are responsible for putting into operation decisions made by the decision makers. Usually these networks are characterized by midlevel personnel and first-line supervisors whose *personal and social relationship* figures heavily into perceptions of self and each other's legitimacy and worth. In many industrial organizations these networks include union and nonunion members whose allegiance to the union (or lack of it) contributes to the complexities of carrying out tasks and interacting with others who must help them carry out tasks. Within this type of formal network we find that many technical and secretarial personnel are active participants, although they may never be given credit for it.

Problems experienced within decision-implementing networks include disputes between union and nonunion workers over contracts, rights, treatment of subordinates, and levels of authority and supervision. We also find evidence suggesting that *personality conflicts* may seriously interfere with the ability of the network to induce cooperation among those parties who are responsible for implementing the decision. The presence of personality conflicts also tends to inspire the formation of personal loyalties and commitments instead of loyalty to the firm and commitment to the well-being of the project or even the organization. And, as you might expect, among decision-implementing networks there is a problem with information flow. Because much of the communication between persons is *lateral*, a lack of an effective chain of command may exist. In these cases, just as Max Weber observed long ago, the likely outcome is that *illegitimate lines of authority* will evolve among charismatic, manipulative personalities.

Here again, we caution you to recognize that although all organizations are characterized by the presence of decision-implementing networks, not all of them experience the most severe forms of abuse presented here. But some do.

Telemediated Networks   Among many contemporary organizations, networks are formed by linking computers and telephones and video screens to allow persons in different locales to communicate. This fact produces a new kind of network—the telemediated network.

Telemediated networks create the opportunities for sharing information, knowledge, and persuasion. They also assume that persons participating in them will be motivated to do so. Early reports from participants tend to indicate that although they appreciate the communicative freedom telemediated conferences and networks allow, they also create feelings of reticence about communicating, reluctance to share important data, and suspicions about how the data might be used.[38] One participant summed it up this way:

> In this building you learn to know who you can talk freely to, who you can trust. Hell, I don't know the guy on the screen from Adam—he's just a name on the chart. For all I know he could be my competitor next week. I bet he thinks the same way about me. So the result is that we speak in a kind of vague code to each other, never really getting to the heart of issues, never really cooperating as fully as we probably should. But the problem is that we don't know each other well enough to trust each other with important information. You can't expect people to form conference-call relationships without figuring out that they will be new and different relationships altogether.[39]

Despite the corporate rhetoric advocating the astonishing abilities of telemediated decision making, there are, nevertheless, simple human problems associated with using them. Perhaps these problems will diminish over time, as persons learn how to develop long distance relationships more effectively. But then, again, perhaps they will not.

Formal networks exist because they have to in order to conduct the business of the organization. They are seldom, even rarely, formed because of natural causes—perceived mutual interest, friendship, loyalty, trust, and so on—and instead, must be looked upon as being artificial. By the term *artificial,* we mean that people in these networks probably would not, if given the choice, choose to associate with the other persons in them. The networks exist, and relationships in them develop, because they must.

Now let's examine relationships that are created naturally—informal networks.

Informal Networks

Recall our introductory example concerning Will and his friends. What brought these persons together to exchange information? Clearly, they were not involved in decision-making, decision-implementing, or telemediated networks. Their example allows us to discuss the presence and meaning of another form of organizational network—the informal network.

Informal networks originated with the discovery of a *grapevine* which was responsible for passing messages between and among levels of hierarchy. Studies found that when managers/supervisors allowed messages to flow naturally "through the grapevine," more people possessed the information, even more than those who would read a formal memo or report.[40] Perhaps, more importantly, the *accuracy* of the received messages is consistently demonstrated to be between 78 to 90 percent.[41]

A *grapevine* is a network based on the freedoms of speech and choice. Freedom of speech ensures that whatever information, knowledge, or persuasion is available, it will be discussed among persons who have an interest in it. Freedom of choice allows for individuals to choose to whom they will communicate, or not to communicate equally among all persons, information, knowledge, or persuasion. The result is a network based on contacts, friendships, and eavesdroppers.

The presence of informal networks in organizations is a natural phenomenon. However, from the organization's perspective, this is a phenomenon with at least as much of a propensity for good as for evil. For example, although the accuracy of a received message is genuinely high, the messages passed through grapevines aren't always legitimate. Rumors, gossip, and speculation often are communicated in the language of fact, and once a statement is perceived to be factual, the more likely it will be repeated as a fact. People who base relationships on friendship seldom *question* the precise wording of rumors or gossip; they tend to be more concerned about the effects of the statement on themselves, and their jobs, than on the truth value of the actual words. Hence, from an organizational point of view, information that passes through the grapevine may be accurately received—unfortunately, it may be *in*accurately grounded. But how much information really is conveyed by gossip?

The International Association of Business Schools (IABC) conducted a study of over 45,000 hourly workers across the United States to discover how information was generated. The results of this study indicate that about 39 percent of all information is generated by gossip, second only to direct communication between and among workers and managers on issues related to the completion of tasks. In this study the relationship between the accuracy of the information and organizational reality was 52 percent.[42] As you can see, gossip is a major source of information in organizations, and furthermore, it has a slightly better than 50/50 chance of being true. Now, if you were going to base your decisions on information you received through the grapevine, would you be willing to stake your reputation on something that has *only* a *slightly better than pure chance* likelihood of being correct?

Some researchers make clear distinctions between the two types of informal communication (gossip and rumors) characterizing informal networks. Let's examine them in more detail.

Gossip and Rumors   Although these terms are often used interchangeably, each one actually defines a specific type of communication.[43] *Rumors* refer to vague or ambiguous situations and speculations about the future in which the ability of the communicators to substantiate the data is limited or absent.[44] For example, Will might learn that in addition to expanding the technical writing department, certain cuts may be made among the part-time graphics staff. Because this information is speculative, it is difficult to check out. And even if Will was able to check it out (with Rhonda, e.g.), she might not be able to tell him (if she was under pressure not to disclose the information), or she might not have heard the rumor herself (in which case it would seem that Will has access to decision makers which she doesn't have). And potential fact contributes to a second important definitional characteristic of rumors—they rely on *collaboration.*[45] A rumor must be articulated by one party, received by another party, and *together* they must collaborate on its importance and meaning.

Gossip differs from rumor in three important respects. First, although the truth of rumors usually cannot be verified, gossip produces information that may or may not be verified. Second, although rumors generally deal with the organization or department or professional, gossip tends to focus on individual employees' personal affairs. Third, rumors tend to produce *serial* communication among its hearers and tellers, whereas gossip tends to be perceived as *social exchange,* based on its commodity value.[46] For example, Will might *use* information he has about Rhonda's romance with a financier to gain power or status among his peers. Possessing gossip is more valuable than possessing rumors.

With these differences in mind, we return to our examination of the uses and meanings of gossip and rumors in informal organizational networks.

Informal Networks and Social Control   Several researchers discuss rumors and gossip as forms of social control.[47] In this sense *social control* refers both to the overt and covert mechanisms used to gain and maintain adherence to a particular, or preferred, way of doing things and recognizing power and status. For example, rumors are one major way in which the culture of any organization is communicated to newcomers. Specifically, this can be accomplished by explaining corporate histories *while* speculating about future opportunities, or naming names of power figures *while* detailing how a report is to be done. Rumors serve as social controls when they combine a personal view of the company with any otherwise relevant information. The result is a sharing of a personal perspective on the organization, a preferred way of doing things, and recognition of the power and status of others.

From a management perspective, rumor as social control has positive value. A rumor can be started by a manager, who, by placing information into the existing grapevine, can be sure it will find its way around. Hence, advance notice of layoffs or pay raises can become grist for the rumor mill—allowing, in the former case, some employees to look for work elsewhere (a humane rumor), and in the latter case, persuading employees who might be investigating opportunities for work elsewhere to remain (a persuasive rumor).

Second, rumors often serve as barometers of organizational health, increasing when the company is experiencing instability and change and decreasing when the environment becomes more stable.[48] The more you hear rumors, the more likely unstabilized situations are characterizing the organization. And, as the rumors diminish, you can assume that stability is reestablished. In this sense rumors provide a "sense of the place" which informs understandings about what is going on and why. Even if the rumors aren't entirely accurate, their presence in any organization serves as an indicator of the stability of the firm.

Gossip may also aid social control. Specifically, gossip can be targeted for a particular person. Let's suppose that a manager wants Candy to know that she is being promoted during the next review period. Further, suppose he can't tell her this information directly without risking his own future. However, he can praise her work to others who will in turn tell her about it, thus signaling to her the possibility of reward.

Perhaps the best way to sum up this section is to borrow a statement from Keith Davis: "No administration should abolish the grapevine. It is as permanent as humanity. It should be recognized, analyzed, and consciously used for better communication."[49]

Now that we have discussed formal and informal networks, we need to examine one final aspect of communication processes in organizations. These are the processes know as *rituals,* or those communicative situations that mark particular understandings of peculiar importance to persons in organizations.

RITUALS: LEARNING THE ROPES

All communication processes can be seen as ways in which any organization attains personal meaning for its employees. From talk designed to accomplish tasks to talk designed to spread gossip, communication processes are the lifeblood of any company, because they allow the company to do what it does. However, in this section we want to focus on the influence of special communication processes on the individuals experiencing them. Specifically, we will discuss the processes known as *rituals,* processes that create senses of arrival, full participation in the organization, belonging, and exclusion.[50]

Rituals of Arrival

Rituals of arrival refer to communication processes that let a newcomer know that he or she needs to learn the ropes of an organization before an individual identity can be recognized and respected by others. It's as if the members of the organization are saying "You have just *arrived* here from Planet Zero for all we know, and you have to learn what cuts it here if you plan to stay around."

Rituals of arrival include what appear to be, from the newcomer's perspective, strange and often "off-putting games." For example, one common ritual of arrival is known as "privileges." This ritual explains that newcomers aren't accorded the same privileges as everyone else; in fact, privileges must be earned. Depending on the nature of the given organization's culture, these rituals may include where you can park your car, which washroom you can use, and access past computer security clearances. Although they often seem to get in the way of progress and personal happiness, these rituals separate the newcomer from everyone else and ask for demonstrations of loyalty, desire for membership, and trustworthiness before rituals of arrival are officially removed.

Rituals of Full Participation

Rituals of full participation refer to verbal, nonverbal, and analogic perceptions of meaning about an individual's knowledge and place in the organization. As everyone who has been an employee recognizes, you are expected to participate in a wide range of work and social activities; however, *full participation* in them seems available only to persons who have demonstrated their leadership and understanding. These are the persons "in the know" who seem to exert informal and formal control over the organization and with whom relationships beyond casual friendliness are virtually impossible.

These rituals make most employees feel like just employees. They are designed to do exactly that. They say, in effect, "you can work here, be rewarded like anyone else, but there is nothing special enough about you to warrant full participation in decision making or in my cocktail parties." Mostly, these rituals are enacted through (1) *unwillingness to communicate* when communication is not only possible, but necessary; (2) *gestures of dismissal* in reference to a suggestion for change, or recommended plan of action; (3) *analogic signals* that indicate you don't possess the stripes to behave as a leader yet or that seem to comment on your mental capacities, judgment, and character as if something observed in them has been found lacking. In sum, these rituals let you know that you aren't ready to be treated for who and what you claim to be, or desire to be.

Rituals of Belonging and Exclusion

In literature classes you have studied the theme of "rite of passage," perhaps in Salinger's *The Catcher in the Rye,* or Roth's *Goodbye Columbus.* In these tales you discover that there are times when demonstrations of belonging are given by others and their ritual enactments are vital to the future identity and well-being of the character. By comparison, similar situations occur in every organization, and we refer to them here as *rituals of belonging.*

Some rituals of belonging resemble fraternity initiations. You are finally invited over to the boss's house for dinner, where he shows you the trophy room lined with awards, each one explained in reference to a battle won in the company. You are asked to keep these bits of information to yourself, to maintain the secrecy of the knowledge. In return, a bond is established between you and the boss, making you feel like you have finally been accepted as a person.

Other rituals of belonging concern work groups, or teams. In these settings you may be "set up" by the group, given some impossible task (e.g., locating a left-handed screwdriver or completing a computer program in a language you cannot decipher), and when you demonstrate how hard you are willing to try to do it, even though it can't be done, the group comes to your "rescue," and a good laugh is had all around. During the laughter you may feel both embarrassed (after all, any idiot would know there is no such thing as a left-handed screwdriver!) and elated (because, after all, the group rescued you), and the result is a sense of *transcendence*—you have "become" one of them, and forever separated yourself from those who will never be accepted.

The opposite of rituals of belonging are *rituals of exclusion.* These rituals are expressed in forms of digital and analogic communication that informs individuals that their talents, character, or personalities will never be accepted in this organization, or at least by this particular work group. Rituals of exclusion include informal invitations to group activities (going out for drinks after work, weekend get-togethers, etc.) that exclude one or two persons, and formal sanctions concerning the use of equipment, machinery, or office space that accord special privileges to some and not to others.

As you can see, rituals are important sources of communication in any organization. They allow the continuation of practices during times of struggle and change, providing an informal source of social and professional control. In short, they provide an individual with a sense of the place and a sense of their worth and identity within the place that ultimately matters a great deal to all of us.

SUMMARY

Communication processes *are* the organization. They create, maintain, modify, and change who, how, why, and what work gets accomplished and are responsible for defining the organization and its personnel to each individual member. Hence, communication processes are the organization; by observing and analyzing them you can arrive at an understanding of any organization.

This chapter investigated communication processes in organizations. First, we defined the nature of information exchange and encouraged you to view communication as a *commodity/investment,* to examine communication for its *digital and analogic* properties, and to see how communication is a *goal-oriented* process. With this method of "triangulating" your understanding of communication processes, you can learn how to analyze ongoing organizational patterns and outcomes.

Second, we investigated the four basic functions of messages in organizations. *Task* messages are those attempting to do the work of the company. *Integration and differentiation* messages are those providing a sense of belonging and individuality that is vital to the social and task processes. *Maintenance* messages contribute to the smoothness (or lack of it) of the operation and express levels of understanding and power relevant to the company. *Adaptation* messages refer to how the communication processes within the organization respond to the need for change and modification, both within and outside the organization.

Third, we discussed communication problems in organizations, describing serial, perceptual, and semantic distortions, as well as information overload and underload.

Fourth, we dealt with communication networks. We first described network functions and compositions. Then we detailed differences between formal and informal networks and the functions they serve in organizations. Finally, we discussed rituals in any organization that provide special understandings to employees.

This chapter provided a broad view of organizational processes, from private to public communication environments and actions. In Chapter 5 we explore one variety of communication activity toward which your understanding of this material should be directed—the interpersonal relationships and processes that characterize any organization.

ENDNOTES

1. Andrew S. Grove, *High Output Management* (New York: Random House, 1984), p. 48.
2. Sandra O'Connell, *The Manager as Communicator* (New York: Harper & Row, 1979), see especially Chapter 1.
3. Equity theories enjoy a long and distinguished tradition in scholarly research crossing many disciplines. For a complete treatment, see Elaine Walster, G. William Walster, and Ellen Bersheid, *Equity Theory and Research* (Boston: Allyn & Bacon, 1978), the major source from which the four propositions used here were developed. See also George Caspar Homans, *Social Exchange: Its Elementary Forms,* 2d ed. (New York: Harcourt Brace Jovanovich, 1972).
4. From Gerald M. Phillips and Julia T. Wood, *Communication and Human Relationships* (New York: Macmillan, 1983); see especially Chapters 7–10.
5. See H. Lloyd Goodall, Jr., "The Nature of Analogic Discourse," *The Quarterly Journal of Speech* 69 (1983): 171–179. See also Jay Haley, *Problem-solving Therapy* (New York: Harper & Row, 1976), pp. 81–99; and the pioneering work by Gregory Bateson and Don D. Jackson, "Some Varieties of Pathogenic Organization,"

in *Communication, Family and Marriage,* ed. Don D. Jackson, (Palo Alto, CA.: Science Behavior Books, 1968), pp. 200–215.

6. H. Lloyd Goodall, Jr., "Truth, Being, and Analogic Discourse in Relational Communication," paper presented at the Eastern Communication Association convention, Ocean City, MD, April 1983.

7. See Tricia S. Jones, "Sexual Harassment in the Organization," in *Women in Organizations: Barriers and Breakthroughs,* ed. J. J. Pilotta (Prospect Heights, IL: Waveland Press, 1983), pp. 23–38; see also Rosabeth Moss Kanter and Barry Stein, eds., *Men and Women in the Organization* (New York: Basic Books, 1978).

8. See Robert L. Scott, "Communication as an Intentional Social System," *Human Communication Research* 3 (1979): 258–268.

9. Eric Eisenberg, "Ambiguity as Strategy in Organizational Communication," *Communication Monographs* 51 (1984): 230.

10. See Henry Mintzberg, *The Nature of Managerial Work* (New York: Harper & Row, 1973), pp. 109–111.

11. See Frederick M. Jablin, "Superior-Subordinate Communication: State-of-the-Art," *Psychological Bulletin* 86 (1979): 1201–1222. See also H. Lloyd Goodall, Jr., "The Status of Communication Studies in Organizational Contexts: One Rhetorician's Lament After a Year Long Odyssey," *Communication Quarterly* 32 (1984): 133–147.

12. See Jablin, "Superior-Subordinate," pp. 1214–1215.

13. See D. Katz and R. L. Kahn, *The Social Psychology of Organizations* (New York: Wiley, 1966).

14. Michael J. Pacanowsky and Nick O'Donnell-Trujillo, "Organizational Communication as Cultural Performance," *Communication Monographs* 50 (1983): 126–147.

15. See Linda Putnam and Michael J. Pacanowsky, eds., *Communication and Organizations: An Interpretive Approach* (Beverly Hills, CA.: Sage 1984). All the essays in this volume contribute to this perspective.

16. For a complete account of this research style and tradition, see Robert Norton, *Communication Style* (Beverly Hills, CA.: Sage, 1984).

17. See R. Richard Ritti and G. Ray Funkhauser, *The Ropes to Skip and the Ropes to Know,* 2d ed. (Columbus, OH: Grid, 1982) for an excellent treatment of these ideas.

18. See Karl Weick, *The Social Psychology of Organizing,* 2d ed. (Reading, MA: Addison-Wesley, 1979).

19. From Lee Thayer, *Communication, and Communication Systems in Organization, Management and Interpersonal Relations* (Homewood, IL: Irwin, 1968), pp. 67–70.

20. See Daniel Yankelovich, *The New Rules* (New York: Random House, 1981); see also H. Lloyd Goodall, Jr. and Gerald Mr. Phillips, *Making It in Any Organization* (Englewood Cliffs, NJ: Prentice-Hall, 1984), especially Chapter 1.

21. See H. Lloyd Goodall, Jr., *Human Communication: Creating Reality* (Dubuque, IA: Brown, 1983), Chapters 3–6 for complete treatment of this systematic process.

22. Jablin, "Superior-Subordinate," pp. 1217–1218.

23. From Kenneth Burke, *A Rhetoric of Motives* (Berkeley, CA.: University of California Press, 1969).

24. Susan B. Shimanoff, "The Role of Gender in Linguistic References to Emotive States," *Communication Quarterly* 31 (1983): 174–179.

25. Constructivism is a general theory of human behavior derived primarily from the work of Harold Kelley and his associates. For a survey of the seminal work in constructivist theory, see Jesse Delia, "Constructivism and Human Communication," *The Quarterly Journal of Speech* 62 (1976); see also Peter L. Berger and Thomas Luckmann, *The Social Construction of Reality* (New York: Anchor Books, 1967).

26. See Basil Bernstein, *Language, Class, and Control* (New York: Oxford University Press, 1972) for a challenging analysis of the ways in which our social and educational institutions reinforce class-specific language codes.

27. These categories are derived from Karlene Roberts and Charles O'Reilly, *Communication Roles in Organizations: Some Potential Antecedents and Consequences.* Technical Report No. 11, Contract No. N000314-69-1054. (Washington, DC: Office of Naval Research, July 1975); see also by the same authors, "Organizations as Communication Structures: An Empirical Approach," *Human Communication Research* 4 (1978): 283–293.

28. See Tom D. Daniels and Barry K. Spiker, "Social Exchange and the Relationship Between Information Adequacy and Relational Satisfaction," *The Western Journal of Speech Communication* 47 (1983): 118–137; see also Barry K. Spiker and Tom D. Daniels, "Information Adequacy and Communication Relationships: An Empirical Investigation of 18 Organizations," *The Western Journal of Speech Communication* 45 (1981): 342–354.

29. Gerald M. Goldhaber, *Organizational Communication,* 3d. ed. (Dubuque, IA: Brown, 1983), pp. 148–149.

30. See Keith Davis, "A Method of Studying Communication Patterns in Organizations," *Personnel Psychology* 6 (1953): 301–312; see also Keith Davis, "Management Communication and the Grapevine," *Harvard Business Review* 31 (1953): 43–49.

31. See Roberts and O'Reilly, *Communication Roles,* 283–293.

32. See Daniels and Spiker, "Social Exchange," p. 119; see also Goldhaber, *Organizational Communication,* pp. 148–151.

33. See Gerald M. Phillips, *Help for Shy People* (Englewood Cliffs, NJ: Prentice-Hall, 1981) for complete treatment of the problem.

34. See Samuel C. Raccillo and Sarah Trenholm, "Predicting Managers' Choices of Influence Mode: The Effects of Interpersonal Trust and Worker Attributions on Managerial Tactics in a Simulated Organizational Setting," *The Western Journal of Speech Communication* 47 (1983): 323–339, for an account of the trust factor contributing to the problem of communication isolation.

35. Roberts and O'Reilly, *Communication Roles.*

36. From Richard V. Farace, Peter R. Monge, and Hamish M. Russell, *Communicating and Organizing* (Reading, MA: Addison-Wesley, 1977).

37. See Roger Jehensen, "The Social Distribution of Knowledge in Formal Organizations: A Critical Theoretical Perspective," *Human Studies* 2 (1979): 111–129.

38. See Irving Janis, *Groupthink,* 2d ed. (Boston: Houghton Mifflin, 1982).

39. These conclusions are based on personal interviews with persons involved in telemediated networks and should be considered, therefore, tentative. However, the problems cited are real; see Robert D. Gratz and Philip J. Salem, "Technology and the Crises of Self," *Communication Quarterly* 32 (1984): 98–103, for an analysis of some of the influences of technology on human communication.

40. Keith Davis, "The Organization That's Not on the Charts," in *Readings in Interpersonal and Organizational Communication,* ed. Richard C. Huseman, Cal M. Logue, and Dwight Freshley (Boston: Holbrook, 1973), p. 228.

41. Keith Davis, *Human Behavior at Work* (New York: McGraw-Hill, 1972); see also Evan Edward Rudolph, *A Study of Informal Communication Patterns Within a Multishift Utility Organizational Unit,* Dissertation, University of Denver, 1971; and Barbara June Marting, *A Study of Grapevine Communication Patterns in Manufacturing Organization,* Dissertation, Arizona State University, 1969.

42. See S. Friedman, "Where Employees Go for Information: Some Surprises!" *Administrative Management* 42 (1981): 72–73.

43. From Betsy W. Bach, "Rumor and Gossip in Organizations: A Review and Analysis," paper presented to Speech Communication Association annual convention, Washington, DC, November 1983.

44. J. M. Suls, "Gossip as Social Comparison," *Journal of Communication* 27 (1977): 164–168.

45. R. Shibutani, *Improvised News: A Sociological Study of Rumor.* (Indianapolis, IN: Bobbs-Merrill, 1966).

46. R. L. Rosnow and G. A. Fine, "Inside Rumors," *Human Behavior* 8 (1974): 64–68.

47. A. R. Rysman, "Gossip and Occupational Ideology," *Journal of Communication* 27 (1977): 64–68.

48. S. Yerkovich, "Gossiping as a Way of Speaking," *Journal of Communication,* 27 (1977) 192–196; see also Bach, "Rumor and Gossip," p. 17.

49. Keith Davis, "Management Communication and the Grapevine," *Harvard Business Review* 31 (1953): 43.

50. See R. Richard Ritti and G. Ray Funkhauser, *The Ropes to Skip and the Ropes to Know: Studies in Organizational Behavior,* 2d ed. (Columbus, OH: Grid, 1982) for a complete and entertaining treatment of these rituals.

three

COMMUNICATING IN ORGANIZATIONS: FORMS OF EXPERIENCE

chapter **5**

Communication Between Persons

Did you ever *not* know what to say?

Have you ever been standing next to someone you wanted to talk to but found that you couldn't speak because you didn't have anything you really wanted to say?

How many times have you argued with someone, reached a stalemate, and steadfastly refused to admit it because you didn't want to give up, or lose face, and yet at the same time you didn't have any other idea of what could be done to end the dispute?

What are you going to say the next time someone subtly insults you?

How will you handle the rumors that you hear? The jokes you don't want to be a part of? The stubbornness of a friend?

These are everyday communication problems. They are important to everyone because they are common to everyone, and yet chances are good that you may spend at least one third of your life in school without ever discussing them productively. If this happens, you could spend the remaining two thirds of your life consistently confronting these common communication problems without knowing what to do. And of that remaining time, a major portion of it will be spent at work, where the inability to communicate effectively in everyday situations can have disastrous consequences for your career.

This chapter is about everyday communication in organizations. It explores how and why persons talk to each other at and about work and provides a method for analyzing interpersonal relationships in organizational settings.

We begin by explaining the nature of interpersonal communication and interpersonal relationships in organizations. In this section we discuss varieties of interpersonal talk, from casual greetings with co-workers to making friends and enemies in the organization to communication between superiors and subordinates.

Second, we describe in detail the four levels of analysis that are important to our appreciation of how interpersonal relationships function in organizations and for the people involved in them.

Third, we examine problems associated with interpersonal communication and interpersonal relationships. In this section we provide a way to analyze conflict and suggest the means to overcome it.

As a result of reading and studying this chapter, you should be better able to approach the meaning of relationships you have at work, be more informed in order to understand communication in them, and to appreciate more deeply the complexities of talk that you otherwise might discount as being only "everyday" business.

THE NATURE OF INTERPERSONAL COMMUNICATION IN ORGANIZATIONS

Interpersonal communication refers to any establishment of meaning between two persons that is mediated by verbal, nonverbal, and/or analogic content. As you can see, the term includes a wide range of possible situations. In this section we define and distinguish five basic situations characterized by interpersonal communication: (1) phatic communions, (2) interviews, (3) making friends and being friendly, (4) being competitive and making enemies, and (5) superior/subordinate communication.

The Phatic Communion

Some communication is "just talk." For example, this morning you may have entered the building and spotted a person whom you almost know. What did you do? Probably you raised your hand, said "Hi!" and went on your way. The person whom you almost know probably returned the gesture and smiled. Both of you were engaged in meeting and greeting behavior, known as the *phatic communion,* but neither of you used the opportunity to engage in real talk, argument, negotiation, or relationship development.

The phatic communion was first described by a team of researchers led by Paul Watzlawick.[1] These researchers were interested in the ways through which communication creates, maintains, and modifies human relationships. The phatic communion represented one end of a theoretical continuum, a point or a *ritual situation marked by the presence of acknowledgment and friendliness,* without the exchanges characterizing other formal types of interpersonal communication. The other end of the continuum is romance/intimacy (see Figure 5.1). You can see that this kind of communication has specific characteristics.

The phatic communion should not be taken lightly. For example, what would you have thought if your acknowledgment to the person you almost know had *not* been returned? Probably you would have been offended. Your sense of being offended would have shaded your opinion of the person, and more than likely affected future interactions with him or her. You might even have determined that the perceived affront was intentional and malicious and decided not to speak to the person again. Or, given your inherent sense of good will and trust, you might have tossed it off as a minor social slight, perhaps an oversight on the other person's part; after all, perhaps he or she really didn't see you.

All these possible interpretations reveal the degree of relative importance

Phatic Communion	Friendliness	Friendship	Romance/Intimacy
Highly ritualized			Highly personalized
Public acknowledgment			Private bonding
Digital communication			Analogic communication
Cultural expectations govern analysis of talk			Acuity in psychology— analysis of talk
Vague goals for talk			Specific goals for talk
Over/Under self-disclosure			Appropriate use of self-disclosure
Trust has not been tested			Trust has been worked out
Future of relationship in doubt			Future of relationship stable

Figure 5.1   Interpersonal communication continuum.

you attach to phatic communions. Despite their highly ritualized nature, they possess social meaning, a sense of public etiquette that can be upheld or violated. If it is upheld, and the person returns your greeting, then all is well. If it is violated, then you engage in a search for meaning. As in most partial analyses of communication events, you become most concerned about, and conscious of, talk when something goes awry.

The phatic communion provides a private sense of participation in a well-established public ritual. It also *reveals membership in a particular community,* and, in some cases, allows for *status differences* to be demonstrated. One of the typical manifestations of status differences in phatic communions is embodied in the use, or absence, of titles (e.g., Mr., Dr., Mrs., Ms.), accompanied by names (e.g. Jones, Smith, Smilowitz). In some phatic circles there may be a Mr. Smilowitz (the boss) and a John (a subordinate), a Mary (a subordinate), and a Dr. Frank Jones (an outsider—probably a consultant). Within each organization's culture these distinctions are established and maintained through phatic communions. They allow the members of the community to acknowledge each other and the stability of their operation while at the same time distinguishing themselves from any nonmembers or outsiders (as in the case of the mysterious Dr. Frank Smith, a man with a title and both names).

Phatic communion may also be examined for evidences of familiarity and friendship among the participants. If greetings are given in a dry, humorless tone, with a high incidence of titles accompanying last names, and the virtual absence of first names, pet names, or initials, then you may infer there is a high degree of impersonality in them, usually a sign of the impossiblity of friendship between the phatic communicators. On the other hand, if you hear a lighter tone, perhaps accompanied by *heh-heh-heh*ing, pet names, initials, or general jocularity, you may infer there is a high degree of friendliness and probably friendship.

The presence of phatic communion, and its accompanying cultural, social, and personal signs and meanings, is an important kind of interpersonal communication in any organization. As a cultural display of acknowledgment, it sums up the relationships among the participants. As an inducement to more personal contact, it is an index of friendliness, a source of inferences about the character, attitudes, values, and behaviors of the participants. And as a source of organizational communication analysis, it is a place in which status differences, the stability of the relationships among members, and the common sense of community may be found.

Some talk may be just talk, but phatic communion is just talk that is *important.*

The Interview

Some forms of phatic communion can be thought of as "preliminary talk." The first time you meet someone in the organization you engage in phatic communion ("Hello. You must be from customer engineering—what should I call you?"), from which other relationship possibilities may emerge. If you decide to pursue other relationship possibilities, you generally will conduct what should be considered an *informational interview.*

Perhaps you think that interviews are only conducted to gain employment, appraise work, or become part of a public opinion survey or poll. Most people's concept of the interview is limited to these formal situations, but if you examine the *purposes* and *content* of initial conversations between persons who are potentially interested in developing a friendly (or romantic or friendship or competitive) relationship, you will find that it is, in fact, an interview.

The *purposes* of any informational interview are: (1) to gain data about the other person, in order (2) to guide all future decisions about how to deal with them, and (3) to compare the person to others you know for clues to their personality, character, and potential. The *content* of any informational interview consists of a connected series of questions and answers, characterized by the pretension of complete absorption in the situation, and marked by social etiquette and congeniality. Of course, the questions and answers may be well-rehearsed lines that carry no real meaning, and the pretension of absorption is commonly used by people to signal their interest when in fact there is little interest. The maintenance of rules of social etiquette and congeniality are comments on the ritual nature of the interview, but they also serve as ways to break the rituals, demonstrate creativity, reveal a sense of humor, or gain power. And, by choosing to violate the rules, the participants communicate their desire for a less formal, less ritualized relationship.

For example, let's say you meet this new woman, and, after exchanging names and departments, you say to her, "Well, so what are your goals on this project?"

She looks you directly in the eyes and says, "I want to find a man, a real man who can fulfill my wildest dreams. . . ."

While we wait for you to clear your throat, what do you think? If you are a woman, you might take this sample of talk as both a violation of the rules for social etiquette and a statement of priorities that might dramatically influence your evaluation of her character. If you are a man, you might think she is "coming on to you," or maybe she thinks you were "coming on to her" and she is letting you know what a fool you are. This little informal interview suddenly acquires new dimensions of meaning and importance. More to our point, however, is the issue of rule violation. As various scholars have indicated, when someone violates a conversational rule, you tend to think them "mad or bad."[2] Either they are crazy for not following the rules or wickedly interesting because they didn't follow the rules (which may mean they don't follow many rules at all).

You conduct informational interviews of this sort on a regular basis. Aside from *initial* interviews, you also conduct *news update interviews* when you check up on people you know to see how they are doing and what's new in their lives. Again, the purposes of your communication, as well as its content, reflect the structures and concerns of formal interviews, despite their informal nature.

A third form of informational interviewing is *counseling.* Virtually everyone, at some time, acts as a career/relationship/problem counselor to other persons within the organization. Some individuals become so well known for their ability to help others solve personal and professional problems that their skills become part of the folklore of the community. Here again, as a counselor, you ask and answer questions designed to gain access to information that can help you reach your objectives. You are engaging in interviewing behavior.

A fourth form of informational interviewing is the *formal discussion of a task with a supervisor or superior.* Generally the superior will ask and answer questions and use the session to see how well-informed members of the task group are and the nature of the individual characters involved. Despite its appearance as a *"discussion* of the task," the structure and content of the communication more closely resembles an informational interview. The superior is using the communication situation to discover and analyze information in much the same way as you might do when interviewing a potential employee about his or her ability to handle the job.

A fifth form of informational interviewing is the *appraisal interview.* These interviews are formal communication situations in which a superior provides a written and oral account of a subordinate's work over the review period. Most organizations use biannual performance reviews, although some companies prefer to do quarterly or yearly appraisals of work. The frequency of the appraisal interview is less relevant than its content. In virtually all cases, the appraisal interview represents a time for serious and frank discussions of work, goals, impediments to work, and perceptions of the task and of others. However, these opportunities are seldom realized because of (1) the *anxiety* usually associated with the appraisal interview[3] and (2) the unfortunate perception of appraisal interviews as places in which discussions of work are directly related to discussions of money and promotions.[4] These two influences are responsible for the general inability of the appraisal interview to be much more than a formal organizational ritual. The superior reviews the performance, the subordinate signs the form or files a grievance, and the real issue is perceived to be money.

The sixth form of informational interviewing is the *exit interview.* These are interviews conducted with departing employees, and can provide frank appraisals of the work situation in which the employee was involved, as well as reveal his or her reasons for leaving the company. Exit interviews have received scant attention in the research literature, and our understanding of them is limited to individual case histories. Little is known about the structure or content of exit interviews, and the rule seems to be that they differ from organization to organization.

A seventh form of interviewing is the *selection interview.* This is the most universal form of interviewing; every organization engages in it to find, through exchanges of communication, the most qualified persons for its jobs. Research indicates that candidates *who most closely resemble* the interviewers in attitudes, values, physical appearance, and behavior tend to make the best overall impression,[5] and the major characteristics of individuals hired for any job are: (1) their general level of confidence, (2) their ability to communicate, especially their articulation and language usage skills, and (3) the way they talk about educational and work experiences related to the position applied for (e.g., use of clear examples to document expertise, use of rational approaches to problem solving and decision making, etc.).[6]

These research findings shed light on the role of communication during selection interviews, but they also seem equally important in our understanding of *any* of the interviewing situations in organizations. People generally tend to feel closer to others who most closely resemble their attitudes, values, physical appearance, and behavior. We tend to use talk as an index of intelligence, rationality, knowledge about a subject, and level of experience in every situation. Perhaps this is as it should be. After all, the interview is a pervasive form of communication in all organizations.

Making Friends and Being Friendly

Most interpersonal communication is conducted between persons who maintain friendly relationships. By *friendly,* we mean that there is a mutual perception of interest, trust, empathy, and cooperation between the participants. However, as the old saying goes, "There are friends, and there are *friends.*" The *degree* of interest, trust, empathy, and cooperation varies with the relationship. Most people make important distinctions among "just friends," "friends," "close friends," and "my best friend," and conduct these relationships with those distinctions in mind.[7]

Making friends and being friendly are not the same. As we discussed earlier, we exhibit phatic communion with most persons with whom we work. These ritual exchanges signal our level of friendliness, indicating that we are capable of "being friendly." We seldom notice these exchanges unless our expectations for reciprocity are violated; for example, you say, "Hi! How are you doing this morning?" to someone who greets this statement with a cold, blank stare and then turns and walks away from you. Unless you are motivated to find out what is wrong, you will probably just "let it pass," and attribute it to the other person's being unfriendly, or troubled. However, if the other person is someone you consider to be a "friend," you will be less likely to let it pass.

Organizations thrive on a spirit of cooperation that often fosters friendships among employees. Although everyone would probably prefer to work among friends, the presence of friendships appears to be at best a mixed blessing to organizations. For example, although researchers generally assume that productivity should be positively related to job satisfaction (which includes relational satisfaction), studies have been unable to demonstrate that the happy worker is, in fact, more productive than the unhappy one.[8] Furthermore, when friendships develop among co-workers who also compete for raises, promotions, and status, the success of one person can mean the demise of others. Research indicates that one of the most tenuous times in a worker's career occurs when she or he is promoted over persons with whom friendships were maintained.[9]

Making friends and being friendly is an important part of interpersonal effectiveness. Certainly we would not encourage you to avoid making friends or being friendly; the point here is far more subtle. You need to *monitor* your relations with others with the awareness of the equipotential for relational satisfaction and dissatisfaction as a realistic outcome of your tenure on the job.

A recent trend in studies of organizational relationships concerns the special problem of men and women who maintain friendships on the job. The problem is deceptively simple if you believe that the gender differences between men and women lead to differences in attitudes, values, goals, and behavior. This perception of difference, rooted in the biological, cultural, and social prejudices with which we mature, often encourages us to use simplistic categories and abstractions to explain more complex attitudes and actions. For example, if a male employee sees a female employee crying, he may attribute her behavior to the "fact" that women are more emotional than men. His attribution may prevent him from understanding the real nature of her distress, and perhaps, more importantly, may create a false sense of dominance over her. Guided by what he unfortunately believes to be a right-minded appreciation of women, he may choose to behave in a wrongheaded way.

Friendships between women and men in organizations are a normal aspect of any company's evolution. However, what appears to be "normal" in an evolutionary sense often causes turmoil among those experiencing the evolution. Because relations between the sexes are learned during adolescence, when the emphasis is less on friendship and more on sexual exploration, the mutual perception of sexual differences may interfere with the development of friendships based on neither romance nor sexuality in later working life. In fact, in a study of over 4000 persons conducted by Phillips, Wood, and Goodall, over 95 percent of the men surveyed indicated that they could not conduct a relationship with a female without sex being an issue, whereas slightly more than 80 percent of the females indicated they did not believe sex was an issue in relationships with men.[10] Many women reported being surprised by sexual invitations and demands from men who they considered to be "friends." And in some cases, women believed they either lost career opportunities or their jobs because of sexual misconduct or misunderstanding.

Making Enemies and Being Competitive

Perhaps you believe that you are incapable of making enemies or of letting your sense of competitiveness interfere with your friendships. This is yet another myth commonly clung to by women *and* men. And, as with the myth of sexless friendships between women and men, it is equally damaging to your understanding of the complexities involved in communicating interpersonally in any organization.

The next time you visit your college bookstore, peruse the titles in the business/career section. In addition to various guides to getting ahead, you will undoubtedly also find many titles dealing with how to overcome interpersonal difficulties at work. Count them. Chances are you will find there are at least as many books written giving advice about dealing with difficult people as there are books about dealing with career success. Do you suppose these books would be published if there wasn't a clearly defined market for them?

People problems permeate most organizations. Persons may not get along with each other, may in fact despise the sight of each other, and yet have to work in close proximity. No job guarantees that you will like the people you work with and for. And among those you don't like, chances are good you will find at least one outright enemy.

Enemy communication is something we know little about. But enemies do communicate interpersonally, and they represent one category of adult experiences available to you in any organization. Now let's focus on a theme that organizations, and the persons who work within them, thrive upon—being competitive.

When you go to work you will usually select your friends from those persons with whom you compete most directly for rewards. Probably, you will spend the majority of your working day interacting with persons who work in the same basic physical space, and who do approximately the same task, for roughly the same amount of money and status. Within this environment you will strive to be friendly, cooperative, ... and competitive. You may like the person who sits at the desk next to yours but you hope you receive the raise or promotion. In this way we compete with our friends, and the sense of competition between or among us is something about which we seldom speak.

Nevertheless, it is *there,* the unseen quest at every conversation. Consider your talk with a co-worker. How much of it includes subtle innuendos indicating the desire to demonstrate greater intelligence, skill, or ingenuity? How many times do you later recall a casual remark and wonder if anything was "meant" by it? As a recent scholarly book puts it, one basic theme of human conversation is *war,* not peace.[11] Listen carefully to the words we chose to use when discussing our talks with others:

"I really *destroyed* that guy in the meeting today!"

"She *demolished* my arguments about cost accounting."

"He is a *treacherous* person, you never know when he will *blow up* on you."

"You should be careful what you say to her. I think she's a *spy* for the boss."

"When he said that to me, I just *exploded!*" And so on.

Our talk is competitive, guided by a sense of war that we seldom articulate. We are constantly doing battle with words, seeing who can undercut the best, overstate the most, get in a word before the fighting starts. For this reason, being competitive is an important part of your understanding of how interpersonal communication in organizations operates.

Superior/Subordinate Communication

The majority of published research about interpersonal communication in organizations concerns the effects of status differences on choices of words and actions and on perceptions of relationships based on status differences.[12] One assumption these studies exhibit is the need to perceive the influences generated by status differences in organizations. For example, how important is the talk initiated by a subordinate to his or her superior? Or, do superiors tend to talk more or less than subordinates? The results of work done in this tradition indicate the following statements to be true:

1. Subordinates tend to overestimate the value and importance of their communication to superiors.
2. Superiors tend to think they spend more time communicating interpersonally with subordinates than they actually do.

3. Superiors tend to value communication directed toward the accomplishment of assigned tasks and duties rather than toward phatic communions or varieties of talk designed to demonstrate friendliness.
4. Subordinates feel high levels of anxiety about talking with superiors; the higher the rank of the superior is, the more anxiety they feel. These feelings of anxiety often interfere with their ability to communicate effectively.
5. Superiors are more likely to initiate interactions with subordinates. They are also more likely to be less satisfied with these episodes than are subordinates.
6. Superiors believe they communicate more effectively than their subordinates believe they do.
7. The more influential the superior within the organization or professional field is, the more likely subordinates will try to communicate with them. As superiors lose their perceived influence, there is a corresponding loss in attempts at communication with them by subordinates.
8. If a superior is perceived to have "too much influence," openness decreases between superiors and subordinates.
9. Successful communication between superiors and subordinates appears to be a "given case" phenomenon. No consistent trait, characteristic, or feature of communication style, personality, or professional expertise has been found to be effective in every situation.

As you can see, research about superior/subordinate communication provides insight into everyday situations. It helps explain, for example, why a boss might forget what a secretary told her, even though the secretary also told her boss it was important—unless the boss initiated the interaction, most likely she would not perceive it to be very important. It also helps explain why you might feel somewhat uneasy discussing a problem with an instructor—differences in status tend to create feelings of anxiety that contribute to strained communication.

You should approach these generalized findings with caution. As Benson points out, what is absent from most of the research literature is any consistent understanding of *power* and status. It might be easier to measure status, but power is usually at least as important as status in organizations.[13] Furthermore, as Goodall argues, to perceive status differences in every relationship all the time is to behave neurotically. This does not mean people aren't aware of status differences, but the importance of status differences might be grossly overestimated.[14]

Now that we have discussed the varieties of interpersonal experiences in organizations, let's deal now with how individual analysis can be accomplished.

LEVELS OF ANALYSIS FOR INTERPERSONAL RELATIONSHIPS

In addition to the varieties of interpersonal relationships we experience at work, there are also different *levels of analysis* we use to understand those relationships.

Interpersonal relationships are analyzed at four levels—the cultural, organizational, social, and personal levels.

When using the term *levels of analysis* we are referring to the *kinds of information* we employ to make sense out of our communication with others.

There are four levels of analysis—four kinds of information—typically available to organizational employees: (1) cultural, (2) organizational, (3) social, and (4) personal. In this section we describe each of these levels of analysis and show you how these different kinds of information contribute to different understandings of your relationships with others.

The Cultural Level

As pointed out throughout this text, the term *culture* is important to any interpretation of organizational relationships, and to the organization itself. *Webster's Dictionary* defines a culture as "the integrated pattern of human behavior that includes thought, speech, action, and artifacts and depends upon man's capacity for learning and transmitting knowledge to succeeding generations."[15] From this general definition you can see how a culture can be described by its most prominent features: pattern, human behavior, thought, speech, action, artifacts, transmitting knowledge to succeeding generations. These focal points in the definition give us a way of seeing what a culture consists of and how it attains meaning for insiders and outsiders.

But a culture is more than the sum of its parts. Examining the communication and artifacts of a culture might provide insights into *what* a given culture believes to be important, but it does not provide a way to see *how* people within the culture used the artifacts and communication to create cultural understandings and meanings. It is similar to looking at an organizational chart, collected interdepartmental memos and reports, and the organization's physical environment to describe how decisions are made within the organization.

An anthropologist, Ward H. Goodenough, encourages us to view culture slightly differently. For him, a culture "consists of standards for deciding what is, standards for deciding what can be, standards for deciding how one feels about it, standards for deciding what to do about it, and standards for deciding how to go about doing it."[16] He believed the meaning of any culture must be located in shared standards that allow the communication and the artifacts to be used in particular ways, and not in other ways. As you can see, this would be a difficult, if not impossible, task if all you had to go on was the organizational chart, memos, reports, and the physical building or plant. The problem would be that the *information* you used to perform the analysis would have no starting place—no sense of the human standards within the organization that have evolved over time and through the efforts of specific decision makers.

A culture, then, encompasses a way of making decisions.

In the following discussion we describe two ways in which culture enters into decision-making processes. First, we show how *different* cultural understandings function to *divide* people by allowing communication decisions to be rooted in different standards. Second, we show how *shared* cultural understandings function to *unite* people by allowing communication decisions to be rooted in commonly held standards.

Culture as Divider   Think of a culture as standards, both overt and subtle, used to guide human decision making, and you begin to get a sense of how the cultural level of analysis operates. Now consider how *different* cultural understandings can interfere with communication decisions. For example, let's say you meet a new employee and your job is to orient the person to the company. What happens?

First, you are affected by each other's nonverbal communication. You notice each other's race, size, shape, coloring, clothes, and general demeanor. All of these sources of information are used *in reference to* previous cultural understandings you have developed over time. During this mutual appraisal you may be exchanging names and basic information about your employment in the company, and you gain access to other cultural data—the sound of each other's voices, the way words are pronounced—and again, you compare the data you are receiving to other data you have about persons of this type. In effect, you are creating a *cultural profile* of each other, trying to fit each other into a preexisting pattern of information that helps you make decisions about how to act and what to say. These "first impressions" are very important because they guide your decision making about each other; however, research indicates they are also highly fallible. Because you are relying on cultural standards that are abstract categories (e.g., white southern female; articulate black male; etc.), the inferences you make tend to be culturally specific rather than person-specific.[17] Simply put, you are treating a unique human being as just another member of a general category of persons about which you have predetermined attitudes, values, and beliefs. The standards you are using are cultural standards; they inform your decision making and shape how you create impressions in your own mind about each other.

Let's continue the example. Suppose you are asked to show Mary Jo, a new employee, the company. After the initial greetings are completed, you walk down a long corridor to a set of partitioned offices. As you walk, you say, "Here is the finance department, and you need to meet Ed, the guy who really runs the place." Your initiate nods in nonverbal agreement. "Ed, this is Mary Jo—I'm sorry, I'm no good with names, what's your last name again?"

"Thomas." She smiles at Ed.

"Yeah, Thomas. You'll be Mary Jo around here anyway."

Let's stop the example here and examine what has taken place. First, you have given her several important clues to the culture of this particular organization. You have informed her that Ed is the informal power figure in the finance department, and perhaps that she didn't make a good enough first impression to leave the imprint of her last name, and that, in fact, last names are not important in this company. However, you may have a bad memory. You may have used your bad memory to create an understanding that is invalid. Or, you may simply be letting her know that women are treated as inferior species in the finance department.

The issue centers, then, on how Mary Jo Thomas is going to make sense of these possibilities. How are her cultural understandings going to shape her responses to these people? What should she believe, and what should she do?

Let's say Mary Jo Thomas is a feminist; furthermore, that she left her last job because of the poor treatment accorded females from the males. Perhaps the conversation takes this turn:

"You may have forgotten my last name, but I haven't." Mary Jo smiles at Ed. "I'm pleased to meet you, Mr.?"

"Wilson, Ed Wilson, Miss Thomas." Ed offers his hand, which she shakes firmly. "I understand you are the new auditor."

"Yes, I am. And I understand you have some serious difficulties in your auditing group. Should we talk about them now, or should I continue with the company tour?" She rolls her eyes menacingly at you.

Let's stop the example again. What has occurred? Clearly, Mary Jo Thomas is asserting herself, and at the same time letting both males know she intends to be treated professionally. Moreover, she has signaled her displeasure toward your actions and her boredom with your guided tour. She is interested in getting down to work.

However right-minded Mary Jo Thomas appears to be in this scenario, she is nevertheless allowing her previous negative associations with males to interfere with this interaction. Also, she is ignoring the cultural signals she is receiving from both Ed and you. Let's pick up the conversation.

"Well, I'd love to get down to business, but I'm sure the company tour is important too. Why don't you drop by sometime later today?"

"Fine." Mary Jo Thomas checks her watch. "Shall we say around two?"

"If that's okay with you two that's fine with me."

"I'm sure we'll be finished with the company tour by then," you say.

"Can't that wait? I'm anxious to get started." Mary Jo looks at Ed and seems to ignore you.

"Fine with me," you say. "Ed, I'll need those reports before noon. Maybe you can go over them with Ms. Thomas so she can see how we do things around here."

"Okay, Bob."

Mary Jo Thomas looks confused. "But I thought you were just a person giving me the standard tour. . . ."

"I was," you reply. "But I'm also in charge of the finance division. Welcome aboard, Ms. Thomas. And I'll be sure not to forget your name."

End of scenario.

We have pointed out that most people don't analyze communication until something goes wrong. In this case Mary Jo Thomas may realize the need to do some serious thinking about her behavior. If she does, she should begin her analysis at the cultural level, where the standards informing the judgments of all three persons involved in this example were based.

Cultural level analysis begins with an assessment of *the attitudes* of the participants that shape their choices of behavior and an investigation of *the scene* in which the action occurs.[18]

The attitudes   Kenneth Burke advises us to examine an attitude as a vocabulary, out of which "emphases, standards, desires, kinds of observation, expression, and repression" form a way of understanding an occupation as a kind of culture.[19] The sum total of attitudes prevalent in any organization form an *ideology,* to the extent that Burke suggests the terms *ideology* and *culture* are synonymous.[20]

In reexamining our previous organizational example, you will find that Mary Jo Thomas did not possess the cultural understandings that would have aided her initiation. Because her talk violated these taken-for-granted assumptions, word might get around that she didn't possess the proper "attitude" for the job. In this way, the complexity of an organization's culture can be seen in the ordinary judgments passed by people like Ed. From his perspective, as Kenneth Burke would put it, the new woman's attitudes were inappropriate—she didn't fit in.

The scene   Every culture owns and inhabits a physical and psychological space. When discussing an organization's culture, we include consideration of its physical properties: buildings, offices, machines, work spaces, corridors, conference rooms, and symbols. These are the places in which the work of the organization is accomplished, the environment of human purposes directed toward organizational objectives.

Within these environments you will find important clues to the organization's culture. How the offices are sized and separated, where important machines are located, the symbols used to convey the name of the organization and the status of its inhabitants, and even the letterhead on the company stationery are sources of cultural knowledge. If you think about these spaces and symbols as simply the "workplace," you miss an important opportunity to understand the meaning of culture.

For this reason, we believe you should think of an organization's environment as *scenes*—as places in which action occurs, dramas of work are played out, and heroes, heroines, and villians contribute to a shared reality. In short, we are asking you to think about an organization's environment as scenes, or stages, on which dramas are acted out.

Consider the last time someone recounted a situation to you. Try to remember his or her use of language and the level of involvement with the plot. Chances are the person told a story as complete as a Greek tragedy or an Elizabethan drama, with an opening, some rising action, a climax, and perhaps, if the scene called for it, some resolution or ending. The telling of the story is the key. The individual wasn't objectively describing a neutral environment; this was his or her life he or she was talking about—full of passion, intensity, power, and ambiguity.

When you acquire a dramatic appreciation of working in any organization, there is no *environment,* but instead, there is a *scene.* The term *scene* refers to the physical and psychological setting as it is enacted by participants in the drama —it is the *interpretation* of the situation, an interpretation charged with cultural *attitudes,* expressed in a vocabulary that *belongs* to it.

The terms attitude and scene describe much of any organization's culture. For this reason, it is vital to remember that the cultural level of analysis requires access to the thoughts, passions, and actions of the persons who work in the organization. Through an appreciation of their language use and meaning, as well as the artifacts they manipulate and pay tribute to, we can acquire a fuller appreciation of culture. Moreover, *cultural level understandings must inform all other levels of analysis.* From attitudes come a perspective on the language of scenes, out of which other levels of analysis evolve.

One note of caution is in order. Mary Jo Thomas didn't possess cultural understandings of our organization. Hence, her attitude would be alien to the scene. Truly, she might not be able to understand the meaning of what happened to her because she doesn't yet possess the language capable of accurately describing it. This is an important issue because of what Kenneth Burke calls a corollary to any attitude, which is, as he puts it, a "trained incapacity," or "terministic screen." These terms refer to the power our attitudes have to shape and control our understanding. From Mary Jo Thomas's point of view, she "made a stupid mistake," but from Ed's point of view, she "violated the unwritten law," and "doesn't fit in." Because each one of them has a distinct perspective, or attitude, toward the scene, they also have a "trained incapacity" to see the scene from the other's point of view.

Culture as Uniter Communication has the equipotential for cooperation or competition, for dividing or uniting persons. In the previous pages we demonstrated how communication rooted in different cultural understandings functioned to divide persons, to create a spirit of competition instead of cooperation.

In this section we focus on the more positive aspects of an organization's culture by demonstrating how shared cultural understandings promote *identification* among persons which contributes to shared organizational realities and feelings of unity.[21]

Let's begin with a familiar example. You are responsible for initiating a new employee, Ms. Mary Jo Thomas, into the finance section of your organization. You greet Ms. Thomas at the reception desk, and both of you engage in the kinds of nonverbal analyses described earlier. Imagine, if you can, that you are a black male, she is a white southern female, and although your cultural backgrounds are dissimilar, you share a professional commitment to the world of finance.

"Good to see you, Ms. Thomas. Your first name is Mary Jo?"

"That's right. And your first name is . . .?"

"Just call me Bob. Everyone does. In fact, around here first names are used exclusively."

"That sounds friendly."

"We think so. We like to believe that we are a kind of extended family—after all, we spend at least eight hours a day here."

"I see." Mary Jo looks a bit confused. "Are you from the personnel office? I was told someone would show me around, but I wasn't told whom to expect."

"No, I'm the head of the finance division." You smile.

"Oh, well, I'm *sorry,* I . . ."

"No need to apologize. Sometimes I wish I did work in personnel—those guys never have to deal with the hard facts numbers provide. Shall we go?"

"Yes, I mean, go ahead."

"I understand you know Sally Deerfield."

"Yes, I do. She and I went to school together."

"She says good things about you. In fact, her recommendation meant a lot to me. Around here we like to get personal recommendations from employees we already know and trust. It helps to eliminate the problems of hiring people who just don't fit in."

"I see. Well, I'm sure glad Sally recommended me."

"I'm sure you'll do just fine. I want you to meet Ed, the guy who really runs this place."

This time our initiate got off to a better start. Mary Jo was properly deferential to Bob, even though she didn't know that he was her boss. Furthermore, Bob may have been more tolerant even if she had been less deferential simply because his attitude toward her had already been shaped by a trusted employee—Sally. Despite their many cultural differences, both Bob and Mary Jo shared an association with Sally, and through this human connection a source of *identification* was articulated.

Obviously we have manipulated this scene. The purpose here is to alert you to two important facts concerning cultural level analysis and communicative decision making. First, *nothing exists until it is communicated.* To share anything in common requires communication of commonality. Bob and Mary Jo share Sally in common, but until Bob said so, that possible source of unity did not exist in Mary Jo's mind, nor in her *relationship* with Bob. Communication brings unity and identification into existence.

Second, *identification can transcend cultural differences by creating new sources of unity that are culturally more relevant than are the differences.* Despite racial and hierarchical differences between Bob and Mary Jo, their common relationship with Sally was more relevant to decisions guiding their choices of communication than were the differences. If both parties in a relationship recognize the increased relevance of a shared attitude, relationship, or understanding, and use this recognition to guide communication decisions, the result can be unity where division previously existed.

Summary of Cultural Level Analysis

We have devoted a good deal of space to indicating the importance of cultural level analysis of communication. We do this because the culture of any organization is the starting place for any informed understanding of interpersonal communication and interpersonal relationships within that organization.

In summary, a culture is composed of standards that influence thoughts, passions, actions, and judgments—a way of making decisions about communication. There are two channels through which cultural level analysis proceeds: (1) *nonverbal channels* carry information about a person's race, size, shape, physical appearance, clothing, and level of articulateness, and about an organization's physical environment, machines, offices, symbols, and use of space; and (2) *verbal channels* carry information about interpretations of personal and organizational attitudes, scenes, and sources of identification and division.

Communication is the vehicle of cultural level analyses, and communication is always capable of uniting or dividing persons based on cultural understandings, misunderstandings, perceptions, and misperceptions. Although culture is vital to any appreciation of communication, certain communication choices can *transcend* cultural divisions by pointing out sources of identification relevant to the given scene. Because of trained incapacities and terministic screens in any organizational culture, these transcendent sources of identification are perhaps the only viable means for humans to overcome their cultural biases.

Now let's examine the second component in your understanding of interpersonal communication—the organizational level of analysis.

THE ORGANIZATIONAL LEVEL OF ANALYSIS

When thinking about any organization you may mentally create structural categories: purpose and objectives of the firm, chain of command (hierarchy), types of work done in the company, relative authority or power found in particular departments, and the like. When you begin thinking this way, you are engaging in an organizational level of analysis—a level characterized by a focus on *the systematic accomplishment of tasks.*

In this section we examine the ways in which the organizational level of analysis proceeds, from assessment of goals to assessments of work flows, in order to help you see how consideration of the organization provides important information about interpersonal relationships. We describe (1) the formal goals and objectives of the company, (2) the levels of command or hierarchy, (3) the types of work accomplished within the company and the relative authority or power in those departments, and (4) the flow of work through the organization, with special attention to the human relationships responsible for getting the job done.

Goals and Objectives

Understanding the goals and purposes of any organization are important in your assessment of the *functions* of interpersonal communication. Every human relationship can be characterized as *task related* or *socially oriented*—these relationships function to accomplish organizational goals or social objectives.

In most organizations, however, you will find that some relationships combine task and social functions. For example, there appears to be some evidence suggesting when task and social functions are combined, communication within the organization is enhanced.[22] This research focuses on the *network* characteristics of organizations and assumes that combinations of task and social functions contribute to communication flows through an organization. Furthermore, this research seems to be in line with other work suggesting persons are happier when they receive information about the company, the job, and each other. However, we have very little evidence of long-term organizational effects. For instance, when social and task functions become a routine, expected characteristic of work relationships, and the relationships change (e.g., one party receives a raise/promotion, one party moves to another company, or the relationship deteriorates), the organizational *network* may be adversely affected. Hence, the relationship between communication functions and organizational effects may be tenuous.

You need to learn *to discover the purposes of an individual's communication within the contexts of his or her task and social functions.* This will improve your understanding of relationship and communication functions at the organizational level of analysis. You learn to see that Quintin is not just another systems analyst whom you know at work; he is also responsible for solving programming problems assigned to the investment group and maintains strong social relationships with his superior, Helen, and perhaps two or three other systems analysts from other departments. The goals and objectives dimension of the organizational level of analysis encourages you to view each person in relation to his or her task and social functions. From this kind of analysis you can learn to: (1) define social and task functions within relationships, (2) assess the relative importance of social and task functions for your relationships with others, (3) understand how your communication might travel through the organization (who talks to whom about what), and (4) establish relational priorities to enhance your job performance and career possibilities.[23]

Levels of Command/Hierarchy

All humans are, as Kenneth Burke puts it, "goaded by a spirit of hierarchy, and rotten with perfection."[24] As we have consistently pointed out, perception of and responsiveness to status differences in any organization are major topics of the organizational communication research tradition.[25] Hierarchy is an important feature of the organizational level of analysis, because part of our understanding of other people is based on *how we stand in relation to them,* in terms of physical appearance, social skills, educational attainment, professional field, popularity, importance, wealth, health, and even knowledge of trivia. When Burke writes that we are "goaded by a spirit of hierarchy" he is suggesting that we treat superiors differently from how we deal with inferiors and that we desire to be more like superiors than like inferiors. In part, this "natural" ambition is responsible for the human creation of the chain of command in any organization, which is a symbolic invention allowing one person to tell other people what, how, and when to do something. The implied payoff for this sort of behavior is the promise of advancement, a relationship, or more money, which allows subordinates to *identify* with superiors.

Research has demonstrated that both social and task perceptions are involved in evaluations of hierarchy.[26] For example, Vito may be your superior, but from your point of view he may also be a vulgar person who dresses badly and is undereducated. This helps explain why you defer to him at work on task-related issues but demonstrate social superiority—by getting a sense of oneupsmanship in conversations with him, by laughing *at* rather than *with* him, and so forth. He may be your superior, but your communication with him enables you to "feel" superior in social matters.

Conducting an examination of the hierarchical dimension of the organizational level of analysis encourages you to: (1) define relationships in terms of hierarchical positions within the company, (2) make distinctions in how you respond to the communication of others when hierarchy is concerned, (3) see the interdependence of task and social judgments in considerations of hierarchy, (4) look for inducements to help you "identify" with superiors, and see your career in terms of graded or stepped advancements, and (5) withhold or release information in conversations based on your assessment of how the content of the talk may influence others' perceptions of you in relation to the company hierarchy.

Types of Work and Relative Authority/Power

The third dimension of the organizational level of analysis asks you to categorize the types of work carried out in the company and to assess the relative authority and/or power of persons responsible for doing the work. The objectives of this dimension are to discover: (1) the relative *status* of work categories (e.g., physician, nurse, technician, temporary staff), (2) the *legitimate authority* given to both categories of work and individuals in those categories, and (3) the *power* held by individuals, both formal and informal.

This part of your analysis is important because relationships are affected by status, authority, and power in any organization. Some persons with whom you might want to build a friendship may not be available for contact because the status differences between you are too great. Other persons may be open for relational contact, but association with them can overshadow your ability to gain authority and/or power in the company.

Most persons don't normally consider power, status, and authority to be present in their relationships.[27] In fact, the power dimension of organizational relationships is often cited as the most overlooked, underestimated variable in any assessment of organizations.[28] Because we have already dealt with authority and status elsewhere in this book, we will concentrate on power in the following discussion.

Power is a component, a very important one, of any human relationship. Researchers have isolated three types of power that operate in human relationships:[29]

1. *Complementary power relationships* can be described as relationships that exhibit one dominant, strong personality and one submissive, weaker personality. We call these relationships *complementary* because the behavior of either party *completes* the power needs of the other party. Just as it takes students to be defined as an instructor, and workers to be defined as a manager, the power distribution in complementary relationships is often found in the formal authority of the organizational or social hierarchies.

2. *Symmetrical power relationships* can be described as relationships displaying *equal distributions of power needs* and *equity* in the behavioral balance of the relationship. Some organizations, through their bureaucratic structures, don't encourage symmetrical relationships because hierarchical needs would be violated; usually in these agencies only members holding approximately the same rank and tenure can create equitable relationships of the symmetrical variety.

3. *Courtship/mentor power relationships* can be described as relationships based on *initial differences in power* that are narrowed over time through mutual negotiation and goal-seeking and that can attain either symmetrical or complementary status as the relationship matures.

These three types of power relationships describe possibilities. Virtually every person in an organization maintains all three types of power relationships. You may conduct a complementary relationship with a superior/subordinate, a symmetrical relationship with a colleague with whom you maintain a friendship, and a courtship/mentor relationship with someone who can help you gain knowledge and status in the company. As you can see, each type of power relationship might serve a function within the organizational hierarchy.

Flow of Work and Human Relationships

The fourth dimension of the organizational level of analysis concerns the flow of work in a company and the varieties of human relationships that contribute to the flow. As you already know, work accomplished in any organization depends on formal and informal communication networks. In this section we focus on the *purposes* interpersonal communication serves to *help and inhibit* the organization's ability to accomplish its tasks efficiently.

First, let's examine problems associated with work flow. Our assessment of organizations with whom we consult or provide training have shown us the following types of work flow problems:

1. *Too much bureaucracy—lack of personal quality in human relationships.* Some organizations are too formal. They constrict communication between and among levels of hierarchy, and therefore contribute to work slowdowns and stoppages by their stubborn insistence on bureaucratic detail and nonpersonal intervention. Two specific kinds of relational deficiencies develop: (1) *groupthink,* in which decisions are made based on power relationships and the will of the group and outside sources of alternative wisdom, data, or perspective are not sought nor encouraged;[30] and (2) *distorted communication,* in which the content of memos, reports, conversations, and group meetings doesn't correspond with the organizational realities. The purpose of distorted bureaucratic communication is to protect yourself by concentrating power over the small details of your assigned job; this tends to prevent reliance on others, which in turn doesn't encourage a sense of cooperation and cohesiveness.

2. *Too little formal organization—too much reliance on individual initiative and interpersonal relationships.* The opposite of too much bureaucracy is too little formal organization. Work flow is inhibited because individuals' personal relationships prevent proper exercises of power, authority, and control, and because personal problems and feelings take precedence over organizational goals and objectives.

3. *Political alliances.* Our experience demonstrates that in any organization you will find individuals who form political alliances. These relationships can shape corporate policies, change organizational objectives, and manipulate raises, promotions, and careers. However, some political alliances constrict communication among levels of hierarchy, thus contributing to work flow difficulties.

4. *Intimate involvement.* Love may make the world go 'round, but it tends to make an organization go crazy. Our experience indicates that *whether the intimate involvement is real or imagined,* the effects on work flow can be dramatic. It takes time to gossip, and the need to tell a friend about so-and-so may lead to wasted time. Furthermore, when intimacies develop, third parties tend to feel uncomfortable in the presence of the overt affection—excuses are found to leave the office when the lover arrives, thus preventing work from being accomplished. Finally, intimacy can breed jealousy, envy, and general discontent.

All of these forms of human relationships, or the absence of them, create work flow problems in organizations. Now let's examine the characteristics of interpersonal relationships which contribute to productivity:

1. *Relationships characterized by equitable exchanges and open negotiations.* Relational satisfaction depends on a mutual sense of fair exchange—a perception of equity. This does not mean you will always get your way; it means that both partners have sources of power and authority in the relationship which are mutually respected. It means that goals for the relationship are mutually constructed, and communication is generally directed toward accomplishing those goals. And it means that when things go wrong, and inevitable conflict arises, open negotiation of the problem characterizes the communication.

2. *Personal problems do not seriously block work flows.* Everyone has problems. Virtually everyone shares personal problems with co-workers. To advocate never discussing personal difficulties at work is untenable; instead, we have observed that mutual understanding and sharing of personal data can contribute to productive relationships by identifying needs. However, when personal difficulties prevent work from being accomplished, the organization, and the humans involved in the relationship, tend to suffer.

3. *Relationships display an awareness of competition and an overarching sense of cooperation.* Too often competitiveness and cooperation are seen as mutually exclusive terms; in fact, organizational reality dictates that both competition and cooperation characterize most human relationships. You compete for the rewards offered by the organization, and you cooperate to accomplish organizational and personal goals. When competition or cooperation dominate the relationship, the organization either loses its competitive edge or its cohesiveness. For this reason, communication exchanges should exhibit an awareness of the competition for rewards, but a unifying sense of cooperation which can lead to mutual achievement and organizational satisfaction.

Summary of the Organizational Level of Analysis

The organizational level of analysis focuses on the processes and relationships required to carry out tasks in any company. Because all organizations are characterized by status, authority, and power differences, these dimensions of human relationships must be analyzed for their influences on the ability to develop interpersonal relationships with individuals, the kinds of exchanges which should characterize productive human relationships in the organization, and the possible effects of developing, maintaining, or dissolving relationships at work.

Now that we have discussed the organizational level of analysis, we need to focus on the social aspects of interpersonal relationships in any organization.

The Social Level of Analysis

Communication creates social relationships. In organizations many interpersonal relationships are social in nature, and task-oriented in function, which means they serve to connect individuals in ways which contribute to the attainment of task objectives. In this section we want to increase your awareness of these interrelated dimensions of social relationships in organizations.

Functions of Social Relationships in Organizations

Relationships do not simply "exist." They exist in relation to some goal, purpose, or unsatisfied desire; in short, they serve to carry out individual and organizational functions. In this section we describe three basic functions for social relationships in organizations: (1) belonging and affiliation, (2) affection, and (3) power.[31]

First, people need to feel a sense of belonging and affiliation in any organiza-

of conflict. Blake and Mouton consider two factors to be important in any decision concerning management style: (1) concern for people and (2) concern for production of results. The conflict management grid demonstrates communication strategies that take into account these two concerns. The following discussion describes the communication style inherent to each one of these conflict management strategies.

Withdrawal (position 1.1) combines a low concern for people with a low concern for the production of results. This strategy demonstrates *avoidance behavior,* which in turn communicates fear, apathy, and insensitivity. This strategy is perhaps the worst possible choice under most conflict conditions because nothing happens and nothing is resolved. The problem remains, the uncertainty about human responses to it remains; nobody wins and everybody loses.

Research on the withdrawal strategy shows that the individual electing this approach tends to be a poor planner (disorganized), an infrequent planner (harried), who is unaware of a superior's attitudes (insensitive), relatively uncommunicative (closed as opposed to open communication style), and not very helpful to co-workers, superiors, and subordinates.[36] Given these negative characteristics, it is safe to assume that the withdrawal strategy is the least desirable one for productive, efficient, communicative individuals in an organization.

The *smoothing* (position 1.9) conflict management style describes an individual who relies on feelings of happiness instead of accomplishment of results to measure productive behavior. This person may be highly communicative, friendly, and even charming, but seems unable to deal directly with conflict. Instead of analyzing the problem and working systematically toward its resolution, the smoothing person will appeal to the sense of belonging, familiarity, and togetherness of the work group and produce inducements such as the use of first names or nicknames, humor, reminders of past favors, and glossing over the real problem. This strategy tends to encourage short-term feelings of cohesiveness among the arguers, but also tends to continue the conflict rather than to resolve it. In this approach, the smoother wins a brief sense of happiness at the expense of long-term satisfaction and productivity.

Forcing (position 9.1) is a strategy relying on legitimate authority and interpersonal power. In Blake and Mouton's terminology, it combines a high concern for production results with a low concern for people. The result is almost always a win-lose situation. Based on your earlier appreciation for the importance of *equity* in any organization and any relationship, you can see why a win-lose outcome is inevitably inequitable.

For this reason, the forcing strategy is not desirable, except in those rare situations *where a particular outcome must be secured in a short period of time at all costs.* The deadline that must be met, the report that must be delivered, or the delivery of goods on schedule to ensure the maintenance of the contract are all situations common to any manager. During these crucial times the forcing strategy, undesirable as it is, may be the only way to accomplish the goal. When this occurs, the manager employing this strategy *must make restitutions to the losers* as soon as possible or else risk costly inequities that can seriously impede work.

The *compromise* (position 5.5) strategy reveals a method of *reducing* conflict rather than *resolving* it. The communication of compromisers tends to display bargaining techniques, such as offer/counteroffer, give-and-take, and appeals to the common good of the organization. Compromise is status quo in labor/management negotiations, where the outcome can be announced as a "victory" for each side. Actually, both sides generally are less satisfied with the outcome than they had hoped for initially. Thus, compromise represents a middle ground for the arguers, a place for minimal satisfaction and sense of accomplishment.

Compromise once enjoyed greater status as a technique for reducing conflict. However, research demonstrated that most compromises *appear* to be more equal than they actually are.[37] In fact, compromise always favors the party in the dispute with the *least to lose.* In some situations the party with the least to lose has authority or legitimate power and could exercise it if he or she wanted to. In other situations the party with the least to lose enjoys informal power or social status within the organization, and the other party's unwillingess to compromise would result in wide organizational disharmony. In either case the situation could easily turn into a win-lose rather than a compromise if the party with the power used it. Because this threat can be perceived, what passes for compromise actually tips the balance scales toward the power holder.

Optimizing (position 9.9) represents an attainable ideal. It balances a high concern for people with a high concern for production results and encourages rational decision making and careful articulation of communication processes involved in the decision.

Using the optimizing strategy requires an *open communication climate.*[38] Organizations fostering productive planning, organizing, and coordinating functions, and encouraging open communication between superiors and subordinates can optimize conflict situations. Instituting the optimizing conflict strategy usually requires clear identification of the problem, clear articulation of the goals of each party in the conflict, and identification of common values, and systematic resolution of the conflict. The arguers avoid placing blame for the problem on each other and attempt to mimimize status differences in order to prevent power threats to interfere with the decision-making process. They are also aware of their own biases and prejudices and actively try to overcome them while working through a solution to the problem. Optimizing is clearly the best possible strategy for dealing with conflict in any organization, when the situation allows for it. However, it depends on a positive communication climate and the willingness among the arguers to rely on rational argument over abuses of power, status, and standing in the organizational culture.

Conflict is inevitable in any organization. Managed poorly, it can lead to disharmony within the culture, disruption of working relationships, and negative organizational outcomes. Managed positively, it can lead to new and creative ways of dealing with problems and persons and can reveal methods for improving communication within the organization's culture.

SUMMARY

In this chapter we dealt with interpersonal communication in organizations. We demonstrated how four levels of analysis can be useful in systematic understandings of relational goals and possibilities within specific organizational cultures. These levels are: (1) cultural, (2) organizational, (3) social, and (4) personal. Each level of analysis asks specific questions and provides sources of insight capable of informing your decision making.

We also analyzed the role of interpersonal conflict in organizations. In this section we defined conflict, discussed its essential characteristics, and provided a nine-stage pattern for analyzing how communication creates, constitutes, and manages conflict. Finally, we used Blake and Mouton's conflict management grid to reveal five methods for dealing with conflict: (1) withdrawal, (2) smoothing, (3) compromise, (4) forcing, and (5) optimizing. We advocated the optimizing strategy and discussed how the general organizational culture and climate contribute to productive conflict resolution.

ENDNOTES

1. See Paul H. Watzlawick, Janet Beavin, and Don D. Jackson, *The Pragmatics of Human Communication* (New York: Norton, 1967).

2. Susan B. Shimanoff, *Communication Rules Theory and Research* (Beverly Hills, CA: Sage, 1980).

3. Gerald L. Wilson and H. Lloyd Goodall, Jr., "The Performance Appraisal Interview: Examination and Reinterpretation," paper presented at the Southern Speech Communication Association annual meeting, Winston-Salem, North Carolina, April 1985; see also Jeffrey S. Kane and Edward E. Lawler, "Performance Appraisal Effectiveness: Its Assessment and Determinants," in *Research in Organizational Behavior,* Barry M. Straw, ed. 1 (Greenwich, CT: Jai Press, 1979): 425–478; and John F. Kikoski and Joseph A. Litterer, "Effective Communication in the Performance Appraisal Interview," *Public Personnel Management* 12 (1983): 33–42.

4. See Donna Bogar Goodall and H. Lloyd Goodall, Jr., "The Employment Interview: A Selective Review of the Literature with Implications for Communication Research," *Communication Quarterly* 30 (1982): 116–124.

5. Barry Z. Posner, "Comparing Recruiter, Student, and Faculty Perceptions of Important Applicant and Job Characteristics," *Personnel Psychology* 34 (1981): 329–339. See also E. C. Mayfield et al., "Selection Interviewing in the Life Insurance Industry: An Update of Research and Practice," *Personnel Psychology* 33 (1980): 725–739; and especially, Lois J. Einhorn, "An Inner View of the Job Interview: An Investigation of Successful Communication Behaviors," *Communication Education* 30 (1981): 217–228.

6. See Michael Hanna and Gerald Wilson, *Communicating in Business and Professional Settings* (New York: Random House, 1984), pp. 209–219 for comprehensive review.

7. Gerald M. Phillips and H. Lloyd Goodall, Jr., *Loving and Living* (Englewood Cliffs, NJ: Prentice-Hall, 1983).

8. See J. E. Baird and J. C. Diebolt, "Role Congruence, Communication, Superior-Subordinate Relations, and Employee Satisfaction in Organizational Hierarchies," *Western Journal of Speech Communication* 40 (1976): 260–267.

9. See H. Lloyd Goodall, Jr., and Gerald M. Phillips, *Making It in Any Organization* (Englewood Cliffs, NJ: Prentice-Hall, 1984).

10. Gerald M. Phillips and Julia T. Wood, *Communication in Human Relationships* (New York: Macmillan, 1983); see also Phillips and Goodall, *Loving and Living.*

11. George Lakof and Mark Johnson, *Metaphors We Live By* (Chicago: University of Chicago Press, 1980).

12. H. Lloyd Goodall, Jr., "The Status of Communication Studies in Organizational Contexts," *Communication Quarterly* 32 (1984): 133–147.

13. J. Kenneth Benson, "Innovation and Crisis in Organizational Analysis," *Sociological Quarterly* 18 (1977): 3–16.

14. See Goodall, "Status of Communication." 133–147.

15. From *Webster's New Collegiate Dictionary* (Springfield, MA: Merriam, 1973), p. 227.

16. Ward H. Goodenough, *Culture, Language, and Society* (Reading, MA: Addison-Wesley, 1971), p. 22.

17. From Gerald R. Miller and Mark Steinberg, *Between People: A New Analysis of Interpersonal Communication* (Chicago: Science Research Press, 1975).

18. These terms are derived from the many writings of Kenneth Burke, to whom we owe a special debt of thanks.

19. Kenneth Burke, *Permanence and Change,* 2d. rev. ed. (Indianapolis: Bobbs-Merrill, 1965), p. 238.

20. Kenneth Burke, *Counter-statement* (Berkeley, CA: University of California Press, 1931), p. 191.

21. For a thorough review on the literature of organizational identification, see Phillip K. Tompkins and George Cheney, "Account Analysis of Organizations: Decision Making and Identification," in *Communication in Organizations: An Interpretive Approach,* ed. Linda Putnam and Michael E. Pacanowsky (Beverly Hills, CA: Sage, 1983), pp. 123–146.

22. Network studies assume that interrelationships are important to communication effectiveness; see Terrence L. Albrecht and Vickie A. Ropp, "The Study of Network Structuring in Organizations Through the Use of Method Triangulation," *Western Journal of Speech Communication* 46 (1982): 162–178.

23. Barry K. Spiker and Tom D. Daniels, "Information Adequacy and Communication Relationships: An Empirical Investigation of 18 Organizations," *Western Journal of Speech Communication* 45 (1981): 342–354.

24. Kenneth Burke, *Language as Symbolic Action* (Berkeley, CA: University of California Press, 1966).

25. H. Lloyd Goodall, Jr. "Status of Communication," pp. 133–147.

26. Frederick M. Jablin, "Superior-Subordinate Communication: State of the Art," *Psychological Bulletin* 86 (1979): 1201–1222.

27. See Gerald M. Phillips and Julia T. Wood, *Communication.*

28. J. Kenneth Bensen, "Innovation and Crisis," pp. 1–21; see also Phillip K. Tompkins and George Cheney, "Unobtrusive Control, Decision-making, and Communication in Contemporary Organizations," paper presented at the Speech Communication Association annual convention, Louisville, KY, November 1982.

29. See Paul Watzlawick et al., *Pragmatics;* for an analysis of the courtship/mentor power relationship, see H. Lloyd Goodall, Jr., *Human Communication: Creating Reality* (Dubuque, IA: Brown, 1983), Chapters 7, 8.

30. See Irving Janis, *Groupthink,* 2d. ed. (Boston: Houghton Mifflin, 1981).

31. These categories are drawn from the work of Alfred Shutz; see his *The Phenomenology of the Social World* (London: Heineman, 1972).

32. These advisories are drawn from the research done for H. Lloyd Goodall, Jr., and Gerald M. Phillips, *Making It in Any Organization* (Englewood Cliffs, NJ: Prentice-Hall, 1984).

33. Chris Argyris, *Integrating the Individual and the Organization* (New York: Wiley, 1964).

34. Allan C. Filley, *Interpersonal Conflict Resolution* (Glenview, IL: Scott-Foresman, 1975).
35. Robert R. Blake and Jane S. Mouton, "The Fifth Achievement," *Journal of Applied Behavioral Science* 6 (1970): 412–426.
36. Ronald J. Burke, "Methods of Resolving Superior-Subordinate Conflict: The Constructive Use of Subordinate Differences and Disagreements," *Organizational Behavior and Human Performance* 5 (1972): 393–411.
37. Bertram H. Raven and Arie W. Kruglanski, "Conflict and Power," in *The Structure of Conflict,* ed. Paul Swingle (New York: Academic Press, 1970), pp. 69–109.
38. See R. J. Burke, "Methods of Resolving"; see also Jay W. Lorsch and Paul R. Lawrence, eds., *Studies in Organizational Design* (Homewood, IL: Irwin, 1975).

chapter 6

Communication in Groups

THE NATURE OF GROUP COMMUNICATION IN ORGANIZATIONS

Varieties of Group Experiences
Formal Work Groups / Problem-solving and Decision-making Groups / Informal Groups / Quality Circles

Levels of Analysis for Group Relationships
The Cultural Level / The Organizational Level / The Task and Social Levels / The Fantasy Level

AGENDAS AND GROUP WORK

The Standard Agenda for Decision-making Groups
Understanding the Charge / Phrasing the Question / Fact-finding / Establishing Criteria and Limitations / Brainstorming / Testing Alternatives / Preparing the Final Report

The Delphi Technique / Less Formal Agendas / Constructing a Sample Agenda

MANAGING RELATIONSHIPS IN THE GROUPS

Goal-setting / Analyzing Group Members / Analyzing Group Setting / Predicting Outcomes / Preparing for Discussion / Resolving Conflicts

Group communication in organizations is one of the results of specialization in the workplace. We are hired as specialists: department managers, project supervisors, systems analysts, product designers, technicians, or operators. And although we may have skills beyond our job descriptions, we are often expected only to work in areas authorized by our legitimate roles in the organization. Some organizations may have a policy of asking employees to work outside their main area of expertise, but such assignments are temporary or soon become part of the legitimate job requirements. Some tasks may lie beyond the capabilities of any individual, however they extend themselves beyond ordinary duties. In such a situation, the best results come from a group of specialists acting in harmony. Thus, groups are essential to bring the best combination of specialists together for multidimensional tasks outside the expertise of any individual.

Although you might feel capable of working on your own, most organizations require you to coordinate your activities with a wide range of other employees. Here lies the central problem of group communication. The task-oriented purpose of groups in organizations should make working in these groups easy, but every group is a social entity. The social nature of groups within the organization brings every nuance of social interaction into play in this allegedly task-oriented situation. So, although you may be willing to coordinate your activities as co-workers, working effectively in a group also requires social awareness and social skills. This chapter shows how effective group communication in organizations meets both task and social needs.

First, we examine the nature of group communication in organizations. After describing different types of likely group experiences, we explore some possibilities in the analysis of group relationships. Second, we discuss the use of agendas for task-oriented group work. Third, we focus on managing social relationships in the group, moving from goal-setting to conflict resolution. After reading this chapter, you should have a better understanding of the role of group communication in organizations and also be able to analyze a given situation to plan for more effective communication in a specific group.

THE NATURE OF GROUP COMMUNICATION IN ORGANIZATIONS

Varieties of Group Experiences

Groups can offer many different experiences to their members, ranging from routine to extraordinary. We will discuss three types of task groups: (1) formal work groups such as the routine group associated with a particular job, (2) the problem-solving group brought together for a specific problem, and (3) decision-making groups in which members coordinate different types of expertise. We will also look at two types of informal groups emerging from an organization: (1) informal communication networks and (2) quality circles, a unique compromise between formal and informal groups.

Formal Work Groups   Formal work groups are fundamental within any organization. The most widely accepted definition of the principal tasks facing an organization should include production, manufacturing, and marketing, or sales. Thus, the task group can be concerned with any and every aspect of an organization's operations in these line functions. Since the staff functions of the organizations support line functions, tasks associated with staff operations such as accounting or personnel are equally vital to organizational operations. In terms of organizational functions, task groups are the operating unit for the organization's daily activities. The organization almost never functions as an entity, but subdivides the organization's functions that are represented by task groups.

The organization may appear to be comprised of individual employees, each pursuing private and corporate goals. But in achieving their objectives, employees are thrown together with others in task groups. The task group is thereby derived from the departmental structure of the organization by the specific funtions of its members. In describing the task dimensions of group communication, Johnson states "the task dimension is the relationship of group members to the work they are to do," often expressed in symbolic form.[1] If the group's work is to produce an output using symbols, a report being a common example, then the task group is working on a metasymbolic level, using a symbol system to discuss the best way to produce further symbolic forms.

Benne and Sheats[2] identify eleven task-oriented roles for group members, applying behavioral labels to group activities: initiator, information-seeker, opinion-seeker, information-giver, elaborator, coordinator, orienter, evaluator-critic, energizer, procedural-technician, and recorder. These labels only identify communication-oriented functions for group members, communication behaviors common to decision-making and task groups. Regardless of the group's job, these types of behavior indicate that the group has the communication characteristics of a task group. If you look at the group from the organization's point of view, a task group is expected to display a set of behaviors identified by Michalak and Yager[3] as "the human performance required to achieve specific management objectives, the tools and conditions needed to perform the job, and the skills and knowledge required of the employee." The task group is the model for formal group communication within the organization and is part of the routine duties associated with every job.

Problem-solving and Decision-making Groups   The problem-solving or decision-making group is a formal group working on a special problem or issue within the organization. Although every employee may be eligible to serve in a problem-solving or decision-making group, the specialized nature of such groups limits their membership to those with specific expertise. Both of these groups are formal components in the organizational communication network, but each has a different function.

The problem-solving group is likely to be created to deal with an unusual problem, a crisis impacting the organization as a whole, such as the threat of a strike by labor or a contract being canceled. Problems concerning one department within the organization may call for problem-solving techniques but can usually fit into the scheduled agenda of existing task groups. Thus the problem-solving group environment contains enough danger to the organization to overcome members' personal differences and departmental loyalties. If members cannot work together effectively, the organization may well suffer to the extent that all employees are affected. This is a threat situation in which the problem must be overcome before ordinary internal squabbling can safely resume.

Problem-solving and decision-making groups are similar in their purpose, dealing with special problems beyond the scope of routine task groups. But problem-solving and decision-making groups may differ in power and their relationship to the task authority. The problem-solving group may not always deal with problems perceived as threats that demand a plan of action. Lesser problems call for resolution through decision making. The decision-making group produces a recommendation for a higher authority to take action, but this product of group communication is often less urgent and powerful than a problem-solving group's recommendation. For example, the group selected by the CEO (Chief Executive Officer) to resolve the problem of slow and distorted communication between offices in different cities is likely to get more attention than the group deciding which of three sites to use for long-term storage of surplus materials. The focus of the problem-solving group is on a special problem, a situation that is unique enough to require the attention of this particular group. The group's capability to solve the problem gives it some power of its own. On the other hand, decision-making groups receive their task from an authority who is delegating decision-making responsibilities to the group. The authority can accept the group's decision or abrogate the group's authority and make the decision independently.

Informal Groups   We have been discussing groups created by the organization as part of the formal communication network. But informal communication networks produce equally significant groups through affiliations between formally disparate members of the organization.

Every opportunity for social contact is a likely beginning for an informal group. The informal group lies outside the control of the organization and offers a chance for individuals to form relationships without taking organizational membership into account. The informal group has the potential to ignore formal organizational aspects of status such as job title, seniority, and legitimate authority. This potential is limited by the real power of superiors over subordinates that carries over from the workplace.[4] Thus the informal group is likely to communicate about issues unrelated to organizational tasks while maintaining awareness of distinctions in organizational status. Social groups endorsed or created by the organization, such as the bowling team or management club, are only quasi-informal. In fact, informal communication is possible only in groups where members have no formal organizational relationship, as in community groups and church groups.

Quality Circles   An excellent example of a quasi-informal group is the quality circle. Created as a forum for discussions about productivity between production level employees and management, the quality circle brings everyone connected with a work situation into contact so that open interpersonal communication is possible without regard for formal communication channels. It is significant to note from research that quality circles work best in organizations that already have a climate that fosters communication from the production level up to management through formal channels.[5] As an informal group, a quality circle facilitates interpersonal contact and personal communication between participants. The personal nature of relationships is influenced by formal organizational relationships, especially since meetings occur at work during the regular work-day. But the fact that quality circle participants are volunteers demonstrates their commitment to personal involvement in informal communication. Because most quality circles are trained in decision-making and problem-solving techniques, members have these techniques available as neutral, sanctioned ways to communicate outside the formal communication network. Furthermore, if the quality circle is given responsibility for solving problems in productivity, the prestige of the group will give it credibility and some power within the organization.[6]

Thus, the quality circle shows that the informal group can be put to work on behalf of the organization without imposing the limitations of formal communication networks. Informal groups like quality circles use the informal communication network's tendency to seek efficient, personally rewarding relationships outside formal channels to increase employee participation in task-related communication.

Levels of Analysis for Group Relationships

The social and task dimensions of group communication create and maintain relationships on many levels within both formal and informal groups. In order to understand group communication in more detail, we divide the study of group communication into five levels of analysis: (1) the cultural level, (2) the organizational level, (3) the task level, (4) the social level, and (5) the fantasy level. Each of these levels can be analyzed as the principal function for group communication in organizations, but, in reality, all levels operate simultaneously as significant parts of organizational communication.

The Cultural Level   By observing a group that has been active for many meetings, you can see it has clearly defined procedures for task resolution and social maintainance. This well-established group seems to perform effectively by getting its work done within a reasonable time with a minimum of nonproductive conflict. If you ask the question, "How is this group communicating?" you'll likely find two important types of language use. First, the structure of the talk is well organized with clear rules for who talks, what sequence of turns they take, and how the group knows when to quit a topic and to go on to the next one. Second, the content of the talk is adapted to the individual members, so that members seem to understand each other quickly with little confusion about what their words mean or imply. These two characteristics indicate that the group has a well-developed, efficient group culture—an organized way to conduct task and social affairs.

We discuss the culture of the organization in Chapter 5, treating organizational culture as a product of interpersonal communication. The culture of a group within the organization reflects the procedures and value system of the organization's culture. The group shares the organization's awareness of the boundaries on it as a scene in which organizational attitudes need to be maintained. Adherence to their organizational identification gives every group a relationship with the organization as a whole, a common ground of shared beliefs and practices that defines every group member as a member of the organization.[7] This continuity of identification between group members and the organization is one reason informal groups so rarely escape the influence of the formal organizational hierarchy and communication network.

But group cultures do exist within the organizational culture, and are identifiable by the structure and content of their talk through sociolinguistic analysis.[8] The details of relationships within the group can and should be understood in studies of group communication.[9] Pragmatic linguistic's explanation of the effect of context on language use and meaning connects the group identity to the external context provided by the organization, thus analyzing the influence of context on communication.[10] Sociolinguistics turns this relationship between culture and communication around, and finds that language use determines group culture. Both of these approaches to group culture reflect earlier findings that certain types of talk may indicate closeness between group members, a behavior that is evidence of psychological membership as well as of vocal participation.[11]

As Duncan has stated, each member "hears his own words and then learns what those words mean because he can observe how they affect others as well as how they affect him."[12] These observations are the basis for shared meanings that are specific to a particular group. Such socialized language use forms a group dialect when analyzed as a set of idiosyncratic language patterns.[13] From the members' point of view, group communication is a result of the demands of the context and the other members for the appropriate behavior that demonstrates knowledge and compliance with the rules for group membership. In terms of effective organizational communication, the group that can communicate as a social unit is likely to be more efficient and productive in their task-oriented communication.

The Organizational Level   The group operates within the organization in the same way as an individual member operates within the group. The group provides the environment for the member and the organization provides the environment for the group. Thus, the organization could be regarded as a collection or assembly of group-sized subunits, each containing specialized personnel working on a routine task, a special problem, or a specific decision for later implementation. The primary issue for group communication on the organizational level is to coordinate the various groups that operate within the organization.

Coordination of the groups' external environment calls for attention to four basic aspects of group communication. First, how effectively is the group connected to the organization's formal communication network? If the group has access to all the information and other resources needed to resolve its task, then there should be evidence that the formal communication system is being used. Formal channels to other groups within the organization may operate through key group members, but the formal communication network should permit communication between groups as well as communication between each group and the organization. The means of access to the formal network is also significant since cumbersome channels or formats for communication reduce the group's effectiveness.

Second, does the group connect with the informal communication network? The capability of the group members to exploit their informal communication potential may influence the group's effectiveness. The group's relationship with the informal communication network would be essential if the formal communication network was deficient in any way. A productive group with little reliance on informal relationships with the rest of the organization could indicate that the formal network is adequate for the group's needs. Whether further informal communication would enhance the group's capability would be difficult to assess, but network analysis focuses on the frequency and degree to which units like groups are interconnected within the organization.[14]

Third, how does the organizational system supply the group with required inputs in the form of information and resources like time, money, and personnel? The organization functions as the support system for the group, providing members with both the impetus for their group work and the means of resolving their task. If you recall the principles of exchange theory from Chapter 5, groups within organizations will collectively evolve accepted systems for apportioning resources. Within the group, resource allocation is intended to permit members to maximize outcomes equitably for the group and for themselves as individuals. Within the organization, this same principle of equitable resource allocation can become the basis for deciding how to allocate resources among groups so that each group can equitably maximize outcomes. For example, NASA research labs working to get a person on the moon routinely shared their data so that each lab could work with the others' data and the organization could succeed as a whole. If information had been kept within individual research labs, the rate of progress of the entire organization would have been too slow to get to the moon within a reasonable time.

Fourth, how are group outputs integrated into the organization? The group can deliver the outcome of its work through formal and informal communication networks. Analysis of group interaction on an organizational level should indicate a clear target audience for a group's activities. The group can direct its activities toward a clear purpose when the audience receiving the group's report is known to the group. If formal channels are prepared to accept the group's output, then the group also has a clear idea about the format for their reports. The group's relationship with the organization is thereby controlled by formalized inputs and outputs, but only to the extent that the formal communication network permits the group to do its job.

The Task and Social Levels   The stated purpose of group relationships usually reflects the work environment by focusing on the task facing the group. Since communication patterns emerge to facilitate the group's intent, the nature of the group's task is likely to have an effect on the group's communication patterns.[15] The interaction between the task and the group can be evaluated through techniques like task analysis, precise detailing of task frequency, competence, and significance. But this type of information about the nature of group tasks is of limited usefulness when the impact of the group is ignored.

Analysis of task-oriented relationships can be productively combined with analysis of social relationships in a task group. Including some indication of the task group's social dimensions helps account for two significant factors beyond the task itself. First, the group's specific orientation toward the task needs to be determined in each case. Second, this group's task orientation is likely to be balanced by social orientation that is dedicated to maintaining the group as a social entity. The dynamics of these forces within a task group are more likely the measure of a group's task capability than of any measure of the task itself. The role of communication in group processes is a good example of the interdependence of task and social functions. Effective analysis of the factors contributing to task output also recognizes the relationship among language use, group identity, and task performance.[16]

Group identity can also be explored by observing and analyzing communication as it is used in group interaction. Robert Bales has been developing a technique for the analysis of group interaction for over 40 years. His work with interaction process analysis (IPA) began in 1942, evolving into a system using an outside observer or an observer-participant. These observers can record and analyze group members' communications in terms of both task and social orientation. This technique is now called SYMLOG, a system for the multiple level observation of groups, and data can be processed with convenient computer programs to produce maps of the group's task and social coorientations.[17] We will go into more detail about this system in Chapter 10 when we discuss assessment of group climates. The most significant contribution of techniques like SYMLOG is that the group is perceived as an amalgam of task-oriented behaviors that are coordinated with social forces. Differences in performance between groups may depend on the demands of the task or individual members' response to the task and the group. Avoiding fixed standards of competence suitable for routinized task performance permits adaptation to social forces and specialized task requirements.

The Fantasy Level   Individual perceptions of group relationships are bound to be influenced by our interpretations of overt behavior in the group. Although we may claim to "say what we mean," other members apply individual interpretations to group members' intentions and meanings. As recognized in the work of Bormann and others, this basic attribute of communication and individual perception can be magnified in group communication when symbols used in talk cannot be controlled and individual fantasies can develop without the speaker's knowledge.[18] The symbolic possibilities can stimulate communication among group members, where a member's meaning for an utterance is picked up by other members, who amplify or distort the intended meaning of the original utterance. This level of analysis of group relationships is thereby focused on fantasies that are generated by members and played out by the group.

This situation parallels the digital and analogic levels of communication that were discussed in Chapter 4. Communication in the group also has a digital component referring to the information carried by our words, which is accompanied by an analogic component that gives meaning to the message because of the relationship between the participants. The analogic meaning attributed to a specific message reflects the meaning of the relationship between communicators as much as the words of the message itself. So nonverbal cues such as tone or style of delivery become as important as verbal cues such as word choice. But even word choice can operate on the analogic level to stimulate group fantasies. A good example of this phenomenon in groups comes from Janis's study of groupthink.[19] Group members' long association and history of success both contribute to the fantasy that the group is invariably correct in its decisions, invulnerable in conflict with other groups, and besieged by enemies who don't agree with the group's stated position. The fantasy theme of the group being embattled and under siege produces a collective desire to suppress internal disagreement, reduce diversity of thinking, and lower the creative, problem-solving capability of the group by limiting options in decision making to protect the group.

Individual members are also likely to engage in fantasy about their performance in the group itself. Bales and Cohen found three perceptions of individual behavior in the group, two in the mind of the individual member and one perceived by others.[20] The individual member projected an idealized version of what would be best to do, using that image of perfection to set up expectations for how his or her actual behavior will be perceived. Thus, the individual uses an imaginary ideal form to establish what appears to be realistic expectations about others' perceptions. But the response of the group to what is perceived as the actual behavior is what leads to perceptions of task or social orientation in the individual member. Here the group faces a possible mismatch with the member's expectations and its judgment of the quality of actual behavior. Thus, fantasy on a group or an individual level can influence members' responses to each other and the relationships that are so important to the group's task and social functions.

AGENDAS AND GROUP WORK

Group work always requires some form of organization to coordinate members' activities. Both decision making and problem solving need procedures for conducting their activities. If the group is left to its own initiative, members will construct an agenda or plan of action from procedures they have used in similar situations in the past. We discuss three types of well-tested agendas derived from productive problem-solving and decision-making groups: the standard agenda, Delphi technique, and less formal agendas. All of these techniques organize group work in a format that is suitable to reach group goals. Group members are responsible for defining the actual application of each type of agenda, but we describe the characteristics of each agenda as it is commonly used.

The Standard Agenda for Decision-making Groups

The standard agenda is a decision-making technique that regulates group discussion in an orderly and efficient manner. Based on the observations and analysis of John Dewey in his influential book, *How We Think,*[21] the standard agenda in its current form is derived from the work of Gerald Phillips.[22] The fundamental assumption behind the idea of a standardized agenda is that a decision-making

Use of the standard agenda can help a group come to decisions that are of good quality.

group is primarily a task group that should follow a task-oriented procedure. The orderliness of a planned agenda is intended to organize group discussion around the task, and the standardized nature of this agenda is intended to bring consistency to all decision-making groups.

The standard agenda regulates social forces in the group to the extent that individual goals and interpretations of the task are reduced to an understanding of task and goals shared by the group as a whole. As a task-oriented technique for collective thinking, the standard agenda reduces personal conflict while maintaining the opportunity for discussion and participation by all members. Dewey's belief in the potential for logical, orderly conduct in human interaction may make the standard agenda seem insensitive to individual needs and goals. But the greater need for genuine group participation to utilize the group's resources fully makes the standard agenda ideal for groups without an existing agenda or for groups with strong personal conflict. This is a seven-stage process that should be followed in order to attain maximum efficiency in decision making.

Understanding the Charge   The first stage of standard agenda calls for the group to examine the task with which it has been charged. Each member is likely to have a different understanding of what the task means. Thus, the discussion in the first stage is focused on defining key terms that are important to the task but ambiguous in meaning. All members should participate by comparing their interpretations of what the task means and discussing their differences until a clear meaning for the task is determined. The group should decide as a whole on definitions of key terms in any documents relating to the task and should share an understanding of their joint responsibilities and expectations in pursuing that task. If the group has just been formed, the level of participation in this stage sets up an expectation for full participation in later discussions. Awareness of individual differences and compromise within the group also prepares group members for discussion and compromise in later stages of decision making.

Phrasing the Question   The understanding of the task and its meaning to the group gained in the first stage can be consolidated in the second stage of the standard agenda. In this phase the group phrases a question to guide future discussion. The advantage of having a clearly phrased question is twofold, mainly acting to keep the group focused on the task as it was interpreted in stage 1, and also to guide the group away from talking about the topic. The question has the further function of indicating to the group when their task is complete. When the question has been answered, the problem is resolved, regardless of unfinished business unrelated to the task.

Fact-finding   In order to answer the question, the group generally needs to do research in two general areas, the past and the present. Research into the past involves using records of similar problems or tasks, each acting as precedent for a similar solution in the present. But if the current situation differs significantly from the past, precedent will not apply and research must focus on the exact nature of the current situation. Field research can determine the nature of a problem through surveys and interviews, using further interviews with expert authorities to determine how the problem might be solved. Research assignments are relatively efficient with standard agenda, since the task and the group's needs have been clearly defined in stages 1 and 2. Research may indicate that the group's definition of the task needs to be revised in light of new information, so an occasional result of fact-finding is a redefinition of the task and the question.

Establishing Criteria and Limitations   Once fact-finding appears to be complete, the group can turn toward the solution. Dewey observed that efficient groups knew in advance what they were looking for in a solution.[23] Thus, the group can put its expertise from fact-finding into effect by establishing a set of criteria for an ideal solution, one that would have every desirable feature indicated by its research. As these criteria are recorded, they commit the group to a synthesis of its research into a coherent statement describing the ideal solution. This profile of the ideal solution can then be set aside for future use.

The limitations set in this stage are limitations on the group, reflecting realistic concerns the group might have about the extent of its ability to solve the problem. Common limitations come from limited resources like time, money, and information. Additional limitations may be less tangible but equally important, the power of the group, the willingness of the organization to accept the group's decision, and the morality of the solution. All these limitations balance the profile of an ideal solution to set up a standard for what a good but realistic solution might entail.

Brainstorming   At this point the group may have begun to commit itself to a specific decision or solution; however, the creativity inherent in the individual perspectives and expertise of the group members hasn't yet been tested. Brainstorming is designed to generate a set of alternate solutions that are taken from a less logical level of the group's understanding of the problem. Using the process of free association to stimulate articulation of thoughts from a less than conscious level, brainstorming has been employed by decision-making and problem-solving groups since it was first accepted by think tanks such as the Rand Corporation. The group can move directly into brainstorming without doing further research. A relaxed mind after a good night's sleep is the only requirement.

As group members offer answers to the guiding question, they should follow four basic rules: (1) Decide on a procedure for maximum participation of all members, by either taking regular turns in order or guaranteeing that each person will be permitted to make one brief suggestion before any other person starts speaking. (2) Offer suggestions as spontaneously as possible, without long explanations or evaluations. (3) Have everyone in the group participate, making as many suggestions as possible without giving criticisms. (4) Record answers as quickly and unobtrusively as possible, so that the recording process doesn't impede the group's thoughts. After every member's suggestions have been recorded, the group can be more confident that a wide range of potential solutions will be available to supplement more carefully considered logical alternatives.

Testing Alternatives   This stage leads to selecting the final solution by testing alternatives against the criteria and limitations from stage 4. A match between one of the alternate solutions and the criteria would indicate an ideal solution. But this event is rare, and the group is more likely to find part of the ideal solution in several of the alternative solutions. By combining these alternatives, the group can create a composite solution that closely matches the requirements of the ideal solution while remaining within the limitations on the group.

Preparing the Final Report   Once the solution has been constructed, the group can use information discovered in previous stages of the standard agenda to prepare the group's final report. If the report is to stand alone as a self-explanatory document, standard agenda is especially useful in providing the details of the processes leading up to the decision or solution. Discussion during the first stage about the nature of the task can be recounted to provide background on the nature of the problem as interpreted by the group. If the memo containing the official charge to the group is appended to this section of the report, then the report can be used easily by others in addition to the charging authority.

Working from notes taken during the subsequent stages of the standard agenda, the group can proceed in preparing the report through fact-finding, detailing the question being addressed and the types of research employed. If the group's work is successful, the report can serve as an informative precedent for work of the same nature. If the group has failed, the report can indicate what subsequent efforts should be avoided in its research for a similar task. The criteria and limitations are an excellent source for arguments on behalf of the solution. If the group used clear criteria for its decision, then the same criteria are good reason for the charging authority to accept the composite solution and reject other alternatives. Thus, a report prepared from standard agenda leads the organization of the group's discussions into the organization of the report, producing a logical, orderly treatment of the task. The quality of the standard agenda-based report will reflect the quality of the group's participation in oral discussion. The next decision-making technique eliminates much of the influence of oral discussion skills and the personalities of group members.

The Delphi Technique

Experienced group decision makers recognize the influence of strong personalities on the course of group discussion. The articulate, charismatic group member becomes just another expert chosen by the charging authority for job-related knowledge in groups using the Delphi technique.[24] A Delphi group's decision also eliminates the influence of differences in status, permitting members from any level of the organization to participate freely. By limiting the group communication format to written memos, and by channeling all communication directly between each member and the charging authority, the Delphi technique works through the centralized direction of the charging authority. Group members never know the rest of the group unless the charging authority reveals their identities. This decision-making technique follows a four-step process.

1. The charging authority chooses the group members, setting up lines of communication and describing the task or problem.
2. The charging authority sends a memo detailing the situation and the problem. The group member responds with a memo taking a position on the problem, a memo seen only by the charging authority.
3. The charging authority sends a memo to each of the group members, including the positions taken by each of the other members. Members can now respond by changing their original positions on the problem, but each change must be explained. These responses go back to the charging authority.
4. The exchange of memos must continue until the group reaches consensus on its solution or decision.

The Delphi technique does eliminate the influence of skill in oral communication, but it replaces that influence, to some degree, with skill at written communication. Thus, the most effective participation in Delphi-style discussion comes from skilled writers. This situation is mitigated by the experience gained from participation and the examples provided by other participants.

Less Formal Agendas

Decision making also has a natural evolution that follows a less formal agenda. The naturally occurring phases of decision making are similar regardless of the situation, leading many researchers to identify the same informal decision-making agendas.[25] The phases of informal decision making are summarized as a four-step process; orientation, conflict, emergence, and reinforcement.[26]

Phase one: orientation For each group member, the first meeting of any group is ambiguous about the task and the other members. In order to reduce ambiguity, those who intend to become group members exchange information about themselves and their perceptions of the task. If there is disagreement about the task while the identities of other members is still unclear, rules for politeness and appropriate conduct with strangers prevent conflict over the task. But as soon as members are oriented to the identity of the rest of the group, the group can move on to the next stage of informal decision making, conflict.

Phase two: conflict Decision-making groups know that eventually the members will have to produce a decision representing the entire group. Although one member may want the group to endorse his or her individual opinion, the individual expertise of other members often gives no one member the capacity to dominate the discussion and decision making. Working from the assumption that maximum participation yields the highest quality decision, a decision-making group can expect productive results from natural conflict. By testing each other's claims in conflict over facts, values, and policy decisions, the group can move from individual perspectives on the task toward a joint decision.

Phase three: emergence The group's conflict over facts, values, and policies may diminish as members arrive at an agreement over facts and values, leaving only policy decisions. By starting with agreement over facts, members can work from a relatively objective beginning point to the more personal issues involved in conflict over values and priorities. Finally, if the group can generate a set of criteria by which to judge alternative solutions, then consensus over the final solution to the problem can emerge. The emergence phase permits the group finally to resolve the task, make the decision, and compromise individual differences.

Phase four: reinforcement Once conflict has been resolved and the decision has emerged, the group has completed the task-oriented phases of its decision making. But continued association among group members as a final report is prepared offers an opportunity to build social solidarity in defense of the decision. By demonstrating their willingness to cooperate in their commitment to the group's decision, each member increases group cohesiveness. The reinforcement phase adds social force to the rationale for the decision that has already emerged.

Constructing a Sample Agenda

A sample agenda can be the most useful tool a group discussion planner can produce. As a model for any task-oriented discussion, a sample agenda should be constructed to establish a routine for meetings. The traditional practice of running meetings according to parliamentary procedure may be acceptable in some organizations. But the lack of familiarity of all potential group members with these procedures requires an agenda format that meets four basic requirements:

1. The agenda must be complete, including all the topics you intend to cover. The primary purpose of the agenda is to prepare participants for the meeting, permitting them to consider issues carefully and gather resources for the meeting. The topics should also be stated in terms that are easily understood by every member. Cryptic agendas promote confusion and perhaps suspicion.

2. The agenda should set objectives for the meeting, detailing the tasks to be attained. A clear description of what you expect the participants to do will help them prepare to act appropriately and efficiently. All group members should know how they will be expected to participate.

3. The agenda should specify the time allotted for each piece of business. A stated time limit lets participants know how much discussion to expect and acts as a safeguard to prevent the group from exceeding reasonable time limits.

4. The agenda should follow a pattern with logical topic development. The natural past to present flow of old and new business can be combined with topic schedules that work from problem to solution or from cause to effect. Once the order of topics has been published, avoid wandering through the topics in another order. Special, late-developing topics can be added, but members will work most effectively if they are notified of all topics prior to the meeting.

A basic agenda derived from parliamentary procedure would follow this pattern:

1. Call the meeting to order at the appointed time.
2. Have the minutes of the previous session accepted as written or amended to show an accurate account of the last meeting.
3. Include as old business an issue from a previous meeting if it requires further discussion. But old business can also be tabled for a later discussion if it impedes pressing current topics.
4. Introduce new business as indicated by the agenda circulated to all participants well before the meeting. New business might require more time than you planned, and you might want to carry some topics forward to the next meeting rather than delay discussion of the next items on the agenda.
5. Adjourn the meeting at the time promised by the agenda. If participants know that your time limits are observed, they will try to get more work accomplished in the time allotted.

Now that we have sketched the guidelines for a sample agenda, we now consider issues in managing relationships in the group.

MANAGING RELATIONSHIPS IN THE GROUP

Effective management of relationships in groups is derived from a careful consideration of how the group responds to your ideas. In many discussion groups a preplanned outcome is uncertain but planning will help guide the group in the direction you desire. Relationships among group members can be managed to achieve your goals without destroying the autonomy of the members or the creativity of the group. Victor Vroom indicates that subordinates can have the most significant role in decision making when the problem is structured and the group members share organizational goals.[27] This situation calls for analysis of the relationships in the group to promote goal setting and organize group discussion. This six-step process should maximize well-organized discussion focused on organizational goals: (1) goal-setting, (2) analyzing group members, (3) analyzing group settings, (4) predicting outcomes, (5) preparing for discussion, and (6) resolving conflicts.

Goal-setting   Goal-setting can reduce the ambiguity of relationships in the group by creating task-related goals for each group member. If each member's function in the group discussion is specified during the first meeting, perhaps in the agenda circulated prior to the meeting, then nobody will have a chance to find his or her own personal goal. Once a task-oriented set of assignments has been accepted by the group members as part of the charge, the group has limited the grounds for legitimate discourse. This limitation makes conflict resolution easier in later discussions by limiting topics for argument.

Analyzing Group Members   Most group members will have a history of previous group performances that you can assess to determine their potential as group members. But the unique nature of each group situation and combination of members may alter normal individual characteristics. Thus, any analysis of group members should examine the group as a system of interacting forces. Each member's capacity for task-oriented and social behavior should be matched with the potentials of other members to anticipate the general group climate. Members with strong orientations toward social or task-oriented group functions may complement each other or produce conflict between their individual goals. But a group with only one perspective will lack the diversity essential to a creative group.

Analyzing Group Setting   The situation for group discussion extends beyond the nature of the members' areas of interest. Two types of settings lie beyond this mental group topology: the organizational setting and the physical setting. The organizational setting is the most difficult to analyze, since the real role of the group in organizational decision making may not be understood until after the group's decision has gone into effect. But the immediate organizational setting can be determined in terms of two factors: (1) the place in the organization occupied by the group's members and (2) the significance attributed to the group's task and goals by the organization. The group is constrained by the organizational setting in terms of power and prestige.

On a more concrete level, the group must operate in a physical setting that promotes effective decision making. The setting should permit group members to reach their goals with as little impediment as possible. Thus, the setting should be convenient to the information and task-oriented facilities necessary for the discussion. Selecting the setting should take the physical comfort of the group members into account, but maximum comfort might not produce optimum conditions for efficient work if the group is too comfortable. Physical distraction can come from that luxurious lunch as well as from the room that is too hot or too cold.

Predicting Outcomes   If you know all the factors operating on the group members, and also have a reasonable expectation of how members will influence each other, then you can predict the outcome of group discussion. It would be more reasonable to combine a systems approach where you can envision a likely chain of events, as in PERT (Program Evaluation and Review Technique), with evaluation of how contingent one event is on other events. Predicting outcomes then becomes a matter of breaking down the group discussion into stages of development, such as we have done in the standard agenda, the Delphi technique, the and natural decision-making agendas. As the group moves through each stage of discussion, the remaining possible outcomes become increasingly more probable because of agreements and commitments made in earlier stages. Predicting outcomes thus reflects your awareness of the group's development as a social and task-oriented entity. The more behaviors you can label and catalog in terms of a decision-making model, the more informed your judgment about the outcome of discussion will become. Accurate prediction requires you to learn what communication behavior means to the group in terms of task resolution and social development.

Preparing for Discussion   In order to manage relationships in groups, you need to prepare for each discussion as carefully as if it were the first meeting. Basic leadership functions like preparing and distributing the agenda give you an opportunity to plan the discussion format. Attention to goal-setting and potentials for interaction between the setting and the group's members will give you a sense of what strategy should yield the intended outcome. Additional preparation for discussion evolves as the group itself progresses. Adapting your original planning to changing conditions and unexpected developments in the task and the group calls for a review process after each meeting in which you examine your role and its influence on the group's performance. You have many options as manager and mediator of group relationships.

Resolving Conflicts   Intragroup conflict is one of the most troublesome by-products of relationships within the group. Conflict resolution is treated in detail in our discussion of interpersonal communication, but your main options are clear. You can define the conflict as behavior that is unacceptable in the group meeting and avoid it to the degree that members cooperate. Or, you can work with those involved to define and resolve the dispute. In this role, you manage relationships as a mediator.

Defining the nature of the conflict can distinguish between conflict over facts and conflict over values. In addition to identifying the basic nature of the problem, the definition process itself establishes control over group members by structuring their relationship in terms of a procedure that is recognized as the way the group resolves conflict. Getting involved with this process commits the members to the potential for some conflict resolution. Conflict over facts is often settled by exchange of information or definitions of key terms. Such conflict originates in poor listening behavior or in incomplete explanations of what each member means.

Conflict over values may be much more difficult to resolve. If the value-oriented conflict is based on a concern for what is good or bad, right or wrong, moral or immoral about an idea, then the disputants may be able to define their problem strictly in terms of the task. A task-oriented definition of values focuses on organizational goals and values, replacing individual value systems with the value system of the organization. The key to this type of substitution process is the disputants' willingness to give up temporarily their own values while working in the group on an organizational issue. If their personal involvement in the dispute is so great that the conflict exists between them as individuals, then losing the argument may entail a great loss of self-esteem. You can objectify the situation by making it a business matter, indicating that personal grievances are inappropriate. But such personal conflict is best avoided by keeping the disputants from any further contact with each other. The productivity of the group should not suffer to gratify an individual member's desires.

SUMMARY

This chapter examined communication in groups within organizations, seeking an explanation of how different types of groups communicate to reach their task and social goals. The degree of task orientation and social orientation in formal and informal groups was discussed, with special emphasis on the influence of the organization on all types of group experiences. After describing the varieties of possible group experiences, we offered an explication of group relationships on different levels of analysis. The group was assessed as an autonomous cultural entity and as a unit within the organization. Members' communication was found to be accessible on the task, social, and fantasy levels.

In a discussion of the use of agendas in group work, we offered three alternative agendas. The standard agenda represents the primarily task-oriented approach. The Delphi technique reduces the influence of group members' oral communication capabilities by working only through written communication. And the natural decision-making agenda represents the normal evolution of decisions in groups operating without special planning. Finally, we presented guidelines on agenda planning and managing relationships within the group. By applying the principles and findings from this chapter to groups you may encounter in the future, you will be able to use this information to enhance communication in the decision-making or problem-solving group.

ENDNOTES

1. Bonnie M. Johnson, *Communication: The Process of Organizing* (Boston: Allyn & Bacon, 1977), p. 208.

2. Kenneth D. Benne and Paul Sheats, "Functional Roles of Group Members," *Journal of Social Issues* 4 (1948): 41–49.
3. Donald F. Michalak and Edwin G. Yager, *Making the Training Process Work* (New York: Harper & Row, 1979).
4. Frederick M. Jablin, "Superior-Subordinate Communication: The State of the Art," *Psychological Bulletin* 86 (1979): 1201–1222. Also see Audrey C. Sanford, Gary T. Hunt, and Hyler J. Bracey, *Communication Behavior in Organizations* (Columbus, OH: Merrill, 1976).
5. Ron Zemke, "Honeywell Imports Quality Circles as Long-term Management Strategy," *Training* (August 1980): 91–95.
6. Ed Yager, "Quality Circle: A Tool for the 80's," *Training and Development Journal* (August 1980): 60–62.
7. Kenneth Burke, *A Rhetoric of Motives* (Berkeley, CA: University of California Press, 1969).
8. J. A. Fishman, *Language in Sociocultural Change* (Stanford, CA: Stanford University Press, 1972). See also J. A. Fishman, *The Sociology of Language* (Rowley, MA: Newberry House, 1972), and J. A. Fishman, ed., *Readings in the Sociology of Language* (The Hague: Mouton, 1972).
9. J. McGrath and I. Altman, *Small Group Research* (New York: Holt, Rinehart and Winston, 1966).
10. John Searle, *Expression and Meaning: Studies in the Theory of Speech Acts* (New York: Cambridge University Press, 1979).
11. William Labov, *Sociolinguistic Patterns* (Philadelphia: University of Pennsylvania Press, 1979). See also R. T. Golembiewski, *The Small Group* (Chicago: University of Chicago Press, 1969).
12. H. Duncan, *Communication and Social Disorder* (New York: Bedminster Press, 1962).
13. Gillian Sankoff, *The Social Life of Language* (Philadelphia: University of Pennsylvania Press, 1980).
14. E. M. Rogers and R. Argawala-Rogers, *Communication in Organizations* (New York: Free Press, 1979), p. 125.
15. D. Katz and R. L. Kahn, *The Social Psychology of Organizations* (New York: Wiley, 1966). See also C. Facheaux and K. MacKenzie, "Task Depending on Organizational Centrality, Its Behavioral Consequences," *Journal of Experimental Sociology and Psychology* 2 (1966): 361–375.
16. George H. Mead, *Mind, Self, and Society: From the Standpoint of a Social Behaviorist* (Chicago: University of Chicago Press, 1934). See also R. Cattell, "Concepts and Methods in the Measurement of Group Syntality," *Psychological Review* 50 (1948): 48–63. See also Burke, *Rhetoric of Motives.*
17. Robert F. Bales, *Personality and Interpersonal Behavior* (New York: Holt, Rinehart and Winston, 1970).
18. Ibid., pp. 137–138. See also Ernest G. Bormann, "Fantasy and Rhetorical Vision: The Rhetorical Criticism of Social Reality," *Quarterly Journal of Speech* (December 1972): 396–407.
19. Irving Janis, *Groupthink* (Boston: Houghton Mifflin, 1982).
20. Robert F. Bales and Stephen P. Cohen, *Symlog: A System for the Multiple Level Analysis of Groups* (New York: Free Press, 1979).
21. John Dewey, *How We Think* (Boston: Heath, 1910). See also J. H. McBurney and K. G. Hance, *The Principles and Methods of Discussion* (New York: Harper & Row, 1939).

22. Gerald M. Phillips, *Communicating in Organizations* (New York: Macmillan, 1982). This advocacy of standard agenda is offset by R. Y. Hirokawa's article "Group Communication and Problem-solving Effectiveness 1: A Critical Review of Inconsistent Findings," *Communication Quarterly* 30 (1982): 134–141.

23. Dewey, *How We Think,*

24. N. C. Dalkey, "The Delphi Method: An Experimental Study of Group Opinion," Rand Corporation Memorandum RM 5888-PR (June 1969).

25. T. Scheidel and L. Crowell, "Idea Development in Small Discussion Groups," *Quarterly Journal of Speech* 50 (1964): 140–145. See also B. A. Fisher, "Decision Emergence: Phases in Group Decision-making," *Speech Monographs* 37 (1970): 53–66. See also M. S. Poole, "Decision Development in Small Groups 1: A Comparison of Two Models," *Communication Monographs* 48 (1981): 1–24, and M. S. Poole, R. D. McPhee, and D. R. Seibold, "A Comparison of Normative and Interactional Explanations of Group Decision-making: Social Decision Schemes Versus Valence Distributions," *Communication Monographs* 49 (1982): 1–19.

26. B. A. Fisher, *Small Group Decision-making* (New York: McGraw-Hill, 1974).

27. Victor H. Vroom, "A New Look at Managerial Decision-making," *Organizational Dynamics* (Spring 1973): 66–80.

chapter *7*

Public Organizational Communication

THE FUNCTION OF PUBLIC ORGANIZATIONAL COMMUNICATION

THE PUBLIC DEFINED

MODELS OF PUBLIC ORGANIZATIONAL COMMUNICATION

The Publicity Model / The Public-Information Model / The Two-way Asymmetric Model / The Coorientaion Model

AN ORGANIZATION'S PUBLICS

Recognizing Publics / Grunig's Situational Theory / Using the Grunig Theory to Define Publics / Predicting Communication Behaviors of Publics / Developing Communication Strategies

TYPES OF PUBLIC ORGANIZATIONAL COMMUNICATION ACTIVITIES

Writing, Editing, and Producing / Conducting Press Conferences and Interviews / Conducting Special Events / Providing Speakers / Conducting Research and Evaluation

MEASURING PUBLIC ORGANIZATIONAL COMMUNICATION EFFECT

Stages of Evaluation / Evaluation Methods
Qualitative Research / Difficulties of Qualitative Analysis / Quantitative Research

Evaluation Questions

William T. Love built a canal in the state of New York that came into the possession of Hooker Chemical Company. You may not have heard of Hooker Chemical but perhaps you have heard of its parent company, Occidental Petroleum. This abandoned canal was determined to have an impermeable clay bottom and sides. It suited its company's purposes perfectly because it could be used safely, and well within governmental regulations, for the disposal of chemical wastes. So, for 11 years—from 1942 to 1953, Hooker disposed of chemicals in this safe and efficient dump site. Hooker sealed the waste material at the site with the same impermeable clay that had proved so efficient for containing the chemical in the canal.

The area around the canal had begun to attract residents by 1953 and therefore the Niagara Falls Board of Education began looking for a site in the area for a school. Under threat of having the property taken over by the board by eminent domain, Hooker decided to cooperate. It deeded the property to the board for $1, with what it thought was an agreement that only surface construction would be approved. The school board honored its agreement, but sold part of the land to several private developers. These developers as well as the city and state did disturb the chemical bed with their construction. Water seeped into the canal through holes in the clay, thereby allowing toxic chemicals to flow out of their bed.

Upon investigating the situation, the Environmental Protection Agency said of the thirty-six residents it examined, they have a greater "risk of cancer, congenital malformations in their offspring, and an increased incidence of miscarriage and abortions."

Examination of both school board documents and newspaper records presented evidence that Hooker repeatedly warned about the danger of disturbing the clay layer at the dump site. Yet, the warnings were ignored. In fact, the Environmental Protection Agency filed in court against Hooker, even though Hooker had repeatedly warned those in authority of the danger. They charged that "Hooker neither warned residents and developers in the vicinity that the contact with materials at the Canal could be injurious, nor did it take any action to prevent future injuries due to exposure of the wastes."

Love Canal is a familiar example of how the activities of an organization have consequences on the publics in its environment. Of course, this is a dramatic case. But it points to a situation where an organization seems to have tried to be responsible to its public; however, it still generated negative consequences. Although the organization you work for may not face such a crisis, all organizations face the potential of problems that are generated from the consequence of their operation within a community. Because of these consequences, a responsible organization must take its publics into account and generate messages fostering cooperation to the best interest of both parties.

This chapter is about public organizational communication. Its purpose is to address the issues of identifying publics and generating communication with them that will create understanding and/or acceptance of a message. First, we define the concept of public and tell how to discover the particular publics an organization may wish to address. Second, we describe four models of public communication. These models serve as a guide to public communication activity for those organizations that adopt them. Third, we examine the concept of linkages and how through a situational theory, communication behaviors of a public may be predicted and acted upon. Fifth, we identify the various kinds of public communication activities an organization might use to present its messages to the publics. Finally, we conclude with a discussion of how an organization's public effort must be evaluated.

THE FUNCTION OF PUBLIC ORGANIZATIONAL COMMUNICATION

Public organizational communication has as its overall purpose the exchange of messages between the organization and its many publics. When speaking of the organization here we mean, of course, a representative of the organization. Often these professionals are found in departments such as corporate communications, public relations, public affairs, public information, or community relations.

The public communication practitioner carries out this overall purpose by identifying the organization's publics and evaluating their attitudes and behaviors in order to execute a program of action to create understanding and/or acceptance of a message. Thus, public organizational communication serves a boundary spanning function in making contact and attempting to influence people and groups who are not members. These people are considered to be beyond the organization's boundary, and thus the term *boundary spanning*. The people involved in this role serve as liaisons between the organization and the publics in its environment.[1]

THE PUBLIC DEFINED

To begin discussing the publics an organization might address, we should define what is meant by the word public. A *public* is a group of people who have a common interest and are capable of engaging in discussion of an issue in order to do something about it. This definition comes from the work of sociologist Herbert Blumer and philosopher John Dewey. We turn to these definitions because of their clear statement of the concept. Blumer[2] suggested that a public is a group of people who:

1. Are confronted by an issue
2. Are divided in their ideas as to how to meet the issue
3. Engage in discussion over the issue

John Dewey[3] defined the term public similarly. He said that a public is a group of people who:

1. Face a similar problem
2. Recognize that the problem exists
3. Organize to do something about the problem

Notice that these definitions would not include the public to which "public opinion poll" usually refers. Blumer[4] has called this kind of group the *mass.* Thus, it might be more proper to call such an activity a *mass opinion poll.*

These definitions don't necessarily suggest face-to-face communication. Members of a public engaged in problem solving may move in a similar direction toward a solution but yet not confer. For example, you may recall the movement against nuclear power plants in the early 1980s. A public, say, environmentalists, became aware of the potential dangers of nuclear power plants, discussed the issue in various communities across the United States, and took action to try to force cancellation of plans for building several nuclear reactors. In this case the public didn't meet face to face.

MODELS OF PUBLIC ORGANIZATIONAL COMMUNICATION

Those who manage an organization's public communication are consciously or unconsciously guided by a model of how the organization ought to relate to its publics. A model guides the public communication activity in specifying relationships and thereby the appropriate communication activity.

We present four models that have evolved over time: the publicity model, the public-information model, the two-way asymmetric model, and the coorientation model. They represent an historical evolution of thought about relationships between an organization and its publics.[5] This doesn't mean that one model is better than the other, nor that earlier models are not used. Each of these models might be useful under certain circumstances and all of them are widely used.

The Publicity Model

The origin of this model can be traced back to the 1830s when press agents began their practice. This activity was spurred on by Benjamine Day's creation of the *New York Sun* in 1834 that sold for a penny. This undersold the usual 6-cent newspaper, thereby bringing the news within the reach of common people. This encouraged those interested in bringing publicity to the average American to print it in the newspaper. Thus, a number of publicity efforts were launched. P. T. Barnum, the founder of the Barnum & Bailey Circus, was foremost in these efforts. He promoted show attractions and made popular the word "jumbo" from his elephant, Jumbo, and the terms "Siamese twins" from joined twins he exhibited.[6] Barnum is representative of those promoting private enterprise, but there were also those promoting social causes. These included causes such as peace, the American Peace Society; the temperance movement; and abolition of slavery.[7]

Eric Goldman[8] dubbed this era "the public be damned" in describing the agents of business and "the public be fooled" in describing those press agents promoting other groups. The emphasis here was on a one-directional message that wasn't necessarily truthful. This model extends the communication models presented in Chapter 1 in that the source is the organization or its spokesperson, and the receiver is a public. Figure 7.1 illustrates the publicity model. The truth wasn't important; the end—the creation of the desired image—justified the effort. Goldman[9] cites an example of this philosophy by quoting an anonymous press agent in 1905, "Ordinarily the business of the press agent is not the decimination

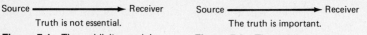

Source ————————▶ Receiver   Source ————————▶ Receiver
  Truth is not essential.   The truth is important.

Figure 7.1 The publicity model.   **Figure 7.2** The public-information model.

of truth, but the avoidance of its inopportune discover." The advent of a change of attitude in public communication brought forth an alternative model—public information.

The Public-Information Model

The twentieth century ushered in the era of big business. Ivy Lee, a journalist who wrote about business, recognized a need to tell the truth. Lee was at the forefront of the public-information movement in public communication. He advocated telling the truth about an organization's activities. His philosophy was simple— if the organization didn't like the truth, it should change its actions so that it could tell the truth. He worked for a number of newspapers, including the *New York Times* and the *New York World* before entering private practice as a public-information practicioner.

Lee formed a firm in 1916, Lee, Harris and Lee,[10] representing many prominent business firms and people. His most famous clients were the United Mine Workers, the Pennsylvania Railroad, and John D. Rockefeller.

Lee viewed the public as rational, and therefore if given enough information, it would come to the right decision on an issue. He concluded that the task of public communication was to supply complete and accurate information. Thus, he viewed the job of the public communication specialist to that of presenting the facts and not to questioning the organization's motives within the limits of public opinion.[11] This model also has a one-way flow (see Figure 7.2).

The public-information model persisted as the only alternative to the publicity model until World War I. During this era a new model of public communication began to evolve that was based on propaganda and persuasion studies by social scientists.

The Two-way Asymmetric Model

The United States entered World War I after an extensive propaganda effort to persuade Americans that the Germans were evil and the Britains correct. One week after the United States entered the war, President Wilson appointed George Creel to head the Committee on Public Information, the agency managing a U.S. government propaganda effort. The committee employed psychological principles of mass persuasion in its highly successful effort to enlist public support, achieving their success by promoting ideas that most Americans held before the war. Its effort was to "codify and standardize ideas already current, and to bring the powerful force of emotions behind them."[12]

Figure 7.3 The two-way aysmmetric model.

Creel's committee gave birth to a new model for managing public communication. This model, called a *two-way asymmetric model* by Grunig and Hunt,[13] had social science as its basis and a communication model that looks like the one in Figure 7.3. The model was two-way, but imbalanced toward the source.

A member of the Creel committee, Edward L. Bernays, who later left the committee for private practice, became the spokesperson for this new model of public communication. His 1923 book, *Crystallizing Public Opinion,* his book published in 1928, *Propaganda,* and his 1952 textbook, *Public Relations,* all articulated his philosophy of public communication.

Bernays's view of public communication encompassed the notion that management needed to be aware of the public's position on the issue. He believed that it was the obligation of public communication specialists to keep management informed, as well as to communicate the organization's view to the public.

Usually managers of public communication approached their organizations about the public by telling management what the publics would accept. There was little or no attempt to tell management how the organization might adapt to the requirements of the situation. Public communication focusing on adaptation is represented by the fourth model, the coorientation model of public communication.

The Coorientation Model

Although a number of managers of public communication have expressed a philosophy that embodies this model, Jack M. McLeod and Steven H. Chaffee[14] have been credited with developing the model. The model recognizes that public communication specialists don't only change the orientations of their publics toward their organization. Instead, it suggests that *both the organization and its publics* jointly orient (coorient) to each other and the parts of their environment they share. Figure 7.4 displays the coorientation model illustrating the relationship between an organization and its publics.

The organizational communication practioner who uses this model would recognize that both the organization and public have an *idea* about certain consequences. Also, each has an *evaluation* regarding the idea—an attitude about the idea. In addition, both the organization (through its members) and the public have a *perception about the other's idea and evaluation* of the situation—that is, what one thinks that the other thinks about the idea and evaluation of it.

Let's consider, for example, a convenience food store owner who is deciding whether to open an additional store in a new neighborhood. The store owner thinks a particular location is good because it is at a major intersection, will provide part-time employment for neighborhood youth, and produce a nice profit. The public, people living nearby, hear of the idea. They see the convenience store as an encroachment of business on a private, residential area, a potential danger

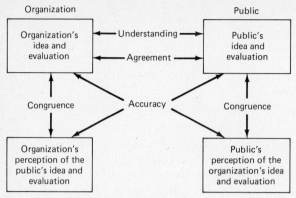

Figure 7.4 The coorientation model.

for small children since it will create more traffic, and a hangout for older children. The store owner evaluates the store site favorably, the public sees it unfavorably.

Now let's turn to the other elements in this model. The word *congruence* is used to express the degree that the organization *thinks* its ideas are similar to those of the public and the degree to which the public *thinks* its ideas are similar to those of the organization. On the other hand, *accuracy* is the degree to which the organization's view of the public's idea and evaluation coincides with the public's actual idea and evaluation. The accuracy of the public's perception would be described similarly. In other words, how near is the guess about the other to what is actually the case. *Understanding* is a representation of how nearly the organization's and public's ideas are the same. Whereas *agreement* suggests the degree to which the evaluations (attitudes) are similar.

Given this terminology and this model, we can look at this situation using the model to help us understand it. As we have already seen, the idea each group has is different. The store manager sees the location as advantageous and the public views the particular location as disadvantageous. Thus, we can conclude that there is no understanding. Although we certainly don't know, we can imagine that each of these parties doesn't currently see the other's point of view. Therefore, accuracy is probably low. We might also suspect that the store owner has a positive evaluation of the idea, whereas the public has a negative view. So there is also a low level of agreement.

Daniel Wackman[15] has conducted laboratory research using this model with dyads. He found that communication between the people increases accuracy, less frequently increases understanding, and least frequently increases agreement. Although research isn't available using this model with publics, we might speculate how communication might affect these elements.

The convenience store owner might hold a neighborhood meeting where he and the members of his public talk about the situation. This discussion should at least increase accuracy of perceptions. The result of having a clearer impression of the other's viewpoint might also lead the way to greater understanding in perhaps modifying each view in the direction of the other party. Agreement, on the other hand, is more difficult to achieve. What will probably happen is that each will hold to its original evaluation of the idea. Finally, congruence is unlikely since we cannot imagine the store owner seeing the ideas and evaluations of the neighbors as similar to his.

AN ORGANIZATION'S PUBLICS

James E. Grunig and Todd Hunt[16] have suggested that an excellent method of determining who the publics of an organization are is to consider the idea of *consequences*. Typically, organizations develop formal communication systems when they believe a public has some consequence on the operation of the organization or the organization is likely to have some consequence on an external public. This relationship is suggested by a model resembling the one in Figure 7.5. It is the perceived consequences that lead to communication between an organization and a public or between a public and an organization.

Let's suppose your local power company believes it could more adequately meet the power needs of the community and do so more cheeply by building a new nuclear power reactor at a site outside the city. The company might well imagine that this would have good consequences for the community. Among several advantages it might provide considerable savings on the individual citizen's power bill, attract new industry because of the lower power cost, and prevent the possibility of "brown out" during the peak electricity draw during summer months. The power company might feel a need to communicate these needs to its consumer public. In addition, the company might be concerned about fears this public might have about nuclear energy and its safety, and the negative consequences the company might have because of this fear. Thus, the arrow in the model is two-way. The consumer public might, indeed, consider these consequences and take action itself. You can imagine various segments of the consumer public organizing to address these consequences. They may fear the safety; they may doubt the need; they may be concerned about how the inital cost of building such a plant might affect their power rates. Because of these concerns, the public might send petitions to the government, picket the company, cut back on power use to "punish" the company, and the like. Thus, consequences are the linkage between an organization and its publics.

Recognizing Publics

The publics of a particular organization may be most easily recognized by considering the idea of *linkages*. *Linkages* is a concept suggested by Milton J. Esman in the report of work with the Agency for International Development.[17] Esman

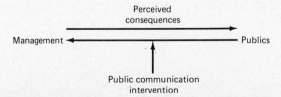

Figure 7.5   Model of public communication intervention.

is concerned about the impact of publics on new organizations in developing countries. He suggests four kinds of linkages: enabling, functional, normative, and diffused.

Enabling linkages are the publics providing authority, control, and regulation that allow an organization to function. These include groups such as legislatures, government agencies, boards of directors, stockholders, and the like. *Functional linkages* connect the organization with publics providing input and receiving output. The input publics include employees, unions, and suppliers of raw materials. Output publics are consumers of products and services. Graduates of universities, clients, consumers, and industrial purchasers are all examples of these publics. *Normative linkages* are represented by organizations that might encounter similar problems and share the organization's interests and values. Often these groups are represented by some formal organization such as the Chamber of Commerce, the American Medical Association, or the Democratic party. *Diffused linkages* are represented by groups that may be subject to consequences of the organization, but they are not necessarily members of any formal group. These are normally groups whose influence on the organization would be considered "public opinion." These publics are identified by general labels such as students, men, women, voters, environmentalists, and the like. Although these groups might also be classified under other linkages, they are placed here because of their diffused nature.

In organizations having formalized public communication programs, these publics are addressed by formal communication efforts and given names. Table 7.1 identifies the usual publics under each of these linkages and the title of the formal communication programs associated with each.

Table 7.1 COMMON PUBLICS AND PUBLIC COMMUNICATION PROGRAMS

Linkage	Publics	Communication Programs
Enabling	Congress	Government relations
	Legislatures	Public affairs
	Boards of directors	Stockholder relations
	Stockholders	Community relations
	Community leaders	
Functional (Input)	Employees	Employee relations
	Unions	Labor relations
	Suppliers	Supplier relations
(Output)	Consumers	Consumer relations
	Industrial purchasers	
	College graduates	
Normative	Associations	Generally no formal programs
	Professional societies	
	Political groups	
Diffused	Environmentalists	Environmental relations
	Community residents	Community relations
	Minority publics	Minority relations

Grunig's Situational Theory

People who manage public communication programs for their organizations probably have no difficulty identifying their obvious publics. A more difficult public to identify is the one relating to a problem or issue. James A. Grunig[18] has developed a theory that provides a set of variables that might be used by those involved in identifying the publics and in creating messages to respond to the publics.

The variables.   Grunig's situational theory suggests that public communication behaviors can best be understood by measuring how members of a public see their situation in relation to organizational consequences. There are three major independent variables—an independent variable explains one or more of the dependent variables. An independent variable is the presumed cause of the dependent variable (the effect). This distinction will become clear as we describe Grunig's theory. These major independent variables suggest when people are or are not part of a public. They are also useful in discovering when people will communicate about an issue. These three independent variables are:

Problem recognition

Constraint recognition

Level of involvement

In other words, the degree to which a group of people recognize a situation (a problem, perhaps), recognize their constraints with respect to the problem, and feel involved—the independent variables—suggests the kind of public they represent (the *effect* or *outcome* produced by the independent variables)—the dependent variable. We might imagine a group of people who have a high degree of problem recognition, who understand their constraints to be minimal, and who have high involvement in the problem. These three independent variables in this combination produce an outcome, an effect, that might be labeled "active public." The active public in this case is the dependent variable.

Problem recognition.   This first variable is derived from John Dewey's theory of human behavior.[19] It suggests that people don't begin to consider a situation unless they discover a felt need to do something. Here they begin to communicate with others as information is required to understand, construct, and confirm the need to act.

In the case of organizations, some member of a public must detect a felt need that might be related to an organizational consequence—a need to act is thereby created, making this person a member of a public. Grunig posits that measuring whether people who the organization thinks are members of a public detect an organizational consequence as a reasonable way to discover if they are members of the public. Figure 7.6 presents an example of questions that might be used to measure this variable.

Remember that the theory says people don't think or communicate about an issue unless they detect a problem. Thus, whether they "stop to think" about an issue would be a logical consequence of problem recognition and an indicator of its presence. The question:

1. First, I would like you to consider how often you *stop and think* about each of the four issues. After I name each of these issues, please tell me whether you stop to think about the situation often, sometimes, rarely, or never. The first issue is:

	Often	Sometimes	Rarely	Never
Deregulation of natural gas	4	3	2	1
Breaking up the Bell Telephone System	4	3	2	1
Chemical disposal sites	4	3	2	1
Acid rain from air pollution	4	3	2	1

Figure 7.6 Measuring problem recognition. (*Source:* James E. Grunig and Todd Hunt, *Managing Public Relations.* New York: Holt, Rinehart and Winston, 1984, p. 150.)

As you can see from this example, one way to measure the presence of this variable is to ask about its effect—a dependent variable. Here the measurement is done by asking about thinking or "information processing" with respect to problem recognition. Other questions might center around a second dependent variable, "information seeking."

Constraint recognition. This variable is represented by the degree to which members of a public see obstacles, constraints, in a particular situation. These constraints limit the person's freedom to affect the situation in any meaningful way. A sample of a simple measure of this variable is displayed in Figure 7.7.

People who perceive serious constraints to having an affect on a situation

Remember that a person feels constrained when he or she, as an individual, cannot do anything about an issue. The following question, therefore, represents a simple measure of that concept:

2. Now, would you think of whether you could do anything personally that would make a difference in the way these issues are handled. If you wanted to do something, would your efforts make a great deal of difference, some difference, very little difference, or no difference?

	Great deal	Some	Very little	None
Deregulation of natural gas	4	3	2	1
Breaking up the Bell Telephone System	4	3	2	1
Chemical disposal sites	4	3	2	1
Acid rain from air pollution	4	3	2	1

Figure 7.7 Measuring constraint recognition. (*Source:* James E. Grunig and Todd Hunt, *Managing Public Relations.* New York: Holt, Rinehart and Winston, 1984, p. 150.)

are probably less likely to seek information, but if they come in contact with information, they will attend to it and process it. If your local power company intends to install a nuclear-powered generator and you believe there is little you can do about it, then you are unlikely to seek information and to process it.

Level of involvement.   Grunig's third variable suggests the kind of communication involvement a member of a public may devote to the situation. Here he assumes that a member of a public who perceives a strong involvement has been driven to seek information and process it, and has recognized low constraints to his or her behavior. Thus, the person has made a commitment to high involvement. Grunig and his colleague describe this process as following this sequence.

> High involvement usually leads to problem recognition because it is difficult to be affected by an organizational consequence without seeing that consequence as a problem. High inolvement decreases constraint recognition because involved people generally try to remove constraints that otherwise would discourage them from communicating and doing something about the problem.

> The involved person most frequently gets rid of constraints by organizing with others facing the same constraints—that is, by becoming a member of an active public. For example, an individual citizen may not be able to do much about air pollution from a nearby steel mill, but a citizen's organization can pressure the government to regulate the polluting plant.[20]

A simple method of measuring level of involvement is shown in Figure 7.8.

Using the Grunig Theory to Define Publics

The Grunig theory can be used effectively to define publics and make predictions about their communication behavior. Grunig used these three variables to identify eight kinds of publics that an organization may encounter. His category system[21] divides the eight publics into two groups—those with high and those

---

The key term used to measure level of involvement, as specified by the theory, is *connections.* Thus, the question asks:

   3. Now, I have a third question about the same issues. For each situation, tell me to what extent you see a *connection* between yourself, personally, and each of the situations. There would be a connection if you believe the issue has affected or could affect you. The first issue is:

	Strong	*Moderate*	*Weak*	*None*
Deregulation of natural gas	4	3	2	1
Breaking up the Bell Telephone System	4	3	2	1
Chemical disposal sites	4	3	2	1
Acid rain from air pollution	4	3	2	1

Figure 7.8   Measuring level of involvement. (*Source:* James E. Grunig and Todd Hunt, *Managing Public Relations.* New York: Holt, Rinehart and Winston, 1984, p. 150.)

with low involvement. Table 7.2 displays the breakdown as well as the type of public. Each public is also designated as having a referent criterion, that is, each believes it has a solution to the situation, or as not having a referent criterion, each believes it doesn't have a solution. Notice the two columns of behavior based on high and low involvement across the top of the table. The other two variables are grouped in combinations in the left-hand column. Grunig has given each of these combinations a behavioral label. In addition, the publics identified by behaviors are given one of three typologies. *Latent public* suggests a group that doesn't recognize the situation as problematic. An *aware public* recognizes a problem, but hasn't acted on it; whereas an *active public* acts to do something about a situation.

Problem-facing behavior is the behavior of a public recognizing that a situation has a particular consequence to an organization and facing no constraints to act on the situation. As an outcome to this situation members of this public are likely to seek and process information. Thus, this will usually be an *active public,* but is an *aware public* when involvement is low.

Constrained behavior results when a public is aware of a problem situation but feels that whatever it does cannot affect the problem. There is a dilemma here because the constraint discourages communication, whereas the problem recognition encourages it. These publics will generally be *aware publics,* but will be either *active* or *latent* depending on the level of involvement they seek.

Routine behavior is the activity of the public that has low recognition of the problem situation but doesn't believe it is constrained. When the level of involvement is high, the public usually has settled on a solution to a problem and actively

Table 7.2   KINDS OF PUBLICS AS DEFINED BY GRUNIG'S COMMUNICATION BEHAVIOR TYPOLOGY

	High Involvement (HI)		Low Involvement (LI)	
	Behavior Type	**Type of Public**	**Behavior Type**	**Type of Public**
Problem-facing Behavior (PF)				
Referent criterion	HIPFR*	Active	LIPER†	Aware.
No referent criterion	HIPF	Active	LIPF	Aware
Constrained Behavior (CB)				
Referent criterion	HICBR	Active	LICBR	Aware
No referent criterion	HICB	Active	LICB	Latent/Aware
Routine Behavior (RB)				
Referent criterion	HIRBR	Active (Reinforcing)	LIRBR	None/Latent
No referent criterion	HIRB	Latent	LIRB	None/Latent
Fatalistic Behavior (FB)				
Referent criterion	HIFBR	Latent	LIFBR	None
No referent criterion	HIFB	Latent	LIFB	None

Source: James E. Grunig, "The Message-Attitude-Behavior Relationship: Communication Behavior of Organizations," *Communication Research* 9 (1982): 171.
   *HIPFR stands for High Involvement, Problem-Facing, Referent Criterion Behavior.
   †LIPER is the Low Involvement situation of Problem-Facing, Referent Criterion Behavior.

supported its decision by seeking information to confirm that decision. Thus the public is active only in the sense that it is engaging in selectively processing information to preserve its solution. Grunig has labeled these publics *active* (reinforcing). When the public has low inolvement, it is a do nothing public and is labeled either *nonpublic* or *latent public.*

A *fatalistic behavior* occurs when the public has low recognition of a problem situation and feels high constraint. This is the apathetic public and is seldom high in involvement. If this group is involved, the involvement is at such a level as to present a *latent public.* Usually this group is not active and therefore is a *nonpublic.*

Predicting Communication Behaviors of Publics

Grunig's research[22] has confirmed the kind of behavior he predicted for each of these publics. This particular study involved identifying publics with respect to corporate-government policy issues. He used four issues that had generated some controversy in the early 1980s: safety of the gas tanks on Ford Pintos, nuclear power, infant formulas, and steel imports. Each of these was considered capable of generating a variety of kinds of publics. For the purpose of this study he divided each public he identified on the basis of whether it believed it had identified a solution (referent criterion) or had not identified a solution (no referent criterion).

Table 7.3 displays the data from this study. The first column shows the percent of the people interviewed fitting into each of the publics. The largest public was the low involvement, fatalistic public, representing 34 percent of those interviewed. The data represented by these numbers in this column show that some publics will be found more often than others. For these business policy issues the high involvement, problem-facing; the high involvement, constrained; and the low involvement, fatalistic publics are the most frequently found publics.

The second and third columns show the percentages of each public that sought and processed information. As you can see from the total probabilities at the bottom, members of publics are about twice as likely to have engaged in information processing than in information seeking. Obviously, people are likely to process information if they happen to come into contact with it but are less likely to actively seek out information.

The remaining five columns show probabilities of communication effects. Message retention refers to a member of a public remembering what he or she heard. In this research a multiple-choice question measured whether the person could remember the stand of a large corporation on the issue. This probability doesn't seem to follow a consistent pattern over the types of publics. This may have been a result of measurement because Grunig used only one question for each issue. The likelihood that a member might have picked out the one particular fact could easily lead to this mixed result.

The pro- and antibusiness cognition column indicates the percent of people having cognitions, rather than having no cognitions, about these issues. This probability was high for all publics, but was highest for the aware and active publics. These are the problem-facing, constrained, and high involvement, routine

Table 7.3 PROBABILITIES OF COMMUNICATION BEHAVIORS AND EFFECTS IN SIXTEEN BEHAVIORAL SITUATIONS

	N	Info. Seek.	Info. Proc.	Message Retention (Percentages)	Pro Bus. Cognit.	Anti-Bus. Cognit.	Attitude	Behavior
High Involvement								
Problem-facing behavior								
Referent criterion	96	77	99	48	95	99	98	52
No referent criterion	18	56	83	44	89	89	94	25
Constrained behavior								
Referent criterion	105	62	92	32	91	93	91	30
No referent criterion	47	49	91	22	81	87	87	13
Routine behavior								
Referent criterion	23	43	83	62	87	100	96	35
No referent criterion	16	19	69	44	53	75	88	19
Fatalistic behavior								
Referent criterion	33	39	76	75	100	94	97	18
No referent criterion	59	29	76	42	75	78	86	10
Low Involvement								
Problem-facing behavior								
Referent criterion	18	61	89	44	89	89	94	11
No referent criterion	9	44	100	22	44	67	89	11
Constrained behavior								
Referent criterion	30	57	87	30	72	93	90	33
No referent criterion	28	46	82	41	89	93	89	18
Routine behavior								
Referent criterion	14	38	75	56	69	75	88	6
No referent criterion	21	24	90	52	48	71	76	11
Fatalistic behavior								
Referent criterion	58	12	58	59	79	88	84	12
No referent criterion	214	20	63	34	57	65	74	6
Total Probability	791	40	79	41	76	83	86	20

Source: James E. Grunig, "The Message-Attitude-Behavior Relationship: Communication Behaviors of Organizations," *Communication Research* 9 (1982): 189.

publics. The probability was lowest for the fatalistic and low involvement routine publics.

The probability of having an attitude was high for all publics, but was lowest for the latent and nonpublics—low involvement/routine behavior and fatalistic behavior publics. This demonstrates that people readily develop an attitude on an issue if they hear about it. The study did not measure how strongly members of the publics held their attitudes, but we would imagine that members of the latent and nonpublics held their attitudes less strongly because they didn't result from active information seeking.

The final column displays the data suggesting probability of behavior. The total probability here is 20 percent. Thus, roughly one in five people surveyed had actually done something about their cognitions. Here, clearly, the most active public is the problem-facing group. Numbers are relatively high for the active and aware publics—problem-facing, constrained behavior, and high involvement /routine behavior—but are low for latent and nonpublics—low involvement/routine behavior and fatalistic behavior publics.

Developing Communication Strategies

Grunig's theory can be useful in planning communication strategies for public organizational communication. Grunig and Hunt[23] have pointed out the five implications of Grunig's theory for developing communication strategies for communicating with publics. After publics are identified the task becomes a decision about the most appropriate message.

Strategy 1. You will notice that some publics do very little information seeking and rarely process information. Here there is very little chance that any message will have an effect. Thus, the strategy is *inaction*. It makes no sense to invest time and money with a public having such a low probability of anyone listening or acting.

Strategy 2. Certain low-probability publics are worth the time and expense necessary to invest in a public communication program directed toward them. Here the key to making this determination is their *linkage*. If the linkage is such that the public can cause severe consequences for the organization—perhaps an enabling linkage, then you can keep them supplied with information. These groups may not pay attention, or may pay only partial attention to the message, and may not retain most of the message, but an organization cannot afford to ignore such groups. This information could inform the public of issues that may lead to problem recognition and a more aware or active public.

Strategy 3. Some publics may process information but will not actively seek information. Here a strategy is needed that will cause the public to take note of the information. Once they have noticed the information, they are likely to process it. *Creativity* is the key here. This is the passive public that must be lured into taking in the message by interest-getting devices such as slogans, photos, illustrations, startling facts, and the like.

Strategy 4.   Active publics must be actively engaged. Here the publics seek information, process the information, and act on it. If the organization doesn't maintain an *active* program to engage such publics, they may go elsewhere for their information. And whatever information they discover, the publics will base their cognitions, attitudes, and behaviors on it. Although the other sources of information may not be hostile to your organization, seldom will they present your organization's view as you would wish it to be presented.

Strategy 5.   Only certain publics are fertile ground for changes in cognition, attitude, and behavior. An *assessment* of your organization's publics will reveal those who are aware and active publics. Here roughly 40 percent of these publics will actually engage in behavior related to the issue. So, if your objective is to change attitudes and behavior, concentrate on the high-involvement, problem-facing publics. Remember, these publics are composed of people who are active in seeking information. This means they will also seek information from other sources and therefore may adopt the attitude represented by these other sources. These publics make reasoned decisions so that messages to them must be carefully formulated.

TYPES OF PUBLIC ORGANIZATIONAL COMMUNICATION ACTIVITIES

The public communication specialist is responsible for managing the organization's communication with its publics through writing and editing documents, releasing information, staging special events, providing speakers, and conducting research and evaluation both to gather information and evaluate the effects of its effort.

Writing, Editing, and Producing

Organizations frequently use the written channel to convey messages to their publics. This enables an organization to communicate with a mass audience in a way that may not be possible through spoken messages. This activity is accomplished through special reports, news releases, brochures and booklets, trade magazine articles, product information, employee newsletters, and shareholder reports.

The audiences that might be a target of such publications are classified as either internal or external. The activity of writing for each of these audiences might be quite different in approach depending on the link to the organization. But there are also some commonalities in this activity. The five basic objectives of this kind of activity are: communication, message retention, acceptance of ideas, formation or change of an attitude, and specific overt behavior.

Because this type of communication is written, it serves as documents presenting the organization and its views. Thus, carefully thought out objectives, attention to objectivity, simple and clearly worded prose, and consistency over time are especially important to this activity.

Conducting Press Conferences and Interviews

The organization may communicate with its publics through the news conference when such an outlet is appropriate. The information must have news value rather than publicity value before an editor will consider sending a reporter. An organization may choose a press conference when it views an issue or an announcement as being complex enough so that a simple news release will not do. The press conference allows an opportunity to answer questions that might not be anticipated in a news release. The question and answer format also allows the organization to avoid being accused of a one-sided statement when announcements are to be made about controversial or complex issues. In addition, some less weighty issues such as the introduction of a new product line are treated in a news conference.

Conducting Special Events

Convention exhibits, anniversary celebrations, special showings of new products, award programs, and tours of facilities are all special events an organization might sponsor. Special events are popular since they often bring large numbers of members of a given public together, and frequently bring them onto the

Public organizational communication specialists often hold a press conference to make a special announcement.

organization's premises. The liabilities of such an event include the consumption of considerable employee energy in planning and carrying out the event as well as the actual dollar cost. In addition, an event that appears to be serving no particular public need or interest may be viewed as merely self-serving publicity calculated to gain free media coverage.

Sometimes an organization will undertake a community project. Although this doesn't fall directly into the category of a special event, it is like a special event in a number of ways—it too is costly and time-consuming. To be successful the organization must have a clear goal in mind that will be recognized by one of its publics as useful. Examples of such projects are joining in on fund-raising for a charity, refurbishing a neighborhood park, or participating in a summer jobs program.

Providing Speakers

Most organizations provide speakers for occasions where a public might make a request. Often the activity is organized through a speaker's bureau. For example, Bell Telephone Company has Teletalkers clubs in major cities serviced by their company. Generally, the company will print a pamphlet identifying the speakers and topics on which they speak. Speakers provide information on new products and services, the history of the company and industry, latest developments in the field, and issues that might have consequences for the particular publics. In addition, many organizations have members who are especially accomplished at a particular hobby or who have traveled widely. Speakers of this type are provided to the publics as a community service.

Conducting Research and Evaluation

Otto Lerbinger[24] has identified four kinds of public communication research activity. These differ on the basis of the particular goal the researcher has in mind. We use Lerbinger's definitions of the research activities:

> *Environmental monitoring* is research conducted to detect trends. The aim is to gather public opinion and information about the social-political climate of the organization.
>
> *Social auditing* is similar to environmental monitoring, but focused on consequences. Here the researcher is interested in detecting the consequences an organization has had on its publics and the extent of correction the organization must make.
>
> *Public relations auditing* is the terminology used to describe research which has as its aim how publics perceive and evaluate an organization. This research seeks to detect publics and answer several questions about these publics. Of primary concern are the standing of the organization with the particular public, the issues that concern the public and the power or impact that public might have.
>
> *Communication auditing* seeks to evaluate how well a particular public communication message got through to the target public. This kind of research takes

two forms. Prior to the delivery of a message content analysis might be employed. If the message is to be written, a readability test could be applied. Once the message is delivered, the result might be measured through a well-constructed survey.

MEASURING PUBLIC ORGANIZATIONAL COMMUNICATION EFFECT

Gone are the days when those who generate messages on behalf of an organization for its publics can do so without having to measure the message's effect. Consider these statements from two practicing managers of public communication for major U.S. corporations.

James Tirone[25] pointed out how important evaluation can be in an essay describing how the Bell Telephone System measures public communication:

In the management of public relations we are ill-advised to assert that we in PR are "different." The corporation is better served, and I think so is the profession, when public relations deliberately attempts to fit itself into the standard procedures of the corporation, by meeting the same tests of performance as other functions and managers.

Robert Marker[26] of Armstrong Cork Company relates how this point was made clear to him by a fellow executive. Marker tells this story of his response to an inquiry about the worth of his public communication effort.

I came prepared with a considerable volume of newspaper clipings, magazine features, and case histories. I pointed out that all this publicity—if strung end to end—would reach from his office located in the west wing of the building, clear across the center wing to the east wing, down the stairs, and out into the main lobby—and there'd still be enough left over to paper one and a half walls of his office. I leaned back in my chair thinking the day had been won. And then it came, the question no one had ever asked before: "But what's all this *worth* to us?" I said it would be difficult to attach a specific value to it. He smiled, "My boy," he said, "I have to attach a value to *everything* in this operation, or else I'm not doing my job. Why don't you go back and write me a memo outlining clearly what this function does for us, and then we'll talk about your operating budget next year."

The question of what a public communication effort is worth is an important one, but even more important to the persons who are doing the communicating is receiving the feedback to know whether they are achieving the desired results from their effort. Research provides the feedback used to adjust messages and carry on a consistent dialogue with the organization's publics.

Researching public communication effect involves more than merely collecting data. It requires understanding the evaluation process and application of research skills. Here our purpose is to describe the evaluation process and discuss evaluation methods. Chapter 8, "Assessment of Organizational Communication," will provide examples of measurement instruments. Those who intend to

Figure 7.9   The evaluation process. (*Source:* Carol H. Weiss, *Evaluation Research: Methods for Assessing Program Effectiveness.* Englewood Cliffs, NJ: Prentice-Hall, 1972, p. 24.)

be actively engaged in this measurement process must acquire the needed research skill to engage in the activity.

Stages of Evaluation

Carol H. Weiss[27] has suggested a model for evaluation research which includes five stages. Figure 7.9 presents these stages.

Specify objectives.   You must specify objectives for a public communication effort in order to be able to measure an effect. Let's suppose your goal is to have your firm's position on deregulation of its industry understood by a certain public. It would be difficult to measure this goal. You might, however, state the goal in terms of objectives, for example, you might say that your objectives are: (1) to create a message that is written clearly enough to be understood and (2) that 40 percent of the people who read your local paper will be able to recall and explain the company's position on the issue.

Measure the objectives.   The next step in this process is to decide how these objectives can be observed and measured. If the objectives haven't been carefully formulated, then the consideration of measurement is considerably complicated. We present some examples of measurement when addressing the issue in Chapter 8.

Collect and analyze the data.   This next step involves administrating the measures selected in step 2 and comparing them to the objectives. Analysis involves consideration of reasons that the objectives have or haven't been met. Where objectives haven't been met, new communication strategies are formulated.

Report the results.   Management is interested in the result of the public communication effort. Here is where you answer the question, "What is this effort worth to the organization?" This step usually is satisfied by a brief report stating the objectives, the plan to achieve those objectives, the extent to which the objectives were met, and what changes will be made as a result of the plan.

Apply the results to decisions.   Evaluation research ought to serve as feedback for an ongoing public communication effort of an organization. But too frequently the practitioner sees them only in terms of justifying the effort. Bad news is therefore buried. Weiss offers several applications of evaluation research:

To continue or discontinue the program

To improve its practices or procedures

To add or drop specific program strategies or techniques

To institute similar programs elsewhere

To allocate resources among competing programs

To accept or reject a program, approach, or theory.[28]

As you can see, there is a variety of considerations the designers of public communication programs have for applying their findings.

Evaluation Methods

The first question faced by the public communication researcher is to decide whether his or her objectives can best be achieved by qualitative or quantitative observations.

Qualitative Research[29]   This methodology doesn't limit itself to what can be counted. Qualitative research describes what can be observed of people in their own worlds. Their written or spoken words are observed, experienced, collected, and studied in order to understand how they view their world. Three types of qualitative data gathering are used in public organizational communication.

  1. *Qualitative observation.* Data are gathered by actually participating in the subject's world while observing and recording the experience. This is managed by either assuming the role of an "onlooker" or "participant." The onlooker merely watches; the participant observer actually takes part in whatever activity the public might be doing. The public may or may not know that it is being observed, but the researcher attempts to gather data without disrupting the normal events in the natural setting. For example, if the power company in your city—as did a particular company in northern Illinois—wanted to know the nature of community concern about nuclear power, it might use qualitative observation. The company might send representatives to meetings of various groups discussing the nuclear power issue. These representatives then would report their impressions to those in the organization who were concerned with its image. These representatives would generally not participate in the groups deliberations. On the other hand, when the researcher is a participant observer, he or she would speak to the subjects, joke with them, empathize with them, and share their concerns.

  Generally, the observer has some preconceived theoretical notions about the data being collected. Using the theory as a guide the person may focus on behavior that will help substantiate that theory. Unlike quantitative researchers, qualitative researchers doesn't limit themselves merely to collecting data about the theoretical ideas of primary interest. When a participant observer, the researcher, as previously mentioned, participates in the group, interacting with its members. All these interactions during this observation are systematically and unobtrusively collected for later analysis.

2. *Qualitative interviews.* This kind of qualitative research differs since the researcher actually intervenes in the structure of the subjects' interaction by asking questions. The question asking may take on one of three formats, but almost always consists of open-ended questions. The power company might select representatives from groups opposed to using nuclear power and interview them. The format of the question asking might be an informal conversation, a general preplanned interview, or a standardized set of open-ended questions. Usually the kind of structure imposed on the question asking is dictated by whether the researcher wants general impressions or specific information.

3. *Focus groups.* This kind of event is more formal than the previous two. Here people, all members of the target public—perhaps members of groups opposed to nuclear power plants, meet in a group interview. The members are chosen so that they are presumed to be typical of the larger public—in this case all groups in the city opposed to nuclear power plants. Usually such a meeting is held off the premises of the organization, in some neutral territory. Once the group is gathered, the researcher proceeds by asking a set of prepared questions. Group members are asked to respond to the questions and to each other's comments. This kind of research has the advantage of gathering data quickly but may be subject to the influence of particularly vocal members. Also, some respondents may not state their true opinions because their view doesn't seem to follow that of the majority.

Difficulties of Qualitative Analysis   Qualitative methods are attractive if they provide the kind of data you need. Their main use is to gather initial impressions and a sense of what is happening. They obviously don't supply hard data that can be used to justify a program and/or show its effect. If you are looking for data to analyze statistically don't select qualitative analysis.

Two difficulties are inherent in qualitative methodology. First, it tends to be more time-consuming than other quantitative methods. For example, you could administer a survey to 100 members of your organization in about 30 minutes. If you were to visit each at his or her work station, it might take a week or more. Second, it is not so easy to remain objective in gathering data through personal interviews as it might be by using more standardized measures. Collecting data in the field through personal interviews introduces the possibility of more "noise" entering the collection process. Personal bias might be introduced and selective perception might take place when the researcher applies his or her own interpretation to editing the lengthy oral responses and dialogues.

Quantitative Research[30]   The aim of quantitative research is the collection of data that describes a situation more objectively than does qualitative research. It also produces data that can be more easily analyzed. This kind of research generally takes either the form of a survey or an experiment.

1. *The survey.* Data are collected from members of a particular public by asking questions or posing statements to be answered on questionnaires or by an oral interview. The power company might decide what information would be helpful in understanding the attitudes of those opposed to nuclear power. They would thus compose specific questions, the answers to which could be counted and tabulated, and then ask these questions of members of the public. The purpose of a survey is to collect information about opinions, attitudes, beliefs, or reactions about issues, policies, procedures, or products. This is undoubtedly the most frequently used method to collect data about publics.

Usually the survey is administered to a sample of a public rather than to every member of the public. The term *population* is used to refer to the group that includes every member of a public. A population might be, for example, all the readers of a local news magazine. Distributing a survey to every reader of a magazine would be impractical because of the time consumed in the process as well as the cost involved. An alternative is to administer the survey to a subgroup of that population representing the larger group. This subgroup is a *sample* of the population.

Two general methods of sampling are used. The first is the *random sample.* Here the idea is to select a sample that will allow you to make statements about the population because you can assume the sample is representative of the entire population. You might select a *simple random sample* of news magazine readers if you had access to a list of all its subscribers. Generally, you would assign a number to each person on the list, then use a table of random numbers to select the sample. (A reference book on research procedures contains such a table.) You might select a *systematic random sample* instead. Here you would select every nth—perhaps the twentieth, thirtieth, or fiftieth—name on the list of subscribers. Finally, you might decide to select a *stratified random sample* by dividing the population into groups of interest. Then you would select a random sample from each group in the population that is part of the overall population. For example, you might divide the list of subscribers by section of the city and then draw a sample from each section. In this case you would want to draw a number of names in proportion to the percent that each section of the town is to the total population.

An alternative and less desirable method of sampling is the *nonprobability sampling.* This method doesn't allow you to make statements about the public, but instead, to make statements about the group you have chosen as a sample. This kind of sampling is done when you don't have enough time or financial resources to draw a random sample and don't need to generalize the results to the whole population. The two kinds of nonprobability sampling used are quota sampling and judgment sampling. *Quota sampling* is like the stratified random sample except that the members are not selected at random. For example, you might wish to poll subscribers to the local news magazine using the same percentage as various groups in the community subscribe. Let's suppose that you know 30 percent of the subscribers are executives. If you were to collect a sample of 1,000, you might select 300 executives from a list put out by the Chamber of Commerce. Although the list you are selecting from doesn't include *all* the executives within your community, you are mainly interested in those who are on that list. In other words, you want only the names of those executives who subscribe to the magazine and who are also on the chamber's list. *Judgment sampling* requires that you know the characteristics of your population and those of your sample. Here you are selecting a sample you believe has the same characteristics as those of your population.

Public communication survey research generally makes use of one of three data collection techniques. Occasionally, *personal interviews* are used. This is only practical if your sample is readily accessible, but this is rarely the case. In order to do a random sample when sampling from a city, you will need to interview people who are located throughout the city. More frequently, the *telephone interview* is used to gather data. The cost in time and energy is clearly reduced and the effort of selecting a sample can be reduced by using a technique known as random digit dialing.[31] The third method of collecting data is the *mail questionnaire*. This has the advantage of being relatively inexpensive, but the disadvantage of a much lower response rate than the telephone interview. Therefore, the mail questionnaire should only be used if the sample is likely to have high interest in your project. Many organizations select a group of people from a particular public and pay them for their opinions over a period of time. This group is called a "panel" and is used to discover how views may have changed over time.

2. *The experiment.* The experiment and the survey differ in that the experiment can establish causes, whereas the survey can only suggest causes. Let's suppose the power company organizes a planned effort to improve its image in the community. It might conduct a survey before and after its campaign and conclude that the campaign caused a change in image. But it may be in error in making this conclusion. The question that always comes up is, "How do they know that something other than their campaign didn't cause the change?" For example, bad news about a competing firm in a nearby community may have caused a change in how the public views the power company in your community. An experiment helps to establish the fact that some competing variable didn't cause the change.

You can see the method used in an experiment to eliminate this doubt by examining Figure 7.10. Notice that before and after measures are taken from both a randomly selected experimental group and a control group. If there is a difference between E_1 and E_2 and that difference is greater than the difference between C_1 and C_2, then you can conclude that your program most likely caused the difference. Measurement of program effectiveness is generally such that it doesn't make using a controlled experiment practical. Instead, you might select a quasi-experimental design or perhaps even a nonexperimental design. Three common designs are the pretest posttest, the posttest only, and the nonequivalent control group.[32]

The *pretest posttest* design requires measuring your group before and after you present your program. You can tell from this design that there was an effect but cannot tell for sure that the effect was a result of the program. The *posttest only* design requires a posttest of both the experimental group and the control group. Here you may discover a difference between the two groups in the direction of the expected change but don't know whether your program was the factor

	Before	After
Experimental	E_1	E_2
Control	C_1	C_2

Figure 7.10 The experimental model.

accounting for the difference. The *nonequivalent control group* design doesn't involve random assignment of people to control and experimental groups. Instead, you identify a control group that is already intact and similar to the experimental group—perhaps a group in a similar city where your firm has an operation. Both of these groups are measured in either a pretest posttest or a posttest only design.

Evaluation Questions

There are two basic types of questions you might use in measuring public opinion and program results. The *open question* allows for a range of unrestricted responses. "What do you know about the XYZ Power Company?" is an example of an open question. You can imagine from speculating about possible answers to this question the variety or responses you might receive. Out of fifty people asked the question, very few of them might mention the same information. Thus, this type of question is suited most to qualitative research or to exploring questions you might ask on a future survey. *Closed questions,* on the other hand, present restrictive responses. Because the responses are specified, you are able to collect data that may be counted and analyzed more readily. Closed questions come in a variety of forms, of which most used are: multiple-choice questions, agreement/disagreement questions, semantic differential questions, and ranking questions. We provide an example of each.

Multiple-choice questions may tap information or attitudes. An information question might be:

Of which political party are you a member?

_____ Republican		_____ Libertarian
_____ Democrat		_____ Socialist
_____ Independent		_____ Other
_____ American		_____ None

How much do you earn in a year?

_____ Under $5,000		_____ $20,001–30,000
_____ $5,001–10,000		_____ $30,001–40,000
_____ $10,001–20,000		_____ Over $40,000

Or the multiple-choice question might call for an evaluation.

How would you rate the service of the XYZ Power Company?

  _____ Excellent   _____ Poor

  _____ Good   _____ Very Poor

  _____ Average

Agreement/Disagreement questions allow the respondent to make choices along a 5-point scale. The middle point on such a scale is considered the neutral point. Here are several examples of agreement/disagreement questions:

Please respond to the following questions by
circling the appropriate response. Do you
strongly agree, agree, neither agree nor disagree,
disagree, or strongly disagree?

The XYZ Power Company provides adequate
service...SA   A   N   D   SD

The employees of the XYZ Power Company are
friendly...SA   A   N   D   SD

The rates for power charged by the XYZ Power
Company are about right..................................SA   A   N   D   SD

Semantic differential questions are composed of questions with a set of polar adjectives (adjectives with opposite meaning). Between each set of adjectives there are seven points to suggest the respondent's experience of the question. Here are several examples of semantic differential type questions:

How satisfied are you with the service of the XYZ Power Company?

       Satisfied _____ _____ _____ _____ _____ _____ _____ Dissatisfied

How important are the following services to you?

  Energy Audits

  Very important _____ _____ _____ _____ _____ _____ _____ Unimportant

  Appliance Sales:

  Very important _____ _____ _____ _____ _____ _____ _____ Unimportant

---

A fifth type of question calls for a *ranking* of several items. Examples of ranking question are:

How would you rank the XYZ Power Company with respect to these other utilities? Mark the most responsible utility 1, the next in responsibility 2, and so forth.

_____ Municipal Water Service

_____ South Telephone Company

_____ XYZ Power Company

_____ Acme Sanitation Service

_____ Central Gas Company

SUMMARY

Public organizational communication is the activity that allows an organization to exchange messages with its many publics. This communication activity involves identifying the organization's publics and evaluating their attitudes and behavior. The goal is to execute programs of action that will create understanding and/or acceptance of a message. This is an organizational boundary spanning function.

A public is a group of people who face a similar problem, recognize that the problem exists, may differ in their ideas as to how to meet the issue, and organize to engage in discussion and do something about the problem. A public need not actually meet face to face to confer.

Public communicators have followed different models in representing their organization's communication relationship with its publics. The publicity model is a one-way communication model including an assumption that telling the truth to the public is not necessarily important. Here the communication is assumed to move only from the organization to the public. The public-information model is also a one-way communication model, but it differs in that telling the truth is important. A third model, the two-way asymmetric model, is grounded on the principles of social science. Those employing this model use social science research on persuasion and look to the feedback they receive from the publics as a guide to formulating messages. The final model, the coorientation model, emphasizes that both the organization and its publics change their orientations toward each other as they communicate. The concern here is an analysis of understanding, agreement, congruence, and accuracy.

One method of identifying publics is to look for groups of people on which the organization has *consequences.* Consequences provide the reason to form the relationship and to communicate. Organizations experience these consequences as *linkages.* There are four kinds of linkages. Enabling linkages bind those publics to the organization that provides authority, control, and regulation, allowing an organization to function. Functional linkages connect the organization with publics that provide input and receive output. Normative linkages are represented by organizations that might encounter similar problems and share the organization's interests and values. Diffused linkages are represented by groups that may be subject to consequences of the organization but that are not necessarily members of any formal group.

James Grunig suggests that relevant aspects of the various publics of an organization can be measured and used to formulate communication strategies. These variables are the degree of problem recognition, constraint recognition, and level of involvement. The first variable suggests that people don't begin to consider a situation unless they discover a felt need to do something. The second represents the degree to which members of a public see obstacles, constraints, in a particular situation. The third suggests the kind of communication involvement a member of a public may be devoting to the situation. A member desiring strong involvement will seek information, process it, and act because of low constraints on his or her behavior.

Grunig's theory can be used to identify types of publics, based on their particular behavior. A public may be described as problem facing when it recognizes the situation as having particular consequences to it and faces no behavioral constraints. These publics are typed as either active, when their involvement is high, or aware, when involvement is low. A public whose behavior is constrained is aware of the problem but feels that whatever it might do cannot affect the problem. This public is labeled aware and either active or latent depending on the level of involvement it seeks. A public whose behavior is described as routine has low recognition of the problem situation, but doesn't feel constrained. When this type of public is involved, it is called active. However, when its involvement is low, it is either a nonpublic or a latent public. The public whose behavior is described as fatalistic has low recognition of the problem situation and feels high constraint. This public is apathetic and labeled either latent, if there is some involvement, or a nonpublic, if there is no involvement. We presented five strategies for communicating with each of these publics, carried out through a variety of communication activities. Typical activities include writing, editing, and producing; conducting press conferences and interviews; conducting special events; providing speakers; and conducting research and evaluation.

Public organizational communication specialists plan and modify programs based on measurement of the program's effect. This process can be seen as stages that follow this sequence:

Specifying objectives → Measuring the objectives → Collecting and analyzing data → Reporting the results → Applying the results

The evaluation itself might employ either qualitative or quantitative methods. Qualitative methods describe what can be observed of people in their own worlds. Major methods are qualitative observation, qualitative interviews, and focus groups. Qualitative analysis may, however, be time-consuming and less objective than other methods of research. This type of analysis rarely generates numerical data. Quantitative methods produce data through either a survey or experiment. In conducting a survey, a researcher draws a sample from a population and the members of the population are either given an oral interview or written questionnaire for response. The data are then tabulated and analyzed.

The experiment involves measuring the effect of an effort with the experimental group and comparing it against a similar group that was not exposed to the program. Both groups are measured before and after the experiment on the relevant measures. These are the data to which a statistical measure is applied to determine if a significant effect was observed.

ENDNOTES

1. Tushman and Scanlan provide additional information on this boundary spanning process. See M. Tushman and T. Scanlan, "Boundary Spanning Individuals: Their Role in Information Transfer and Their Antecedents," *Academy of Management Journal* 24 (1981): 289–305.
2. Herbert Blumer, "The Mass, the Public and Public Opinion," in *Reader in Public Opinion and Communication,* 2d ed., ed. Bernard Berelson and Morris Janowitz (New York: Free Press, 1966), pp. 43–50.
3. John Dewey, *The Public and Its Problems* (Chicago: Swallow, 1927).
4. Blumer, *The Mass,* pp. 43–50.
5. For an excellent example of the history of this area, see Scott M. Cutlip and Allen H. Center, *Effective Public Relations,* 5th ed. (Englewood Cliffs, NJ: Prentice-Hall, 1978), pp. 65–94.
6. John E. Marston, *Modern Public Relations* (New York: McGraw-Hill, 1979), p. 21.
7. Edward L. Bernays, *Public Relations* (Norman: University of Oklahoma Press, 1952), pp. 39–49.
8. Eric F. Goldman, *Two-way Street: The Emergence of the Public Relations Counsel* (Boston: Bellman Publishing, 1948), p. 1.
9. Goldman, *Two-way Street,* p. 2.
10. Ray Eldon Hiebert, *Courtier to the Crowd* (Ames: Iowa State University Press, 1966), p. 46.
11. Hiebert, *Courtier,* p. 317.
12. Curtis D. MacDougall, *Understanding Public Opinion* (New York: Macmillan, 1952), p. 108.
13. James E. Grunig and Charles Hunt, *Managing Public Relations* (New York: Holt, Rinehart and Winston, 1983), p. 37.
14. Jack M. McLeod and Stephen H. Chaffee, "Interpersonal Approaches to Communication Research," *American Behavioral Scientist* 16 (1973): 469–500.
15. Daniel Wackman, "Interpersonal Communication and Coorientation," *American Behavioral Scientist* 16 (1973): 537–550.
16. Grunig and Hunt, *Managing,* pp. 9–11.
17. Milton J. Esman, "The Elements of Institution Building," in *Institution Building and Development,* ed. Joseph W. Eaton (Beverly Hills, CA: Sage, 1972), pp. 19–40.
18. James E. Grunig, "A New Measure of Public Opinions on Corporate Responsibility," *Academy of Management Journal* 22 (1979): 738–764.
19. John Dewey, *Logic: The Theory of Inquiry* (New York: Holt, Rinehart and Winston, 1938); John Dewey, *Human Nature and Conduct* (New York: Modern Library, 1922).
20. Grunig and Hunt, *Managing,* p. 152.
21. James E. Grunig, "The Message-Attitude-Behavior Relationship: Communication Behaviors of Organizations," *Communication Research* 9 (1982): 163–200.
22. Ibid., 163–200.

23. Grunig and Hunt, *Managing,* pp. 158–159.
24. Otto Lerbinger, "Corporate Use of Research in Public Relations," *Public Relations Review* 3 (Winter 1977): 11–19.
25. James F. Tirone, "Measuring the Bell System's Public Relations," *Public Relations Review* 3 (1977): 38.
26. Robert K. Marker, "The Armstrong/PR Data Measurement System," *Public Relations Review* 3 (1977): 51–52.
27. Carol H. Weiss, *Evaluation Research: Methods for Assessing Program Effectiveness* (Englewood Cliffs, NJ: Prentice-Hall, 1972), pp. 24–25.
28. Weiss, *Evaluation Research,* pp. 16–17.
29. For an in-depth discussion of qualitative research methods, see Michael Quinn Patton, *Qualitative Evaluation Methods* (Beverly Hills, CA: Sage, 1980).
30. For an in-depth discussion of quantitative research methods as they apply to public communication, see Roger D. Wimmer and Joseph R. Dominick, *Mass Media Research: An Introduction* (Belmont, CA: Wadsworth, 1983).
31. This technique requires that the last four digits of the telephone number be selected from a table of random numbers. The first three exchange numbers are selected from a listing of these in the telephone book. This technique allows you to reach those with unlisted numbers.
32. Bruce H. Westley, "The Controlled Experiment," in *Research Methods in Mass Communication,* ed. Guido H. Stempel, III, and Bruce H. Westley (Englewood Cliffs, NJ: Prentice-Hall, 1981), pp. 203–207.

four

ORGANIZATIONAL
COMMUNICATION
CHANGE

chapter 8

Assessment of Organizational Communication

DATA-GATHERING TECHNIQUES AND PROBLEMS

Interviews / Questionnaires / Observation

ORGANIZATIONAL COMMUNICATION COST ANALYSIS

ORGANIZATIONAL COMMUNICATION POLICY ANALYSIS

THE ICA COMMUNICATION AUDIT

THE WGW COMMUNICATION AUDIT

Exploratory Interview Guide / Assessing Communication Flow /
Assessing Interpersonal Relationships / Assessing Interviews /
Assessing Group Performance / Assessing Public Communication
/ Assessing Communication Climate

DATA ANALYSIS AND INTERPRETATION

DATA REPORTING

Organizational communication can work efficiently and effectively to help employees reach their organizational and personal goals. Assessing successful organizational communication shows how communication operates to facilitate success in various situations. Such assessments confirm what the organization suspected, that its members are doing a good job communicating, considering the constraints of the situation. The demands of each situation are so different that no simple formula for effective, efficient organizational communication can be applied to every situation. The complexity of each situation requires careful assessment just to determine whether existing communication practices are adequate. Effective organizational communication practices vary with the situation, just as management has adapted its practices to the organization's needs and objectives. Mintzberg's case studies of managerial communication demonstrate how each manager produces communication behavior designed for the demands of the specific situation.[1]

But organizational communication doesn't always work efficiently or effectively in job performance. Communication efficiency may vary according to how individual employees make use of the available communication resources. The same communication opportunities may be used by some employees and ignored by others. The results show in their quality of work. Communication effectiveness is determined by how well organizational communication facilitates successful job performance. Problems in either aspect of communication performance call for assessment of organizational communication by an objective, authoritative observer and analyst.

Assessing organizational communication thereby seems desirable in situations where the organization: (1) changes in size or structure, (2) has problems maintaining past performance levels, or (3) has problems reaching performance goals. Any of these conditions call attention to the role of communication in the organization's operations. Assessment can take many forms, each with its specific purpose. For example, Rothwell[2] identifies five types of assessment: (1) evaluation research to show how current programs compare to preferred programs, (2) action research to establish goals for training and organizational development, (3) critical research to identify the belief system operating in an organization, (4) job analysis to check how closely employee activities match job descriptions, and (5) performance analysis of employee performance according to criteria for competence and excellence. Limiting assessment to communication behaviors simplifies the task but still involves every organizational operation.

In this chapter we focus on techniques and issues related to communication assessment with several forms of audit procedures. We start by discussing data-gathering techniques and problems in interviews, questionnaires, and observation. After considering issues involved in organizational communication cost and policy analysis, we describe the ICA (International Communication Association) communication audit. Based on our own experiences, we offer the WGW (Wilson, Goodall, and Waagen) audit procedure as an alternative or supplement to the ICA audit. Data analysis and interpretation in each of these auditing processes will be compared to show some alternatives in handling data. The chapter closes with guidelines for data reporting and a summary of the basic principles of

structural patterns of interaction determined by task requirements.[4] Networks also display psychological characteristics in their members and the network's organization.[5] Thus, observation should account for structural and psychological forces at work in the organization's communication networks. For this observation to be of use in assessment, the results should lead to accurate evaluation of job performance in terms of communication skills. If observation can provide information about communication practices, a specific behavior can be linked to an observed response and later to attitudes about the communication behavior. The effectiveness of a given communication practice can therefore be evaluated as part of performance appraisal, and observation can produce useful feedback for the organization.[6] We describe two such observation systems in later sections on the ICA audit and the WGW audit. But first let's consider organizational communication cost assessment and the analysis of organizational communication policy.

ORGANIZATIONAL COMMUNICATION COST ANALYSIS

Organizational communication cost analysis is one of the most productive assessments you can make. Knowing what a particular task has cost the organization gives value to communication involved in task resolution. Once communication acquires value to the organization, all concerned are motivated to improve efficiency and effectiveness in the use of this resource. The cost of communication also objectifies and quantifies communicative behaviors, leading to a clearer understanding of how to improve communication processes in the organization.[7] Studies report that 35 to 50 percent of a supervisor's time is used communicating with subordinates.[8] Most of this communication concerns task issues, especially when subordinates need help with their work.[9] Thus, communication cost analysis needs to show how much communication exists between superiors and subordinates, and about what tasks they communicated.

Cost analysis also needs to indicate the other personnel involved in a specific communication situation and what aspects of the task demanded their attention. In order to assess the cost of communication, you will need to answer six types of questions about the situation.

1. Who is involved in the communication being assessed? Who is superior and who is subordinate? Who outside this hierarchy is associated with the communication?
2. What is the task generating the communication behavior? What are this task's objectives?
3. Why are these participants involved in this task? Is this communication part of their jobs?
4. When do these personnel communicate? With what frequency and regularity do they communicate?
5. How do they communicate? What medium or channel do they use, and how does communication flow through their hierarchy?
6. How much does this communication cost each participant? What is the cost in salary, and also in terms of the equity of the situation? Is there an emotional or social cost?

---

1. Describe the task to be costed in terms of behaviors.
2. Identify behaviors involving communication.
3. Describe communication network coordinating communication behaviors.
4. Determine the time spent by each person involved with the task in various communication functions.
5. Value time spent by each person.
6. Compute total cost of communication for the task.

Figure 8.3 Communication cost analysis procedure.

These questions show the issues involved in communication cost analysis. To answer these questions, you need to employ a six-step procedure, summarized in Figure 8.3. Look at the procedure as a whole and then consider what each step in this procedure entails.

The first step calls for interviews to assess the behaviors involved in a specific task. For example, interviewing a manager could tell you what is entailed in producing a performance appraisal—the manager would have to acquire the proper forms, consult records of employee progress, read the employee's self-evaluation, recall personal experiences with the employee, prepare the appraisal forms, schedule a meeting with the employee, meet with the employee to discuss the appraisal, and file the final appraisal forms with the personnel office. Time might be spent communicating in some way in each stage of this task, but communication is the central activity in acquiring information for the appraisal and in the meeting with the employee to discuss the appraisal. You need to analyze the networks from which the manager acquires information to assess the cost of the appraisal process.

Roberts and O'Reilly have devised a simple way to evaluate the networks in which the manager operates.[10] In their study of communication networks in permanently assigned Navy units, they asked three questions to identify the members of three communication networks. To identify sources of expertise, they asked, "When you need technical advice in doing your job, whom are the persons you are most likely to ask?" To identify social contacts, they asked, "With which persons in this squadron are you most likely to have social conversations (not work related) during the course of the day?" And to identify points of contact with the formal organizational hierarchy, they asked, "If you are upset about something related to the Navy or to your job, to whom in the squadron are you most likely to express your dissatisfaction (gripe) formally?" Respondents indicated whom they talked to, the frequency of communication, and the importance to them of each communication.

By modifying these questions to suit the organization at hand, you can also assess the extent of the network(s) involving a particular task. In the case of the manager and the performance appraisal, the task involves a network relating to expertise when information about the employee's technical capability is acquired from co-workers and supervisors. Social networks may come into play when the manager inquires into the employee's social activities at work. The network tying

Network member	$/year	$/hour	Time used	Cost
Manager	36,000	18.0	2 hours	36.00
Supervisor	26,000	13.0	½ hour	6.50
Project manager	38,000	19.0	¼ hour	9.75
Secretary	9,000	4.5	¼ hour	1.13
Employee	21,000	10.5	½ hour	5.25
			Total	58.63

Figure 8.4   Communication cost tabulation.

the manager to the hierarchy provides information about the employee from supervisors, co-workers, and subordinates. Once the manager's points of contact with networks in the organization have been identified, information about the frequency of communication can then be used to establish how much time those involved have spent on the task.

In your interviews, you discover that the manager spent 30 minutes talking to a supervisor about the employee's technical performance after using 30 minutes to read a project manager's report on the employee's efficiency and go over the employee's history in his personnel folder. The manager took 15 minutes to verify her impression of the employee by speaking with the project manager and used a further 15 minutes to dictate her evaluation to the secretary. Meeting with the employee takes 30 minutes, time enough to discuss the appraisal, amend one statement, and set general goals for future performance. The appraisal was then forwarded to personnel for action on its recommended raise. Figure 8.4 shows tabulations of the time spent by each participant and the value of their time to estimate the total cost of this communication. These costs reflect the immediate expense of the human resources involved in the task. Costs for operating the office that supplied the forms, made the appointment, and sent the report to Personnel should be added to the total.

An appraisal is a good example of a task that is comprised entirely of communication. No salable product is produced, and the communication cost must be underwritten by profitable activities. Performance appraisal can be effective in increasing the productivity of every employee. But the efficiency of the appraisal process can be enhanced by communication cost consciousness. If evaluated on the microlevel as examples of organizational communication practices, processes like appraisal can be streamlined for maximum cost effectiveness. For evaluation of the organization as a whole, we turn to the macrolevel and organizational communication policy analysis.

ORGANIZATIONAL COMMUNICATION POLICY ANALYSIS

In his analysis of the communication behavior of five chief executives, Mintzberg examined 1,258 instances of written or verbal communication.[11] Of these communications, 890 used the mail and the remaining 368 were verbal communications. One significant finding in this study was that the managers initiated from

25 to 52 percent of this verbal contact. The manager therefore had control over the form and content of this communication. The manager also involved subordinates in 54 to 77 percent of these communications, making the form chosen for these encounters a model for the subordinate's communication. Through a process of continued modeling down the hierarchy, the chief executive's communication behavior may well become the format or norm for communication in the entire organization. Ouchi's observation of Japanese and Japanese-style organizations shows that a manager can expect compliance with a clearly expressed organizational philosophy.[12] In four of five organizations studied by Mintzberg, the manager was involved in giving information approximately as often as in receiving information.[13] Thus, the interchange of messages between managers and the rest of the organization offers the organization an opportunity to develop a communication policy for transferring information up and down the hierarchy.

Greenbaum separates organizational communication into two levels, communication activities like the appraisal process we discussed in cost analysis and a communication system aimed at implementing the organizations objectives and policies through communication programs.[14] Organizational communication policy analysis calls for you to identify three aspects of the organization's communication system. First, what formal policy statements are part of the organization's commitment to communication programs? Second, how does the corporate philosophy integrate communication into its objectives and policies about corporate activities? Third, how are these formal policy statements modified by informal communication? Answers to these questions combine to describe the organization's communication system and the policies behind it. Figure 8.5 summarizes what you need to do to perform a communication policy analysis of the formal and informal communication system.

The result of policy analysis should be improved formal communication channels, planned communication supported by policy statements. This analysis should also produce greater consistency between the communication practices and the organization's objectives. Policy statements can be adjusted to incorporate features of the informal communication practices, thereby institutionalizing

Formal policy	*Informal policy*
1. Acquire organization chart and documents stating communication policies and organizational objectives.	2. Interview to discover informal channels and unstated policies and objectives.
3. Determine potential formal networks according to policy.	4. Verify what aspects of formal policy are known and in actual use.
6. Plan to adjust formal policy to match objectives and endorse informal practices.	5. Determine actual informal practices that suit organizational objectives.

Figure 8.5 Organizational communication policy analysis.

Organizational communication auditors collect data through questionnaires.

productive innovations while maintaining the actual communication structure. Now that we have considered communication cost and policy analysis as separate enterprises, let's turn to a complete assessment package.

THE ICA COMMUNICATION AUDIT

The International Communication Association (ICA) recognized the need for a comprehensive package of measurement instruments to assess organizational communication. Working from 1971 to 1979, Goldhaber and his associates developed five types of measurement tools.[15] Questionnaires, interviews, network analysis, communication experience reports, and communication diaries have all been used as part of the ICA audit. All five used together constitute the most complete possible audit, but any single technique can be used alone. We don't intend that this description of the ICA audit's features be a complete summary, but refer you to the sources just cited for further information on using these techniques. The ICA audit requires some computer processing of the results and may be limited by constraints in the organizational situation, but all procedures and instruments are reliable and in the public domain since 1979.

The questionnaire survey, which can be used for any of nine topics, is summarized in Figure 8.6.

These questionnaire surveys evaluate the situation in terms of the quantity

Topic

1. Demographic information
2. Amount of information received and needed from selected channels
3. Timeliness of information received from key sources
4. Quality of communication relationships
5. Satisfaction with major organizational outcomes
6. Amount of information received and needed from others on selected topics
7. Amount of information sent or needed to be sent to others on selected topics
8. Amount of follow-up or action taken and needed on information sent to others
9. Amount of information received and needed from selected sources

Figure 8.6   Topics for questionnaire surveys.

and quality of communication. Once the demography of the sample has been established with the first survey, the auditor can evaluate the details of the sample's experiences with the organization's communication practices. Although the communication experience reports can also acquire information about selected examples of communication that is significant to the employee, the questionnaire covers communication experiences in more detail and with greater consistency among all the members of the sample.

Sample Format of ICA Communication Audit Survey

Receiving information from others		
Topic area	This is the amount of information I receive now *Very little Little Some Great Very great*	This is the amount of information I need to receive *Very little Little Some Great Very great*
How well I am doing in my job	**1.** 1 2 3 4 5	**2.** 1 2 3 4 5
My job duties	**3.** 1 2 3 4 5	**4.** 1 2 3 4 5
Organizational policies	**5.** 1 2 3 4 5	**6.** 1 2 3 4 5
Pay and benefits	**7.** 1 2 3 4 5	**8.** 1 2 3 4 5
How technological changes affect my job	**9.** 1 2 3 4 5	**10.** 1 2 3 4 5
Mistakes and failures of my organization	**11.** 1 2 3 4 5	**12.** 1 2 3 4 5
How I am being judged	**13.** 1 2 3 4 5	**14.** 1 2 3 4 5
How my job-related problems are being handled	**15.** 1 2 3 4 5	**16.** 1 2 3 4 5
How organization decisions are made that affect my job	**17.** 1 2 3 4 5	**18.** 1 2 3 4 5
Promotion and advancement opportunities in my organization	**19.** 1 2 3 4 5	**20.** 1 2 3 4 5

Figure 8.7   Questionnaire survey format.

The questionnaires are most useful in establishing current communication practices. Figure 8.7 shows a sample of the format used in the questionnaire about communication from others. Employee satisfaction with the situation may easily be assessed for a variety of topics, and needs for different communication practices identified. Responses about the level of communication required may be used to set goals for organizational development in selected areas. Repeated use of the questionnaires over time may show the rate of change in organizational communication. One weakness of the ICA audit's questionnaires is that the topics and the wording of the questions remain as developed as in the past. A questionnaire using the language of the organization at hand and the topics of interest in the specific case would have some advantage over the fixed ICA format.

Interviews are conducted according to the ICA audit exploratory interview guide. Figure 8.8 shows the questions as represented by Goldhaber.[16] The interview should identify perceptions of the formal and informal communication

---

In the following questions we are talking about communication. Although *communication* can have several different meanings, depending upon the context, we use the term quite broadly to include any message sent or received in your organization.

1. Describe your job (duties, function). What decisions do you usually make in your job? What information do you *need* to make those decisions and from where should you get it? What information do you *actually* get to make those decisions and from whom? Are there formal (written) or informal policies in your organization that determine how you get this information? Should any policies be added, changed, or abandoned?
2. What are the major communication *strengths* of this organization? Be specific.
3. What are the major communication *weaknesses* of this organization?
4. Describe the *formal* channels through which you typically receive information about this organization? What kinds of information do you tend to receive? How often?
5. Describe the *informal* channels through which you typically receive information about this organization. What kinds of information do you tend to receive? How often?
6. How often, if ever, do you receive information about this organization that is of low value or use to you? If and when you do, what kinds of information do you receive? Be specific. From whom do you receive this?
7. What would you like to see done to improve information flow in this organization? Why hasn't it been done yet?
8. Describe the way decisions are typically made in this organization.
9. When conflict occurs in this organization, what is its major cause? How is conflict typically resolved?
10. Describe the communication relationship you have with your immediate supervisor. Your co-workers. Middle management. Top management. Your subordinates (if appropriate).
11. How do you know when this organization has done a good or bad job toward accomplishing its goals? What measures of effectiveness are used in this organization?

Figure 8.8 ICA audit exploratory interview guide.

channels from the user's perspective. This information could be valuable to indicate how well specific communication resources are being utilized. Questions about information flow and decision making might be used to give detailed explanations of problems indicated in questionnaires.

The interviews and questionnaires may be accompanied by network analysis and reports of communication experience. Communication experiences may be reported through the specific communication experience form or via a communication diary. Network analysis identifies the role of individual communicators in a communication network. The degree to which an employee has contact with others may be determined by a questionnaire (see Figure 8.9) subjected to computer analysis. Results of the analysis indicate group membership in a network and status as an isolate separate from the group or a liaison linking groups together. Specific communication experiences are collected with a form (see Figure 8.10) designed to identify examples of high- or low-quality communication. These examples are set against the routine communication behaviors reported in the ICA communication diary (see Figure 8.11). The

During a typical workday, I usually communicate about work-related matters with the following people through the following channels:

	Identi-fication	Formal organizational structure	Informal (grapevine) organizational structure
Executive		How important is the communication?	
Stenographer-secretary	0001	A B C D E	A B C D E
Senior stenographer	0002	A B C D E	A B C D E
Executive secretary	0003	___ A B C D E	___ A B C D E
Assistant executive director	0004	A B C D E	A B C D E
Assistant manager	0005	___ A B C D E	___ A B C D E
Telephone operator	0006	___ A B C D E	___ A B C D E
Executive director	0007	___ A B C D E	___ A B C D E
Administration and Finance			
Assistant director for administration	0008	A B C D E	A B C D E
Typist	0009	___ A B C D E	___ A B C D E
Accounting clerk	0010	___ A B C D E	___ A B C D E
Accounting clerk-typist	0011	A B C D E	A B C D E
Assistant accountant	0012	A B C D E	A B C D E
Senior accountant	0013	___ A B C D E	___ A B C D E
Typist	0014	___ A B C D E	___ A B C D E
Stenographer	0015	___ A B C D E	___ A B C D E

Key: A = not at all important; B = somewhat important; C = fairly important; D = very important; E = extremely important.

Figure 8.9 ICA communication audit network analysis instrument.

While you were filling out the previous section, the questions may have brought to mind a recent work-related experience of yours in which *communication* was particularly ineffective or effective. Please answer the questions below and give us a clearly printed summary of that experience.

A. To whom does this experience primarily relate? (Circle *one.*)
   1. subordinate   2. co-worker   3. immediate supervisor
      4. middle management   5. top management

B. Please rate the quality of communication described in the experience below (circle *one*):
   1. effective   2. ineffective

C. To what item in the previous section does this experience primarily relate? ____ (put in the item number)

Describe the communicative experience, the circumstances leading up to it, what the person did that made him or her an effective or ineffective communicator, and the results (outcome) of what the person did. PLEASE *PRINT*. THANK YOU.

_____

_____

_____

_____

_____

_____

_____

Figure 8.10   ICA communication audit communication experience form.

diary and the experiences provide a subjective, descriptive account of communication practices which are indicated more objectively by the questionnaires and network analysis. Taken as a whole, the ICA communication audit produces data for analysis and evaluation of formal and informal organizational communication.[17] Using these data depends on how well you balance information from questionnaires against anecdotes from interviews and experience reports. Since the interviews give communicators a chance to explain the situation in detail, interviews are the principal source of ICA auditor's understanding of an organization's communication problems. The mass of information derived from the rest of the organization through questionnaires is likely to be interpreted in terms of a relatively small number of interviews. We offer our own assessment procedure, the WGW (Wilson, Goodall, and Waagen) audit as a supplement to ICA audit procedures.

THE WGW COMMUNICATION AUDIT

The WGW communication audit is intended to focus on the results of formal and informal communication. The purpose of the following procedures is to assess the

	Communication							
	1	2	3	4	5	6	7	(etc.)
Initiator								
Self	—	—	—	—	—	—	—	
Other party	—	—	—	—	—	—	—	
Channel								
Face-to-face	—	—	—	—	—	—	—	
Telephone	—	—	—	—	—	—	—	
Written	—	—	—	—	—	—	—	
Kind								
Job-related	—	—	—	—	—	—	—	
Incidental	—	—	—	—	—	—	—	
Rumor	—	—	—	—	—	—	—	
Length								
Less than 3 minutes	—	—	—	—	—	—	—	
3 to 15 minutes	—	—	—	—	—	—	—	
15 minutes to 1 hour	—	—	—	—	—	—	—	
Over 1 hour	—	—	—	—	—	—	—	
Qualities								
Useful	—	—	—	—	—	—	—	
Important	—	—	—	—	—	—	—	
Satisfactory	—	—	—	—	—	—	—	
Timely	—	—	—	—	—	—	—	
Accurate	—	—	—	—	—	—	—	
Excessive	—	—	—	—	—	—	—	
Effective	—	—	—	—	—	—	—	

Your name _____ Date _____
Other party _____

Figure 8.11 ICA Communication diary instrument.

quality of communication associated with the communication resources of the organization. ICA auditing procedures such as questionnaires and network analysis instruments can be used to establish the structure of the organization's communication channels. The WGW audit uses interviews and selected questionnaires to assess further interpersonal and group communication, public communication, and the communication climate of the organization. The information gathered should reflect the experiences of the members of the organization, reducing the bias of standardized questionnaires. Since interviewing is a major part of the WGW audit, we turn now to an exploratory interview guide.

Exploratory Interview Guide

The ICA audit's interview guide focuses on the structure of information channels in the organization. We advocate expanding the exploratory interviews' inquiry into the strengths and weaknesses of the organization in addition to the structural questions. By returning to the interviewee's perception of what is right and wrong about the organization's communication, you are likely to get an account of the situation as the participant sees it. The interviewee must be assured of the confidentiality of the interview and relaxed or committed to the interview by previous questions. Then the following statement and questions can be added to those in Figure 8.8.

You mentioned strengths and weaknesses in the organization's communication. Let's go into that in more detail.

1. What is the best aspect of the way you communicate? Be specific.
2. Why is this a good way to communicate?
3. What is the worst aspect of the way you communicate? Can you give a recent example?
4. Why is this a bad way to communicate?
5. Who is responsible for this communication problem? Why?
6. What is the worst aspect of communication you receive from a supervisor? Give a recent example.
7. Why did this happen?
8. In your communication with your subordinates, what is the best aspect of their communication? Do they all do this?
9. What is the worst aspect of your subordinates' communication?
10. Do you think you have any influence on this communication behavior?

These questions highlight the interviewee's personal experiences. Although you may not get completely honest answers to every question, these probes may reveal who is communicating most effectively in the organization. The performance of the formal and informal channels depends on the ways they are used by every member of the organization. Identifying potential trouble in the organization during exploratory interviews makes later network analysis more informative because you already have some idea who may be blocking or facilitating communication.

Assessing Communication Flow

Assessing communication flow through specific networks and throughout the organization requires combining assessments of the structure of the networks, the roles of their members, and the influences of communication format in the message/channel.[18] The network structure may be assessed according to ICA audit procedures, bearing in mind that information categories need to be adjusted to suit the perceptions and practices of each organization. Depending on the task at hand, an individual may be more than a clearly defined group member, liaison, or isolate. Assessing communication flow calls for you to assess the individual's role in communicating certain types of information through specific channels. Every member of the organization may have varied roles according to the type of information and the channels available. According to the information comprising a message, a group member might also act as liaison or even become temporarily isolate. Thus you may productively begin flow analysis with a specific message, tracing it through the channels that connect various networks.

Communication flow is likely to vary with the formal and informal channels connecting each network. The message may be altered by the channel as parts of the message that are not suited to the available channel are lost. We advocate charting information flow along a time line in order to trace a specific message through a particular series of networks. Types of information that are central to the operation of the organization may be used to test the efficiency and effectiveness of the organizational communication structures. The result of this type of network analysis is a topical flowchart. Charting the flow of various types of information could confirm the roles of key members of the organization. If the situation required a multiple-role person, the networks in operation should provide such an individual for optimum information flow. Network roles could even become parts of job descriptions.

Assessing Interpersonal Relationships

Interpersonal relationships are significant to communication in the organization in two ways: (1) The capacity for interpersonal relationships makes the informal communication system possible. (2) The quality of interpersonal relationships influences the quality of communication throughout the organization. If you are not interested in the details of the relationship, but only in its communicative function, then identifying the informal communication channels through questionnaires should meet that need. But a specific relationship may be impeding communication. Just identifying the relationship as a problem is not enough; you need a methodology to identify the behaviors causing the poor relationship, behaviors that are part of the participants' communication styles.

Chapter 5 discussed the nature of interpersonal communication in organizations. We advocated an effective interpersonal style combining appropriate self-disclosure, supportiveness, goal-setting, and role clarification. These objectives call for a task-oriented communication style with a positive but limited social relationship that is appropriate for work. Robert Bales' interest in interpersonal behavior has led him to develop instruments for assessing the qualities of a task-oriented relationship.[19] Those individuals associated with the organizational member may respond to the questionnaire in Figure 8.12, evaluating the quality of the relationship with a member of their work group.

When the responses are tabulated according to Bales's procedures, the communication behavior of any employee can be described and categorized. By comparing different associates' ratings of the same individual, consistently perceived attributes of that person's communication style can be readily identified. We will go into more detail on this evaluation process in our discussion of group performance. First, let's consider how you can use and assess interviews in the communication auditing process.

Assessing Interviews

Assessing interviews accurately is the key to qualitative evaluation of organizational communication. Analysis of the situation in a specific organization depends on the exploratory interviews. But individual interpretations of the situation are

		(0)	**(1)**	**(2)**	**(3)**	**(4)**

Your Name _____   Group _____

Name of person described _____   Circle the best choice for each item:

		(0)	**(1)**	**(2)**	**(3)**	**(4)**
U	Active, dominant, talks a lot	Never	Rarely	Sometimes	Often	Always
UP	Extroverted, outgoing, positive	Never	Rarely	Sometimes	Often	Always
UPF	A purposeful democratic task leader	Never	Rarely	Sometimes	Often	Always
UF	An assertive businesslike manager	Never	Rarely	Sometimes	Often	Always
UNF	Authoritarian, controlling, disapproving	Never	Rarely	Sometimes	Often	Always
UN	Domineering, tough-minded, powerful	Never	Rarely	Sometimes	Often	Always
UNB	Provocative, egocentric, show-off	Never	Rarely	Sometimes	Often	Always
UB	Jokes around, expressive, dramatic	Never	Rarely	Sometimes	Often	Always
UPB	Entertaining, sociable, smiling, warm	Never	Rarely	Sometimes	Often	Always
P	Friendly, equalitarian	Never	Rarely	Sometimes	Often	Always
PF	Works cooperatively with others	Never	Rarely	Sometimes	Often	Always
F	Analytical, task-oriented, problem-solving	Never	Rarely	Sometimes	Often	Always
NF	Legalistic, has to be right	Never	Rarely	Sometimes	Often	Always
N	Unfriendly, negativistic	Never	Rarely	Sometimes	Often	Always
NB	Irritable, cynical, will not cooperate	Never	Rarely	Sometimes	Often	Always
B	Shows feelings and emotions	Never	Rarely	Sometimes	Often	Always
PB	Affectionate, likable, fun to be with	Never	Rarely	Sometimes	Often	Always
DP	Looks up to others, appreciative, trustful	Never	Rarely	Sometimes	Often	Always
DPF	Gentle, willing to accept responsibility	Never	Rarely	Sometimes	Often	Always
DF	Obedient, works submissively	Never	Rarely	Sometimes	Often	Always
DNF	Self-punishing, works too hard	Never	Rarely	Sometimes	Often	Always
DN	Depressed, sad, resentful, rejecting	Never	Rarely	Sometimes	Often	Always
DNB	Alienated, quits, withdraws	Never	Rarely	Sometimes	Often	Always
DB	Afraid to try, doubts own ability	Never	Rarely	Sometimes	Often	Always
DPB	Quietly happy just to be with others	Never	Rarely	Sometimes	Often	Always
D	Passive, introverted, says little	Never	Rarely	Sometimes	Often	Always

Figure 8.12 The SYMLOG adjective rating form.

necessarily clouded by selective perception and bias. The interviewer can only compare all interviews to arrive at a collective description of a situation. The clearest data available from interviews fall into two categories, descriptions of behavior and attitudes about behavior. If the interviews have elicited examples of good or bad communication practices, then a description of this behavior may be accurately assembled from examples cited in all interviews.

The interviewee's attitudes toward these practices may seem less important than their descriptions. You may feel you know what constitutes effective, efficient organizational communication. But the individual communicator's response to the situation may indicate trouble with the organization and not with the individual. Comparing individual attitudes about different communication practices may give you an indication of where problems occur. If an interviewee approves of most communication practices and can describe effective communication, then that person's perceptions of ineffective communication may also be accurate for the situation. If the same area is highlighted by more than one of these perceptive individuals, then this mutual opinion may be trusted and a significant issue has been identified. Now consider how group communication performance may be assessed.

Assessing Group Performance

The quality of a group's communication shows in its performance. The use of language to facilitate task and social goals for the group links group performance to the communication behaviors of group members. Assessing group performance may be done by outside observers or group members who act as participant observers. Observers from outside are less likely to understand the finer implications of what members mean when they talk, a lack of familiarity preventing accurate analysis until they have spent enough time with the group. The effect of having a stranger observing the group also cannot be ignored. A participant observer has a definite advantage in knowing what group members are really saying while not disturbing the ordinary group interaction. Thus, we advocate assessing group performance by using instruments developed by Bales and Cohen as part of SYMLOG, the system for the multiple-level observation of groups.[20]

SYMLOG assesses group performance by using direct observation or questionnaires to produce field maps of group members' orientation to the task, the group, and other group members. If you plan to use this assessment technique as many in the national SYMLOG applications group have done, please consult the text provided by Bales and Cohen.[21] We can only describe the main points of this system to give you some idea of how a high-quality group assessment technique operates. Figure 8.13 shows a model of the three dimensions of group performance represented in the system. The U/D dimension identifies where a member stands in the group's hierarchy, U-type ratings indicating leadership and D-type ratings indicating followership. The N/P dimension identifies how positively members rate their relationships. The F/B dimension indicates the task orientation of a member; the greater the F aspect of a rating is, the more a member is rated as following a task-oriented agenda. The cube shows how these three dimensions combine to mix leadership behavior with task orientation and degree of friendliness.

A group member can be assessed for contributions to a task group if another member, the participant observer, fills out the rating form in Figure 8.12. Notice how the questionnaire uses descriptions of behavior along with descriptive adjectives to minimize confusion about what you are evaluating. Once a questionnaire has been completed for each group member, the results may be tabulated on the form in Figure 8.14.

The process is simple: (1) put the member's name at the top of the column, (2) transfer the ratings from the questionnaire to the boxes next to the appropriate letters, (3) Add all the ratings with any part U in them and enter in the small box next to "Total-U," (4) Add all ratings with any part D in them and enter in the small box next to "Total-D," (5) Go through the ratings and add all ratings with any part P, enter in "Total-P" box, continuing to do the same for ratings with N, F, and B, (6) Since U/D, P/N, and F/B are opposite ends of each dimension, they need to be averaged to obtain a single rating for each dimension. In each pair, subtract the smaller total rating from the larger one to get a single total rating for each axis and enter the result in the box next to "Total-U/D," "Total-P/N," or "Total F/B." You now have a set of three ratings for each member, ratings that can be transferred to a field map showing the entire group.

Figure 8.15 (p. 225), The Symlog Field Diagram Form, displays the N/P and F/B dimensions on a grid. You can locate the group member you rated along these axes, making a dot where the axes come together. The third dimension, the U/D axis, can be represented by writing the score next to the dot. Once you have

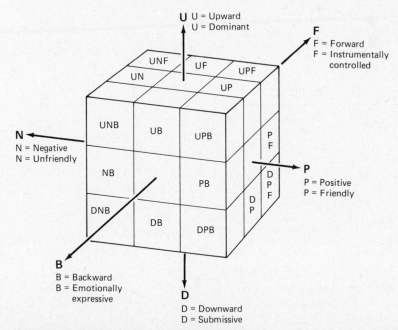

Figure 8.13   The SYMLOG three-dimensional space.

Your name _____

Of what group _____ Present date _____

From what date _____ to what date _____ Page _____ of _____

What method _____ whose perceptions _____ What level _____

Who, or what image→ Direction ↓							
U							
UP							
UPF							
UF							
UNF							
UN							
UNB							
UB							
UPB							
P							
PF							
F							
NF							
N							
NB							
B							
PB							
DP							
DPF							
DF							
DNF							
DN							
DNB							
DB							
DPB							
D							
TOTAL							
U							
D							
P							
N							
F							
B							

Figure 8.14   The SYMLOG directional profile form.

located all the members of the group on the field map, you can begin to analyze their coorientation and performance as a group. The layout of group members on the field map may produce clusters where members are close together. A group can be visually assessed according to this clustering by using the zones in the polarization-unification overlay in Figure 8.16, on p. 226. This overlay is printed on clear plastic and placed over the field diagram with two circles placed around the clusters of members. The arrow at the reference end of the overlay points toward the largest cluster, the reference subgroup. Figure 8.17 on p. 227 shows a typical field map with the overlay in place.

The zones represented by the different parts of the overlay are the bases for analyzing relationships between group members. Subgroups tend to fall into three areas, the reference circle, the opposite circle, and the swing area between the two short dotted lines. Those members within the reference circle represent the main subgroup, indicating by their numbers the predominant attitude of the group as perceived by the rate. The members in the opposite circle are the subgroup in opposition, which may well be in conflict with the reference group. Those in the swing area are uncommitted to either subgroup, and are likely to transfer their support from one subgroup to another. If a swing area member is rated as being on the S end of the central dotted line of balance between subgroups, that member may well be a scapegoat for the group's problems. A

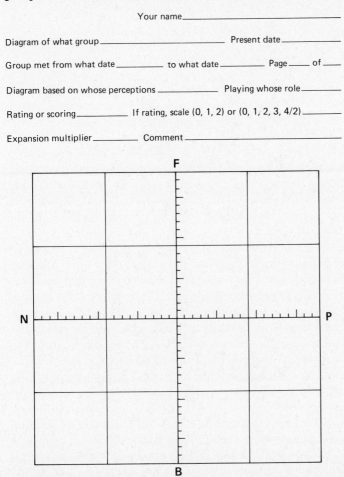

Figure 8.15 The SYMLOG diagram form.

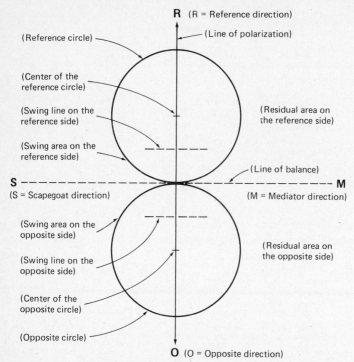

Figure 8.16   The inscription to be made on the polarization-unification overlay.

swing area member rated near the **M** end of the line of balance is often a mediator for disputes within the group. Highly detailed analysis of the relationships between subgroup members can be made by using SYMLOG procedures described in Bales and Cohen's text. Our primary interest in this assessment technique for a communication audit is to give participants feedback on the results of their communication.

The field maps offer useful information about the perceptions of the images created by members' communication behavior in the mind of the rater. You may have all members rate each other, construct field maps of the group, and then compare their perceptions by comparing their maps. The visual impact of the map is strong enough to produce further analysis in discussion of what the coorientations between members might mean. Our experience indicates that productive task groups don't have to share the same coorientation. The dynamics of competition between subgroups may be a good motivator for the group's performance, and can be realized once revealed by consistent mapping. The field maps are most useful in group performance assessment to show members how others see their behavior. The procedure and the map may convince otherwise unwilling members to accept criticism or at least recognize their role in the group and its performance. Unexpected discrepancies between nonproductive members' ratings of themselves on the U/D axis and the ratings made by the rest of the group can rattle the most obstructive group members.

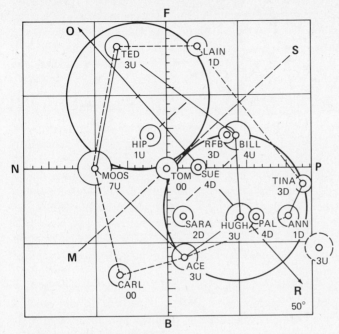

Figure 8.17   Typical field diagram.

One further option with SYMLOG is to use the same procedure but have members evaluate other levels of perception. In addition to rating actual behavior, you may also have members rate ideal behavior to generate a map of their ideal image of the group form. Comparing the idealized group to the maps of actual behavior may lead to useful insights into members' expectations for their groups. Working on a third level, members may also rate themselves and each other in terms of what they perceive as the wished for or intended behavior. Comparison between the rating desired and the actual behavior's rating facilitates goal-setting and assessment of progress toward task and social objectives.

If assessment uses techniques like SYMLOG in addition to interviews and other questionnaires, an image of the organization as a whole should begin to develop out of the detail of individual impressions. This level of information about the organization's communication practices should help with assessment of how the organization itself functions as it communicates with the external environment, addressing itself to the public.

Assessing Public Communication

Assessing public communication is often one of the primary roles of the communication consultant whose specialty is persuasion. A new project may be considered as a chance to modify the organization's image while continuing to sell the product. Managing an organization's image has been treated in detail in Chapter

8. Here we note that assessing public communication is a complex task where you may be asked to produce two types of evaluations: (1) an analysis of the quality of current practices or (2) an analysis of the organization's public communication potential. These analyses are based on two levels of inquiry, establishing the organization's needs and the organization's desires. Here you have to separate sound communication practices from idealized wishes.

First, is there a public communication program that is suitable for the current situation? Since the public communication program has evolved out of prior images and past organizational objectives, the program as it stands can almost always be improved. By identifying public communication practices with interviews and questionnaires, you can see how closely past practices match current needs. If the organization is already committed to careful audience analysis, arguments constructed to suit the audience, and presentational techniques aimed at the requirements of the audience and the product, then you have little work to do. If the organization is badly "out of tune" with current needs, then the assessment immediately becomes a problem of training. We will cover this training issue in more detail in the next chapter.

Second, does the organization intend its public communication to prepare an audience for projects yet unannounced or even unknown? In any quickly growing industry or in a changing organization, public communication may be the first line of attack on new territory, new ideas, and new images. If the organization is already committed to well-planned public communication for its current projects, the people who brought you in to assess the organization may still have something in mind for the future. At the risk of aggravating intraorganizational conflict between them and the status quo, a public communication assessment might focus on the absolute potential of the organization. Rather than limiting planning to current projects, the potential of different organizational resources might be assessed in terms of the possibilities for public communication. The results of an assessment of this nature would not be a presentational strategy but would, instead, be an awareness of where future presentations might originate and what forms they might take.

Assessing Communication Climate

The communication climate of the organization may also be assessed by combining the detailed information from interviews with the data from questionnaires. As an organization level phenomenon, communication climate may be treated as an aspect of the organization's culture. Here we are concerned with identifying what is actually occurring in the organization rather than what organizational philosophy would we like to see. You may assess communication climate by subjecting your data base (derived through interviews and questionnaires) to a further set of questions.

1. What do the exploratory interviews identify as formal and informal communication channels?

2. Do personal examples of good and bad communication practices confirm these channels?
3. Does communication on the interpersonal and group levels show any other good or bad communication practices?
4. Are the stated communication objectives of the organization satisfied by communication practices?
5. Who are the key communicators who establish and maintain communication practices in various levels of the organization? Formally? Informally? Interpersonally? Publicly?

The answers to these questions should help you generate a profile of the organization's communication climate. The more this profile incorporates the experiences and perceptions of those who participate in the daily communication of the organization, the more accurate is this most generalized assessment.

DATA ANALYSIS AND INTERPRETATION

If you have been gathering data according to the ICA and WGW auditing procedures, you will have a remarkably detailed set of examples of organizational communication, statements about the organization's communication practices, and recommendations as to how to improve the situation. Making sense of this information requires some careful thought about appropriate data analysis and interpretation. Data analysis, and its interpretation, balances quantitative versus qualitative analysis to provide an accurate interpretation of the situation. Quantitative analysis produces impressive computer amalysis with numerical values assigned to communication behaviors, but it is even more useful if validated by qualitative analysis of the situation to check on the appropriateness of observation techniques and instruments.

If you use trained observers to count the frequency of specific behaviors, you may analyze the significance of differences in frequency through computation of chi-square statistics. The Statistical Package for the Social Sciences (SPSS) can be used to program a computer to produce chi-square and other statistics from your description of behavior frequency. In their observations of group interaction, Bales and Cohen report success in using trained observers who worked with the SYMLOG behavior categories.[22] The success of trained observers depends primarily on using a methodology that reduces the effect of the individual observer on the observation. A group of observers coding the same sample of behavior should each produce the same observations because of the lack of ambiguity in their technique. If you used participant observers without training to establish their reliability, quantitative analysis is less impressive. The reports of untrained participant observers may be used as qualitative assessments made by experienced participants.[22]

One analysis technique that helps produce consistent coding of written or recorded messages is content analysis. *Content analysis* combines frequency analysis with coding of selected topics to analyze the messages' actual content rather than their meaning. Content analysis may be used with any message—written or oral communication within the organization or public communication, speeches or memos. Stempel identifies the five stages in this process.[23]

1. Select a unit for analysis, a type of message or some part of a message.
2. Construct categories for coding key words, ideas, or phrases.
3. Sample the content of all the available messages or a randomly selected group of messages.
4. Code the sample according to the unit of analysis selected and the code you have devised.
5. Analyze the results by computer using SPSS, or by hand if possible.

Interpreting the results of your quantitative analysis should also take information from interviews and interview-questionnaires into account. The quantitative data usually suffice to establish the frequency or significance of a communication behavior, whereas the qualitative accounts of the situation explain what your assessment means to the organization. The meaning you give to your assessment originates with the experiences of organization members. You can identify important communication problems and explain their significance in terms of how the organization deviates from ideal communication behavior. The value of this interpretation of the situation depends on how well you communicate your findings in your report.

DATA REPORTING

The assessment report supports the basic function of reporting data in a form that is comprehensible and useful to the client. Data reporting is the centerpiece of the assessment report and should be presented as the result of systematic assessment procedures. Thus, an assessment report should include enough information about the assessment itself for the data to be understood without further explanation beyond the report itself. Data reporting thereby becomes a process of terminating the assessment process so that the client can take responsibility for acting on the report's conclusions. Data reporting may productively use a report format including the following sections:

1. Description of the situation
   a. The client
   b. The setting
   c. Problems as stated by the client
   d. Goals for the assessment
2. Assessment procedures
   a. Objectives
   b. Assessment instruments for each objective
   c. Selection of samples and subjects
   d. Plan for implementing assessment procedures
3. Results
   a. Summary of data in raw form
   b. Analysis of data

   c. Analysis of communication practices
   d. Analysis of communication policies
4. Recommendations
   a. Areas for improvement in efficiency or effectiveness
   b. Possible means of communication capability development
5. Appendices
   a. Theoretical assumptions with references
   b. Data analysis techniques

If you prepare an assessment report so that it is self-explanatory, it can remain a resource for the organization long after your audit is finished. The data you collected might be analyzed with different techniques as the organization's needs change. The organization might relapse into a similar situation in the future, and use some of the assessment's conclusions to pull itself out of new problems. The best testimony to an effective assessment report is not only the fact that the organization accepts and implements your analysis and recommendations, but also that the members of the organization continue to implement the assessment techniques you brought to their attention. Their continued interest in assessment will motivate ongoing development in the quality of their organizational communication.

SUMMARY

This chapter has examined some of the issues in the assessment of organizational communication. We described data-gathering techniques like exploratory interviews, questionnaires, and direct observation. After discussing some of the problems with these techniques, we proposed procedures for organizational communication cost and policy analysis. The ICA audit was described, along with additional assessment procedures in the WGW audit. Examination of issues and procedures in data analysis, interpretation, and reporting completed this chapter. If such assessment procedures identify communications problems, you may be asked to design and implement a training program to develop organizational communications capabilities. The next chapter is intended to help you design a successful communication training program.

ENDNOTES

1. Henry Mintzberg, *The Nature of Managerial Work* (New York: Harper & Row, 1973), pp. 230–278.
2. William J. Rothwell, "How to Conduct a Real Performance Audit," *Training* 21 (1984): 45.
3. George Gallup, "The Quintamensional Plan of Question Design," *Public Opinion Quarterly* 11 (1947): 385.
4. G. M. Goldhaber, M. P. Yates, D. T. Porter, and R. Lesniak, "Organizational Communication: 1978," *Human Communication Research* 5 (1978): 77.
5. K. H. Roberts and C. A. O'Reilly, "Organizations as Communication Structures: An Empirical Approach," *Human Communication Research* 5 (1978): 283–293.

6. M. G. Dertien, "The Accuracy of Job Evaluation Plans," *Personnel Journal* (July 1981): 566–570.

7. Rothwell, "How to Conduct," pp. 46–49.

8. F. Jablin, "Superior-Subordinate Communication: State of the Art," *Psychological Bulletin* 86 (1979): 1201–1222.

9. J. E. Baird and J. C. Deibolt, "Role Congruence, Communication, Superior-Subordinate Relations and Employee Satisfaction in Organizational Hierarchies," *Western Speech Communication Journal* 40 (1976): 260–267. See also R. J. Burke, T. Weir, and G. Duncan, "Informal Helping Relationships in Work Organizations," *Academy of Management Journal* 19 (1976): 370–377.

10. Roberts and O'Reilly, *Organizations,* pp. 283–293.

11. Mintzberg, *Nature,* p. 240.

12. W. Ouchi, *Theory Z* (Reading, MA: Addison-Wesley, 1981).

13. Mintzberg, *Nature,* p. 250.

14. H. Greenbaum, "The Appraisal of Organizational Communication Systems," paper presented at International Communication Association Convention, Atlanta, GA, 1972.

15. G. Goldhaber and P. Krivonos, "The ICA Audit: Process, Status, and Critique," *Journal of Business Communication* 15 (1977): 41–56. See also G. Goldhaber and D. Rogers, *Auditing Organizational Communication Systems: The ICA Communication Audit* (Dubuque, IA: Kendall/Hunt, 1979).

16. G. Goldhaber, *Organizational Communication* (Dubuque, IA: Brown, 1983), p. 388.

17. Goldhaber, et al, "Organizational Communication: 1978," p. 85.

18. K. Brooks, J. Callicoat, and J. Seigerdt, "The ICA Communication Audit and Perceived Communication Effectiveness Changes in 16 Audited Organizations," *Human Communication Research* 5 (1979): 130–137.

19. R. F. Bales, *Personality and Interpersonal Behavior* (New York: Holt, Rinehart and Winston, 1970); R. F. Bales and S. P. Cohen, *SYMLOG: A System for the Multiple Level Observation of Groups* (New York: Free Press, 1979), p. 21.

20. Ibid, Bales and Cohen, p. 21.

21. Ibid, pp. 19–37.

22. Ibid, pp. 309–320.

23. G. Stempel, "Constrict Analysis," in *Research Methods in Mass Communication,* ed. G. Stempel and B. Westley (Englewood Cliffs, NJ: Prentice-Hall, 1981), pp. 119–131.

chapter *9*

Communication and Organizational Change

ORGANIZATIONAL DEVELOPMENT

THE ORGANIZATIONAL DEVELOPER

Area 1: Analyzing Needs and Evaluating Results / Area 2: Designing and Developing Training Programs and Materials / Area 3: Delivering Training and Development Programs or Services / Area 4: Advising and Counseling / Area 5: Managing Training Activities / Area 6: Managing Organizational Relationships / Area 7: Doing Research to Advance the Training Field / Area 8: Developing Professional Skill and Expertise / Area 9: Developing Basic Skills and Knowledge

THE ORGANIZATIONAL COMMUNICATION CONSULTANT

What Is Management Communication Consulting? / Consulting Approaches
> The Purchase Model / The Doctor-Patient Model / The Process Model

MANAGING THE CONSULTING PROCESS

Initiating Contact / The Initial Interview / Format for a Proposal / Common Types of Interventions
> Procedural Input / Theoretical Input / Nondirective Counseling / Direct Feedback / Process Session

When Should a Consultant Be Hired? / Ethics of Consulting

Gulf Coast Manufacturing is a small industrial firm employing about 900 people in two small factories located in a southern state. In the previous 10 years of operation, Gulf Coast counted on repeat customers because of the high quality of its product. Within the past year, however, sales are off. Salespeople return to the office complaining that they can no longer compete because the quality of the product has deteriorated. But not only has the quality of the product changed, waste of material has doubled. Gulf Coast has always been considered a good place to work; however, recently there has been considerable turnover and worker unrest. Ten months ago several workers were successful in persuading employees to organize into a local union. The advent of a union has increased the formality of communication between labor and management. Gulf Coast is not handling well the changes it is being forced to face and is in need of professional help. This task usually falls to the organizational development specialist.

This chapter, concerned with communication and effecting and shaping organizational change, focuses on the role of the communication specialist in organizational development. When introducing changes and improvements, in order for its members to work more effectively, an organization must be informed by understanding how people process information, how they present that information, and how the organization and its employees interact with each other. One individual who is uniquely qualified to address the problem of organizational change is the organizational communication specialist.

First, we define organizational development, exploring several models of the process. Next, we investigate the nine activity areas for which an organizational communication professional might be responsible. Then, we examine the communication specialist's part in organizational development. Finally, we focus on the role of the communication consultant in organizational change. Here we explain the various aspects of the process: models guiding the activity, managing the process, intervention activities, when to hire a consultant, and the ethics of consulting.

ORGANIZATIONAL DEVELOPMENT

Organizational development is a process undertaken to improve an organization's adapting, coping, problem-solving, and goal-setting procedures. Warren Bennis[1] suggests further that this process is "a response to change, a complex educational strategy intended to change the beliefs, attitudes, values and structure of organizations so that they can better adapt to new technologies, markets, and challenges, and the dizzing rate of change itself."

The emphasis of organizational development is on people and the changing of their attitudes, values, and beliefs in order to promote organizational goals. David Hampton and his colleagues[2] express this relationship in the following way:

> It is the change in personal values in the system, coupled with the change in ways in which people treat one another, which come first . . . operating procedures, costs, job descriptions, production schedules—the whole rational side

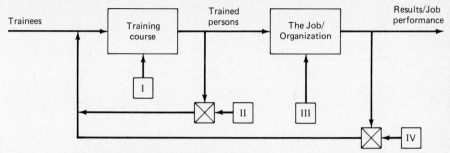

I. Are the trainees happy with the course?
II. Does the training course teach the concepts?
III. Are the concepts used on the job?
IV. Does the application of the concepts positively affect the organization?

Figure 9.4 Adaptive training model with four levels of evaluation. (*Source:* Brethower and Rummler, "Evaluating Training," *Training and Development Journal* 33 (May 1979): 17.)

Area 2: Designing and Developing Training Programs and Materials

People involved in conducting training programs must be able to establish behavioral or learning objectives for the programs they plan. Once objectives are developed, they must determine program content and develop materials that will meet the criteria for the program. The person or persons responsible for designing training programs must be able to generate plans that include the participants, appropriate sequences of courses, exercises, and tests for measurement. Frequently those involved make decisions about developing a training program or buying a program outside the organization.

In an essay written to accompany the ASTD report of areas and activities of the training and development professional, Chip Bell and Tony Putman[10] argue that successful training programs require two kinds of logic: people logic and machine logic. These are the subjective, "perception" part of designing training as well as the objective, "craft" elements. They believe that both are necessary, but the usual emphasis is on the latter.

> The emphasis is typically more on delivery than discovery, more on "training" than learning, ultimately on *doing to* more than *being with.* The transference of knowledge and skill is more valued than the fostering of learner inquiry. The learner is viewed passively, as audience, with an air of detachment and languidness. Frequently, the learner is viewed in a somewhat one-down, dependent position.[11]

We think this argument has merit. Machine logic presents the trainer as a technician, whereas people logic presents the trainer as a counselor. Machine logic is trainer-centered, but people logic is learner-centered. Machine logic suggests that the trainer moves the learner, whereas people logic suggests that the learner moves him or herself.

Training specialists need to know both the logic of the training mechanism and that of the people they serve. The craft elements of the mechanism of designing and conducting a training program are important, and perhaps more easily learned. We present these in Chapter 10, "Designing Successful Communication Training Programs." Here we wish to focus on people logic.

You can learn to use more people logic if you believe that "the primary function of the learning experience is to foster movement and that it is the *learner* who will make that movement."[12] Bell and Putman provide four exemplary questions a trainer might ask if he or she is interested in a people-centered approach. "What impact will my design have on facilitating movement to a new state? Will this role-play create resistance to movement? Will this lecture inappropriately slow movement? Will this handout create confusion and movement in the wrong direction?"[13] Second, the people logic-centered trainer will realize the importance of human relationships in the learning experience. A training design may be incorporated allowing people to share their experiences with each other and thereby develop relationships and enhance each other's learning. Third, the trainer will make use of motivation theory to enhance the learning environment. This might mean using participatory activities at times, as well as other strategies that will introduce variety into the learning experience. This might also mean participants are asked to share what they are learning so that the group keeps track of its progress. Finally, the trainer will recognize the need for an ongoing diagnostic effort, that is, listening to the responses of those being trained for information giving the state of the learner. This allows the trainer to determine if the group is ready to move on to the next activity.

Area 3: Delivering Training and Development Programs or Services

The training specialist must be proficient in a variety of training techniques. Common techniques are behavior modeling, role-playing, simulation, and gaming and laboratory techniques. Discussion and lecture techniques are the most widely used. The trainer must also be able to operate audiovisual equipment such as film projectors and videotape recorders and cameras. Some training specialists are also responsible for teaching managers and supervisors how to train.

Herman Birnbrauer[14] presents a list of self-assessment questions that a trainer might ask him or herself. Figure 9.5 states his questions with respect to the trainer and the creation of climates conducive to learning.

Area 4: Advising and Counseling

The organizational development practioner's primary concern in this area is counseling with managers and supervisors on training and development. This person may also counsel individuals on career development as well as on training and organizational development matters. The training specialist may have the

1. Would you say your results with respect to climate are high or low?

2. Assessing the levels of the trainees quickly and accurately is crucial. Do you adapt to the various learning styles and maintain their participation?
   Always ____ Sometimes ____ Never ____

3. Your expectations and demands are directly related to the level of performance and accomplishment achieved by trainees. Would you say yours are high or low?

4. When you conduct a program, you have influence on the group. Are you aware of yours?
   Yes ____ No ____

5. Would you say it [your influence] helps or hinders?

6. Does the atmosphere you create in your program get trainees physically, emotionally, and mentally involved?
   Always ____ Sometimes ____ Never ____

7. Are you genuinely interested in the success of the trainees?
   Always ____ Sometimes ____ Never ____

8. Are you able to gain their commitment?

9. Can you adapt to their level?
   Always ____ Sometimes ____ Never ____

10. Are you patient with trainees?
    Always ____ Sometimes ____ Never ____

11. Are you fair with trainees?
    Always ____ Sometimes ____ Never ____

12. Are you confident in your skills and ability as a trainer?
    Always ____ Sometimes ____ Never ____

13. Are you cooperative in the training program?
    Always ____ Sometimes ____ Never ____

14. Are you enthusiastic about the program you are conducting?
    Always ____ Sometimes ____ Never ____

Figure 9.5 Self-assessment questions. (*Source:* Herman Birnbrauer, "Delivering Training and Development Programs/Services," *Training and Development Journal* 33 (May 1979): 30.)

additional duty of assisting managers in implementing training and development programs.

Organizations have begun to understand the need for providing advisors and counselors for both subordinates and managers. Employee Assistance Pro-

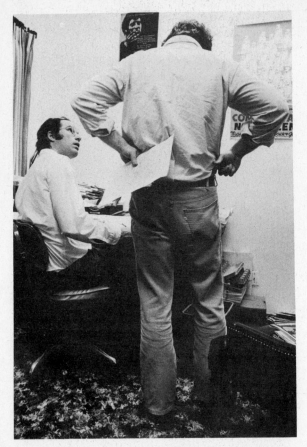

The organizational developer provides advice and counsel.

grams are a common personnel function since management has become aware that it is cheaper to work toward improving employee morale, attitude, and productivity than to terminate employees and train new ones.[15] The effective counselor will utilize skills in conflict resolution, problem solving, team building and process consultation. Chapter 11, "Organizational Communication Career Development," provides help for the organizational developer who is charged with this responsibility.

Area 5: Managing Training Activities

The specialist in organizational development must also be a manager who organizes and staffs the training and development programs and projects. This activity involves arrangement of programs, facilities, budgets, and training personnel. For some programs the manager must secure external instructors and consultants and program resource people. These people and their proposals have to be evaluated and budgeted. Internal instructors must be obtained and evaluated for other programs and often trained and coached. In addition, the organizational development specialist may administer tuition reimbursement programs, arrange for university courses, and make contracts with outside vendors for programs and supplies.

The administrative function of the manager of an organizational development program can be most easily understood by considering the five basic functions performed by managers: planning, organizing, staffing, leading, and controlling.[16]

Planning.   The planning process involves three basic steps: (1) the determination of needs, (2) the setting of objectives, and (3) the construction of a plan.

The *needs assessment* involves four activities. First, you must make a broad preliminary assessment of how training and development can help your organization in its mission. This involves visiting with as many members of the organization as seems wise within your time constraint. Begin with your supervisor and as part of that interview ask whom you ought to visit. Attempt to see employees at all levels of the organization—hourly workers, colleagues, department heads, the chief executive officer. Also read current organizational publications and reports to gain an understanding of problems that may have emerged. This will help you discover what activities the organization has undertaken.

Second, look at the files maintained by the training department for specific information about formal and informal training activities conducted in the past several years. You might make a flow sheet that looks like the one in Figure 9.6.

Third, identify the problems you believe your department might be able to alleviate. Here you might be able to use some of the assessment tools we presented in Chapter 8. Identify key departments that would benefit most from immediate attention. Look for critical situations too. The result of your effort should be a yearlong plan for training and development needs.

Finally, assess the resources of the training department to meet the needs you have identified. What are the costs in staff, materials, equipment, time, space, and dollars? Attempt to be as careful as possible in estimating resource needs. Overestimation may mean asking for additional personnel that you don't need. Underestimation may mean an overworked staff, with too few resources to do the job.

The second step in the planning process is *setting objectives*. Goal setting at this point in the process usually entails adopting program objectives rather than training objectives. Program objectives are more general in nature and don't necessarily specify behavior. An example of a program objective would be:

Program	Objective	Who & how many involved	Methods used	Cost per trainee	Effectiveness of program

Figure 9.6 Training flow sheet.

The first line supervisors (trainees) will be able to structure and conduct a performance appraisal interview in such a way as to achieve both organizational and employee development goals.

One training objective for this program would be:

The trainees will be able to specify Jack Gibb's categories of supportive and defensive behavior and produce an example of each category.

The overall plan would include objectives for the major kinds of organizational development activity: formal courses, workshops, on-the-job training, counseling, and personal and professional development activities.

The third step in planning is the actual *construction of the plan.* This encompasses the two other considerations necessary to carry out the managing task: establishing program priorities and setting procedures and budgeting. You must determine an ordering of your training and development program, going from those interventions that are the most important to those that are the least significant. Remember most training directors rarely have enough resources to do all they planned. Some programs may have to be scratched when you begin the budgeting process.

The budget is the financial scheme needed for carrying out the plan. The most practical way of budgeting is program by program. In this process management is informed of the costs involved to achieve each of the goals you have in mind. Although you may want approval for all your programs, and therefore may try to compute the costs so that it is difficult to cut any particular program, in reality management may have different priorities from yours and may not be willing to fund some of the programs.

How do you figure costs? Jerry Forbes[17] provides a comprehensive list of the costs you may incur:

1. Production of materials such as videotapes, audiotapes, slides, illustrations, photographs, vugraphs, and binders.
2. Course design and development, including staff time, pilot seminars, evaluation, and special developer training sessions.
3. Capital investments, including depreciation.
4. Travel costs, including development travel and train-the-trainer seminars, delivery travel, participant and staff travel, and consultant and subject matter expert travel.
5. Meals, housing, car rental, and laundry costs for staff and participants during the training sessions.
6. Conference room rental and related incidental costs such as refreshments and lunches.
7. Course resource costs, such as marketing guides and promotional literature.
8. Staff preparation time.
9. Delivery of course materials, including reproduction costs per package.
10. Extra copies of materials for file and distribution.
11. Equipment and materials shipping costs.
12. Corporate lost production in terms of average salary per day of training.

13. Delayed income costs.
14. Location costs comparing on-site versus off-site facilities.

You will want to list certain fixed costs separately from program costs. These are secretarial help, ASTD memberships, and library expenses.

Finally, you may wish to develop procedures for carrying out your plan. This would include who will be responsible for what aspects of programs, standard evaluation procedures, and so forth.

Organizing. Organizing requires that the manager combine activities into workable groups, assign groups of responsibilities to the appropriate subordinate, and delegate the authority necessary to complete the required tasks. The process of organizing a training and development department is manifested into two particular kinds of formal documents—the department organizational chart and position descriptions.

The usual way to *describe structure and relationships* is to construct an organizational chart. In a small department, drawing such a chart may not be necessary because there are only a few relationships. These can usually be specified clearly in a short paragraph. A larger department may include seven or eight positions, in addition to clerical staff. Such a department is pictured in the organizational chart in Figure 9.7.

The second area of organizational responsibility for the training manager is *specifying position descriptions.* An example of how the position of training and development administrator might be specified was provided by R. Wayne Pace.[18] Notice that the description of this position is quite broad because the person would have responsibilities for administering an entire department.

1. Prepares a statement of training and development philosophy, policy, and procedures.
2. Prepares a statement of objectives for the department and disseminates them to the staff.
3. Prepares the department's budget and disperses funds to accomplish department objectives.
4. Supervises the work of staff members.

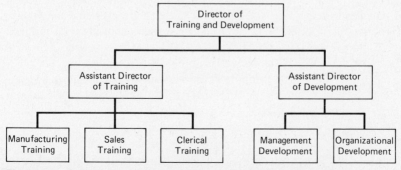

Figure 9.7 Organizational chart of training and development department.

5. Reviews the performance of staff members and recommends salary increases and other personnel actions, such as developmental activities.
6. Prepares periodic reports to inform management about training needs, program effectiveness, and accomplishments.
7. Maintains a continuous analysis of organization training and development needs.
8. Advises top management on manpower requirements and changes in organization needs resulting from changes in the labor market.
9. Develops training programs for technical personnel, secretarial and clerical personnel, and for supervisors and managers.
10. Evaluates training courses available from commercial firms for relevance to the organization's training needs.
11. Arranges for training materials, equipment, and facilities.
12. Trains technical instructors to conduct in-house courses.
13. Assists line managers in conducting job skills and procedural training.
14. Edits written materials prepared by staff members.
15. Supervises and assists in the production of audiovisual and video materials.
16. Develops training manuals, course outlines, handouts, and exercises.
17. Collects performance data from supervisors for use in evaluating the effectiveness of training sessions.
18. Counsels employees on personal goals and job-related training.
19. Establishes prerequisites for entering courses and performance standards for satisfactory completion of courses.
20. Conducts training programs.
21. Promotes training and development opportunities throughout the organization.

Staffing. *Staffing* is selecting, training, developing, placing, and orienting people in appropriate work positions. Gordon Lippitt claims that the human resource development professional can come from a wide range of academic disciplines. He says, "The key to the preparation of an HRD professional is *a mixed background of interdisciplinary education and experience.*"[19] Calvin P. Otto and Rollin O. Glaser found that training specialists are individuals "who have a strong interest in other people," are capable of following detailed instructions, cooperate rather than compete, and enjoy communicating.[20]

Once people are selected, they must be oriented and trained. Both of these tasks happen at the time the individual joins the organization. An orientation ought to acquaint the employee with his or her duties, colleagues, and the organization. Training often takes the form of coaching and consulting with the new professional. Some managers will arrange a team-teaching situation as a first training assignment.

Development differs from training in that it is an ongoing concern. Managers provide the opportunity both for in-service training and to attend professional conferences. Training specialists who begin with a bachelor's degree are often encouraged to return to college for advanced degrees.

Leading. Without effective leadership and supervision of subordinates, planning, organizing, and staffing don't yield a successful department. Leading, as discussed in Chapter 6, also applies here. In fact, much of what we consider in this book pertains directly to leadership. *Leading* is engaging in some behavior that moves the employee to engage in some behavior that will lead to achievement of some goal. Leadership involves understanding human behavior and motivation, utilizing good interpersonal skill, and understanding the communication process.

Management in this function must be able to coordinate, delegate, motivate, and manage conflict. *Coordination* is achieved through issuing instructions that will lead to cooperation in bringing together groups of people and materials in order to achieve organizational goals. Coordination goes beyond the departmental boundary in that training efforts generally involve more than one unit of the organization. For example, the manager often must contact other department heads to arrange for the release of employees for training. Beyond this, the training director often works with organizational managers and others who have the expertise to help in selecting appropriate training materials.

The successful manager must also know when to delegate tasks and when to do them him or herself. Failure to delegate can cause serious problems. For example, one training director we know personally reviewed plans for all training programs and attended training sessions whenever possible. When did this person have time to do the other duties we outlined in the position description? *Delegating* means to assign duties and authority to subordinates. After assigning a task, the manager generally engages only in enough checking to assure that the job is being done.

Controlling.   *Controlling* means to engage in a set of behaviors that will ensure that planned performance (goals) is actually accomplished. This activity involves four sets of behavior: (1) setting performance standards, (2) deciding on performance measurements, (3) measuring actual performance and comparing it to the standard, and (4) taking action either to correct or reward the performance.

Setting performance standards and measurements are frequently not easy tasks, especially when attempting to describe standards for a professional, creative activity. Organizational development and training is such an activity. You will of course measure the effectiveness of the training, which will result in a range of acceptable scores against which to measure. For clerical positions you might set standards such as minimum output, correctness of a typed page, and so forth. Generally, you will find that your organization has some standard evaluation form that will help you in this process.

Measuring results and taking action are accomplished by instituting and carrying out an effective performance appraisal system. This process is facilitated by establishing a training evaluation system and keeping records of training activities, goals, effectiveness of instructors, and the achievement of organizational goals. The performance appraisal interview is the primary arena for taking action on the results of performance review. An effective format for such an interview is the employee-centered problem-solving plan.[21] This plan follows these steps:

1. Ask the employee to prepare for the interview by analyzing his or her performance as compared to assigned duties and performance of others.
2. Establish or reestablish goals related to the specific job.
3. Have the employee analyze his or her performance, including the most successful areas and least successful areas.
4. Summarize any difficulties with performance that came out of the analysis.
5. Assist the employee in selecting a solution by reviewing any suggestions the employee may have for dealing with difficulties.
6. Attempt to get the employee to consider the outcome of the selected solution.
7. Establish new goals, check points, and obtain the employee's commitment to the plan.
8. Plan for training if it appears to be the solution to the performance problem.
9. Plan with the employee for evaluation and follow-up.
10. Let the employee know that you will help him or her improve.

The aim of this plan is to help the employee develop as a problem solver and to meet organizational performance objectives.

A separate interview should be conducted to discuss performance reward, thus avoiding to some extent the subordinate's attempt to pretend to agree with the boss in order to gain a larger raise. Salary adjustment is only one kind of reward available to the manager. Don't forget that sincere recognition of the employee's contributions toward the organizational objectives can serve as a reward too.

Area 6: Managing Organizational Relationships

The activities most often performed in this area are the establishment and maintenance of good working relationships with managers as clients and formal presentations of plans for training and development programs to management. Other activities carried out by the organizational development specialist are preparing and disseminating internal and external training and development program announcements and writing reports, proposals, speeches, articles, manuals, and memos. The human resource specialist may also communicate with governmental and educational committees.

Louise W. Stanek[22] contends that the ability to perform effectively in this area begins with knowing the internal workings of the organization and understanding its place in the community. She expresses the idea this way, "The trainer's first role is company research, looking not only at how the organization works internally, but its place in the larger business community and its relationships with the various regulatory agencies."[23] Stanek suggests that the training and development specialist needs to discover the personality of the organization. This is achieved by seeking the concerns of key people in the organization, discovering the image the organization has and the one it would like to have, and determining the regulations it must meet.

Key persons in the organization can be identified by asking questions. Stanek[24] suggests the following:

1. Who really runs things around here? (This one she suggests is appropriate for an attitude survey.)
2. Who serves on the important committees, such as the executive or finance committee?
3. Whose name do the troops drop when they want to impress their boss or peers?
4. Whom does the press quote most often?
5. Who is most frequently asked to make the keynote address at company functions?

Once you identify the key individuals, meet with them to discover their attitudes and dreams. Where do they see training needs that you might meet? What new programs will be instituted that may require training and development action? Knowing the answers to these questions enables you to help these people solve problems and enhances your organizational relationships.

Area 7: Doing Research to Advance the Training Field

The organizational training and development practitioner experiments with new training and development techniques, interprets data and statistics on training and development, and presents data and statistics in appropriate professional journals and meetings.

Leonard Nadler,[25] in his essay that accompanied the ASTD survey report, draws a distinction between evaluation of training and research. The research evaluation contrast is illustrated in Figure 9.8. This is simplified somewhat, but it makes the distinction clear.

What kinds of issues might be investigated by the training practitioner? There are a number of questions that need further investigation. One area of study might be learning strategies. What strategies work best and under what conditions? Why does a particular strategy fail? How can we achieve better transfer of learning from the classroom to the job? Another area of study is the human resource development field itself. What kinds of people are most successful as training specialists? Are certain kinds of characteristics related to particular roles in HRD? What kind of image does HRD have with management? These questions and many more are in need of the answers research can provide.

	Evaluation	*Research*
Purpose:	What?	Why?
Focus:	Learning objectives	Hypotheses
Approach:	Actual situation	Experimental
Strategies:	Data gathering	Data gathering
Utilization:	To improve program	Varied
	Immediate	Long range

Figure 9.8   The evaluation versus research distinction. (*Source:* Leonard Nadler, "Research: An HRD Activity Area," *Training and Development Journal* 33 (May 1979): 60–64.)

Area 8: Developing Professional Skill and Expertise

The two principal activities under this area are keeping abreast of training and development activities in other organizations and keeping informed about training and development concepts, theories, techniques, and approaches. A less frequent activity is attending seminars and conferences for personal development.

Gordon Lippitt,[26] author of *Organization Renewal,* was asked to respond to this area of the ASTD survey. He suggests several strategies a professional might adopt to ensure continued development. Probably the most important strategy is collecting and utilizing data from those you serve. Most trainers do this if the activity is formal training instead of when the activity is a consultation. Lippit recommends that you take a few minutes after such a meeting and make notes to yourself on how the meeting went. An alternative would be to ask the participant for direct feedback. You might ask, "I'd like to know how well you think what we have said meets your needs," or "Let me know if anything we've talked about doesn't work out for you. I'd like to help as much as I can."

Other sources of development are cotraining, informal sharing of groups with other trainers, exchanging experiences with colleagues, enrolling in learning opportunities, reading programs, and sabbaticals. Consider these options and make a yearly plan of the kinds of activities you will undertake. As Lippitt says, "Truly qualified training and HRD persons should consider their profession as one which requires a constant learning experience."[27]

Area 9: Developing Basic Skills and Knowledge

This area includes skills such as the ability to communicate effectively, to gather data and analyze it, to plan and organize, to set priorities, to problem solve, and to use group skills. Knowledge of training resources, learning theory, and the subject matter being taught are also important to the training specialist. Ideas about developing these basic skills are the substance of this book and numerous other texts about communicating in organizations. We suggest that you acquire for reference one of the basic books in this area.[28]

THE ORGANIZATIONAL COMMUNICATION CONSULTANT

What Is Management Communication Consulting?

Any definition of consulting is subject to the ideal situation in which the client behaves in certain and predictable ways. Often the consultant is torn between what he or she sees as the ideal role and relationship and the realities of the client situation. This sort of uncertainty led Larry E. Greiner and Robert O. Metzger[29] to offer this definition of a consultant in a "half-joking manner":

> Management consulting is an uncertain and evolving process conducted by a foreign intruder who muddles through by performing various problem-solving activities, while trying to maintain high professional standards and still attempting to meet the needs of the client.

This definition, in spite of its cynicism, points to three important facts about consulting. First, the consultant is an outsider. This makes a rather uncertain relationship between the client and organization. Trust must be built for the consultant to be effective. Second, consulting is not an exact science. There are many variables related to each client problem and the complexity of these means that each situation is unique. Each proposed intervention is in part a creative act in that the principles involved must be tailored to the client's situation and need. Third, professional idealism often demand a thorough investigation of the client's situation before any action can be recommended. Clients, on the other hand, are anxious for action on the problem. They may pressure the consultant for action. The consultant often must balance idealism with the pragmatics of the situation.

Against this background of the realism of the consulting profession, we would like to provide a more formal definition of a communication consultant. Our definition is a bit longer than the previous one, but it is necessarily so to capture the essence of the consultant's role.

> Communication consulting is an advisory service, contracted from a trained and qualified professional, to help the client by objectively identifying communication problems, analyzing these problems, identifying and recommending solutions to these problems, and, if asked to do so, assisting in the implementation of these solutions.

Consulting Approaches

The appropriate approach to the consulting activity might follow any one of three models. As a consultant you must assess the situation in order to discover which model will best serve the climate. We describe each model and tell when it is most likely to be the preferred style.

The Purchase Model   This model applies to an organizational situation in which the client has spent the time to analyze a situation carefully, has isolated a problem, but doesn't for some reason believe that the organization is prepared to intervene. Perhaps the organization doesn't have the specific expertise to generate a solution to the problem. Sometimes the organization has attempted a solution, but failed. Or, perhaps the organization doesn't have qualified personnel to provide the needed training. The client approaches a consultant to purchase the service or necessary information to solve the problem, then terminates the relationship.

This model operates on several assumptions that must be valid if it is to be successful. Here are the major assumptions of the purchase model:

- The client has the knowledge and expertise to identify the problem.
- The client can identify the causes and/or describe the situation to the consultant in such a way that the consultant will understand the problem.
- The consultant is hired to recommend and/or implement a solution.

- The consultant has more expertise concerning the solution to the problem than the client has.
- The consultant will implement the solution within a relatively short period of time, with minimal disruption and involvement of the work force.

Of course, the success of this model is dependent on the client's accurate diagnosis of the problem. This presents an important risk in this model and is a potential liability for both the organization and the consultant. If the organization's diagnosis is wrong, then the services it has purchased may not have the desired effect. Thus the organization has wasted the dollars it paid for the service. On the other hand, the organization may blame the consultant for the failure of the intervention. Thus the reputation of the consultant is damaged.

One of the authors had an experience with the purchase model illustrating the potential difficulties that can result from the client's diagnosis of the problem. We were asked to present a proposal for a 15-week training program that would help engineers upgrade their writing skills. We presented a program based on what the training director said the problems were. The program was approved. We were told by several of the engineers, 6 weeks into the training program, that our training didn't meet their needs as *they* saw them. The result of the clients misdiagnosis of need was low attendance, damaged reputations, and resentment.

The Doctor-Patient Model   This model follows the relationship established when a patient sees a physician. The client (patient) complains of some problem (illness) and the consultant (doctor) diagnoses the problem and prescribes a solution. This differs from the previous model in two ways. The consultant is involved in the diagnosis process and generally is not involved in the actual intervention.

William B. Cash and Robert L. Minter[30] suggest that the doctor-patient model operates on the following assumptions:

- The consultant is hired to identify the problem, diagnose it, and recommend a solution.
- The consultant has more expertise regarding the specific problem than does the client.
- The consultant is not expected by management to train the client in diagnostic and problem-solving skills.
- The client expects the consultant to solve the problem in a relatively short period of time with minimal disruption and involvement of the work force.
- The client can be just as committed to implement the recommended solution and to follow up on its progress if the procedures and reward structure for doing so exists.

Clearly, all of these assumptions must be met for success, but failure can often be attributed to three primary difficulties. First, the consultant may get inaccurate information from the members of the client's organization. There is a natural tendency to be defensive when problems exist. Thus, the individual member may try to protect him or herself by distorting or withholding information. Since the consultant is assuming sole responsibility for collecting the data, he or she may not be able to detect this problem as readily as when the consultant and organization are working together to gather data.

A second problem may arise from the client's unwillingness to accept the diagnosis. Again, this may arise out of the nature of pointing out problems. Discovery of certain kinds of problems can lead to defensiveness and unwillingness to accept them.

The third difficulty that may be generated by this model is the inability of the client to implement the intervention. The assumption that the client is as committed to the change as the consultant may not be valid. And even if this assumption holds, the client may not have the expertise to implement the solution even though the client thinks their training and development personnel have it.

The Process Model   This model is highly dependent on client involvement as the consultant and client work jointly on all steps of the intervention. The goal of this model goes beyond the immediate end of solving the problem. Chris Argyris[31] sees one of the goals of the process consultant

> as helping an organization solve its problems in such a way that it becomes more competent in solving the same or a similar class of problems without the continued help of the consultants.

The assumptions upon which this model are based determine its usefulness under particular circumstances. Cash and Minter[32] indicate that the underlying assumptions of this model are:

- The client and consultant jointly diagnose the problem.
- The consultant's role is to train the client in using diagnostic and problem-solving techniques.
- The client has the major responsibility to develop his/her own solution and action plan to the problem.
- Problem solving is more effective when the client identifies what processes need to be improved (e.g., reporting relationships, reward system, organizational structure).
- The client has more knowledge and insight about what will work in the organization than does the consultant.
- The client has more of a commitment for implementating the action plan if involved in the entire diagnostic problem-solving phases.

This model represents an ideal model of the consulting world. No organization ought to be dependent on a consultant for tasks it can do for itself. But the list of assumptions is more rigorous than may be evident from your reading of them. Much more of the responsibility for the outcome of the diagnosis and intervention process has fallen on the members of the organization. Suppose that the members are not skilled at problem solving. Imagine that management is solution oriented and doesn't wish to wait for a careful analysis. Suppose that time is short. Can members be adequately trained to participate fully in this process?

Cash and Minter[33] recommend that a readiness check sheet be performed by both the consultant and client in an attempt to discover if the process-consultation model fits the situation. An example of such a check sheet is presented in Figure 9.9.

MANAGING THE CONSULTING PROCESS

Initiating Contact

The two recognized methods of making contact are *indirect* and *direct*. Indirect methods are at the most unreliable since they result from circumstances. You might become a member of a church in your community and meet a prospective client while participating in an activity at your church. Or, perhaps you join the local chapter of the American Society of Training and Development or the International Association of Business Communicators or perhaps the Public Relations Society of America. At one of their meetings you meet a client. Maybe you agree to make a speech for some civic group and an audience member approaches you after the speech. There is nothing wrong with making yourself known in the community and among professionals. This kind of exposure is a good idea and does lead to consulting work, but it is unlikely to produce enough work to provide a full-time salary.

The second source of contact is direct contact. Direct contact means just that—it is calling on the potential client to offer your services. This is a difficult approach too, but one that is likely to pay off if you are persistent. There are two kinds of direct marketing, *cold calls* and *referrals*.

Greiner and Metzger[34] suggest a method one of them used to establish his consulting practice using cold calls. Here are the six steps that worked for him:

1. Develop a mailing list to the president or CEO of the prospective company.
2. Develop a letter that outlines three or four key industry issues of likely concern to the executive.
3. Mail out no more than ten letters each week, preferably on a Monday and, to keep down your travel expenses, preferably to prospects geographically close to you.
4. Never forget that the *one and only purpose* of the letter is to get that person's attention (your letter will accomplish that by its lucid, brief description of the issues that the administrator most worries about) and that the letter is *not intended to sell anything*.
5. Beginning the following Monday, call each of the letter's recipients for the *one and only purpose* of getting an appointment with that individual; the phone call is *not* intended to sell anything either.
6. Remember that, on an average, you will have to make five calls to each of the ten people before you reach them; most people are busy—not necessarily productive, but busy in meetings, seminars, traveling, sick, or on vacation.

	Yes	No
1. The client has appropriate problem-solving skills required for joint diagnosis with the consultant and others.	____	____
2. The client perceives the need for improvement.	____	____
3. The client is problem-solving oriented (rather than solutions oriented).	____	____
4. The client is willing to learn from the consultant and work group by group through diagnostic problem-solving phases.	____	____
5. The client wants to help in solving the problem.	____	____
6. The client is interested in an "original" rather than a prescriptive solution.	____	____
7. The client will permit the consultant to learn about the work climate through on-location observation, discussions with employees, review of confidential files, etc.	____	____
8. The client and consultant are able to interact effectively at the interpersonal level.	____	____
9. The client and consultant agree that the problem is worth solving.	____	____
10. The problem has high priority with the client.	____	____
11. The client desires to be actively involved in diagnostic phases of the problem-solving process.	____	____
12. The client is willing to commit additional resources (within reason) to aid the consultant in the fact-gathering and diagnosis stages.	____	____
13. The client is trainable (i.e., the consultant feels that the client can, wants to, and has the time to be trained) in using diagnostic problem-solving tools.	____	____
14. The client is open to innovative problem-solving approaches.	____	____
15. The client is willing to work with feedback survey data (such as interview data, or questionnaire data) collected by the consultant.	____	____
16. The client has a high-risk orientation relative to identifying and solving problems through the utilization of participation techniques with his/her work force.	____	____
17. The client is supportive of vertical team-building approaches.	____	____
18. The client is willing to implement mutually agreed upon solutions and action plans.	____	____
19. The solutions are not obvious to the consultant based on past experiences with other clients. Diagnostic work is necessary.	____	____
20. The client and consultant will not be violating professional ethics, laws, or morals.	____	____

Figure 9.9 Process consultation "readiness" criteria. (*Source:* William B. Cash and Robert L. Minter, "Consulting Approaches: Two Basic Styles," *Training and Development Journal* 33 (September 1979): 27.)

Don't get discouraged! However, don't send out more than ten letters each week since you will not be able to follow up effectively beyond 50 phone calls the following week.

Referrals are the bonus from an appreciative colleague or client. Once you establish yourself, people will mention you to their friends who have problems. Sometimes a colleague who consults may pass some business to you also. Clients do come through referral, but not until you have begun to establish yourself as a consultant.

The Initial Interview

If the interview has resulted from a cold call, you will want to follow a different procedure from the one used for a referral. If you followed the recommended procedure just described, you are likely to be talking to someone high up in the organization. This is important because you want to speak with someone who can make the decision to hire you. Here, again, Greiner and Metzger make some specific suggestions. First, thank the executive for taking the time to see you. Second, take about 10 minutes to talk about your consulting firm. Even if you are talking only about yourself, you want to portray the image that your consulting is successful and established. Greiner and Metzger say, "Talk about what you have been doing—your expertise."[35]

Next, suggest that you would like more information about the company so that you can know how you might be useful to them. Greiner and Metzger recommend that you ask questions like these three:

1. What are you most particularly pleased about in your company this year; what's going very well for you now; what is it about your company that is unique and distinguishes it from your competition?
2. What is not going as well? What are the two or three things that you are most concerned about at present?
3. What are some of the things that still need to be done but for lack of time, money, or management you just have not been able to address?

The final step is to ask if you can develop a proposal around some of the issues discussed.

If you have been referred to a particular company, again, be sure that some high-ranking official attends the meeting. Begin by introducing yourself and discussing your consulting firm. Move right into the nature of the problem. Try to get as much detail as possible about the problem so that your proposal can be tailored to the situation. Tell the executive that you will have a proposal on his or her desk in about a week.

Format for a Proposal

A proposal should follow a specific format and be as specific as possible. Keep the body of the proposal down to two to four pages. Put the detail into appendices.

Proposal writing and pricing are not simple matters. We will briefly sketch the format to give you a sense of what is included. You are encouraged to turn to one of the several sources available on the topic.[36] Here is one format for organizing proposals:

   I. Our understanding of the issue
  II. Objectives of the study, project, etc.
 III. Methodology
  IV. Timing and responsibility
   V. Arrangements for our services (costs)
  VI. Benefits
 VII. Summary

Common Types of Interventions

Gerald M. Goldhaber[37] describes five common types of intervention activities used by communication consultants. These are procedural input, theoretical input, nondirective counseling, direct feedback, and process sessions.

Procedural Input　　The word *procedure* suggests a course of action. And this is what it means when we speak of procedural input. It is the direct passing of information on a course of action to the client. This kind of activity is most directly associated with the purchase and doctor-patient models. Sometimes, however, it might be information that tells the client how to investigate the firm's problem situation. When the "how to" becomes assistance in solving a problem, rather than the solution itself, then the process model of consulting is being utilized. A communication consultant, for example, might tell the client how to construct a survey to measure attitudes of one of its publics, show how to draw a sample, and suggest how to interpret the data. This consultant would be following the process model by providing procedural input as long as the person didn't actually do the research.

Theoretical Input　　A consultant may help a client solve a difficulty by providing the theoretical resources to help the organizational problem solvers understand the problem. This is generally a process model consultation since the consultant doesn't actually solve the problem for the client. Suppose after completing a degree that qualified you as a communication consultant, a client asked you to attend several sessions of their management council in order to help improve their meetings. You might attend those meetings and then provide a list of articles and books that addressed the theory underlying the problems you observed. Or, you might instead deliver two or three brief lectures, with discussion following. You have assisted top management by helping them to understand small group communication better. It is up to the individual members to make a direct application to their own group experience.

Nondirective Counseling　　Counseling in this case means working with a member of an organization on a one-to-one basis. Nondirective means that you are not going to offer advice and directives to the client. What you as a consultant are trying to do is to help the person solve his or her own problem by posing questions. The aim of the questions is to cause the person to reflect on the situation more carefully. Generally these questions attempt to get the person to look at the situation in a new way, perhaps examining some aspects of it that escaped the person's attention. Usually the content of the situation would be some communication activity in which the person is engaged.

For example, you might be helping an executive think about his behavior as a leader of meetings. Here are several statements and questions that follow a nondirective approach: "Tell me about any recent leadership situation that you can remember that you would describe as a problem." "How do you think Joe would have described your leadership at this point?" "Why would he say something like that? What would he be trying to get across to you?" "How might you have communicated differently in this situation in order to create a different reaction from Joe?" "What would you need to change in order to behave like that?" "Why would you want to adopt this new way of handling this sort of situation? You can see that the nondirective approach guides the person through the problem-solving process without offering solutions. It is a process model consultation.

Direct Feedback   This intervention technique uses the consultant as conveyer and interpreter of information provided by members of an organization. Often this technique is used with an intact group as a team-building technique. The consultant interviews each member prior to the meeting about his or her reactions to the group and the problems each may have experienced. At the group meeting the consultant summarizes the reactions of each member to the group, filtered of course through the consultant's perception. Then group members are asked to react to the feedback. A variation of this direct feedback technique is direct confrontation. Under this format, the members share their impressions of the group directly to the group with the consultant as group leader. Then they react to each other's comments. Both of these procedures can be threatening to a group and counterproductive if the group is not ready for them. The group has to be mature and willing to try to improve if this intervention is to be successful.

Process Session   This intervention technique has a group focus on its own interpersonal and group processes. It is appropriate for a mature group that has learned how to solve problems. There are a number of different applications that might be chosen by a group. One effective procedure is to have a group devote 15 to 20 minutes at the end of each meeting to discuss how they did as a group. Initially, the consultant may guide a group through such a consideration. Once the group becomes proficient at analyzing its own behavior, the group can take over the process sessions. When group members are satisfied with their improvement, they would discontinue the procedure. Then as a group maintenance function, they might meet once or twice a year away from the place of business to discuss their group process.

When Should a Consultant Be Hired?

There are several situational variables that point to the need to hire an external consultant. The outside consultant should be hired when:

1. Nobody within the organization possesses the expert knowledge to handle the situation.
2. Nobody within the organization possesses the credibility to carry out the assignment.
3. The situation requires an unbiased, independent opinion.
4. It is not feasible to hire a full-time staff member with the expertise to carry out the task.
5. The situation must be handled quickly and there is no time to train an internal person to handle the situation.
6. The issue is too sensitive to be handled by organizational members who have a vested interest in the outcome.

Ethics of Consulting

One of the important factors in consulting is the trust that the client has for the consultant. This trust is enhanced by professionally defensible behavior. Ellis Hays[38] has proposed a classification system for organizational consultant behavior. Table 9.1 presents the relevant sections for your use.

SUMMARY

This chapter discusses communication and organizational change. We began by defining organizational development as a process undertaken to improve an organization's adapting, coping, problem solving, and goal-setting. The emphasis of organizational development is on people and changing their attitudes, values, and beliefs in order to promote organizational goals. Organizational development encompasses a systems perspective and an action research model.

We then examined the possible roles of an organizational developer. The organizational developer conducts activities that are grouped in nine areas. These are: (1) analyzing needs and evaluating results, (2) designing and developing training programs and materials, (3) developing training and development programs or services, (4) advising and counseling, (5) managing training activities, (6) managing organizational relationships, (7) doing research to advance the training field, (8) developing professional skill and expertise, and (9) developing basic skills and knowledge. The managing process, itself, involves five basic functions: planning, organizing, staffing, leading, and controlling.

An organizational communication consultant is an advisor who is trained and qualified to contract services to a client. The consultant helps the client by objectively identifying communication problems, analyzing these problems, identifying and recommending solutions to these problems, and, if asked to

Table 9.1   HAYS'S ETHICAL CLASSIFICATION FOR COMMUNICATION CONSULTANTS

Classification of behavior related to fees

1. Fees must be negotiated and decided upon in advance of the consultancy.
2. Communication consultants will not accept any fees for any referrals.
3. No fees will be accepted from suppliers.
4. Fees will not be tied to any cost reduction.

Classification of information collection

1. The consultant will be able to list the objectives that management has for employing a communication consultant.
2. The consultant will have measures of reliability and validity for all measurement instruments.
3. Communication consultants must attend one official training session every 2 years to update their knowledge of existing information and attitude measurement instruments.
4. No data will be published without the permission of the client.

Classification of analysis or prediction

1. All predictive and analytic statements must be in writing, and a written justification must be given—except in those cases where the client expressly requests the consultant to give only oral reports.
2. Communication consultants must label all analytic or predictive statements as based on quantitative probability theory, expert or personal opinion.
3. Communication consultants must update predictive skills and knowledge of techniques by taking an official short course once every 2 years.

Classification of training activities

1. Training programs should be developed so that the objectives match the needs of the problem analysis results.
2. Training programs should utilize criterion-referenced behavioral objectives.

Classification of personal behavior of consultants

1. Consultants will not seek employment from a client.
2. Consultants will observe all local, state, and federal laws while in the process of consulting.
3. Consultants serving competing firms at the same time will do so only with the knowledge and consent of both.
4. Consultants will read widely in the field in order to pass a yearly refresher test.

Source: Adapted from Ellis Hays, "A Behavioral Objectives Approach to the Development of a Code of Ethics for Communication Consultants." A paper presented at the meeting of the International Communication Association, April 1972.

do so, assisting in the implementation of these solutions. The consultant may adopt the purchase approach, the doctor-patient approach or the process approach.

The consulting process requires an initial contact—through a direct or indirect method, an interview in which the consultant identifies the difficulty, submission of a proposal to the client, and one of several types of interventions. The intervention may be procedural input, theoretical input, nondirective counseling, direct feedback, or a process session. Whatever the method used, it is important to remember that trust is an important part of the relationship. We presented a code of ethics that will guide the consultant in fair consulting practices.

ENDNOTES

1. Warren Bennis, *Organizational Development: Its Nature, Origins, and Prospects* (Reading, MA: Addison-Wesley, 1969), p. 2.
2. David R. Hampton, Charles Summer, and Ross Webber, *Organizational Behavior and the Practice of Management* (Glenview, IL: Scott-Foresman, 1973), p. 850.
3. Bennis, *Organizational Development.*
4. Wendell French and Cecil Bell, Jr., *Organizational Development* (Englewood Cliffs, NJ: Prentice-Hall, 1978), p. 17.
5. Ibid., p. 88.
6. Wendell French, "Organization Development Objectives, Assumptions, and Strategies," *California Management Review* 12 (Winter 1969): 26.
7. Lynda C. McDermott, "The Many Faces of the OD Professional," *Training and Development Journal* 38 (February 1984): 14–19.
8. Tod White, "Increasing Your Effectiveness as a Training and Development Specialist," *Training and Development Journal* 33 (May, 1979): 3–12.
9. Karen S. Brethower and Geary A. Rummler, "Evaluating Training," *Training and Development Journal* 33 (May 1979): 14–22.
10. Chip Bell and Tony Putman, "Mastering the Art of Training Design," *Training and Development Journal* 33 (May 1979): 24–27.
11. Ibid., p. 25.
12. Ibid., p. 58.
13. Ibid., p. 58.
14. For a comprehensive list of self-assessment questions for this area, see Herman Birnbauer, "Delivering Training and Development Programs/Services, *Training and Development Journal* 33 (May 1979): 30–35.
15. Kent Merman, "Advising and Counseling as an HRD Activity," *Training and Development Journal* 33 (May 1979): 44–45.
16. These functions of managers were classified by Henry Fayol as planning, organizing, coordinating, commanding, and controlling in his book, *General and Industrial Management,* trans. Constance Storrs (New York: Pitman, 1949), p. xxi. We prefer to use the categories used by the *Wall Street Journal* to classify its articles that deal with management.
17. Jerry Forbes, "Sales Training and Field Sales: Cost Factors Which Impact Corporate Product ROI," paper presented at Training 80, Sheraton Center, New York City, December 1980.
18. R. Wayne Pace, *Organizational Communication: Foundations for Human Resource Development* (Englewood Cliffs, NJ: Prentice-Hall, 1983), pp. 266–267.
19. Gordon Lippitt, "Developing Professional Skills and Expertise," *Training and Development Journal* 33 (May 1979): 66.
20. Calvin P. Otto and Rollin O. Glaser, *The Management of Training* (Reading, MA: Addison-Wesley, 1970).
21. Michael S. Hanna and Gerald L. Wilson, *Communicating in Business and Professional Settings* (New York: Random House, 1984), pp. 210–215.
22. Louise W. Stanek, "The Care and Maintenance of Organizational Relationships," *Training and Development Journal* 33 (May 1979): 52.
23. Ibid., p. 52.
24. Ibid., p. 57.
25. Leonard Nadler, "Research: An HRD Activity Area," *Training and Development Journal* 33 (May 1979): 60–64.

26. Gordon Lippitt, "Developing Professional Skills," pp. 66–70; Gordon L. Lippitt, *Organizational Renewal: A Holistic Approach to Organizational Development,* 2d ed. (Englewood Cliffs, NJ: Prentice-Hall, 1982).

27. Lippitt., "Developing Professional Skills," p. 70.

28. Ronald L. Applebaum and Karl W. E. Anatol, *Effective Oral Communication for Business and the Professions* (Chicago: Science Research Associates, 1982); Patricia Hayes Bradley and John E. Baird, Jr., *Communication for Business and the Professions,* 2d ed. (Dubuque, IA: Brown, 1983); Michael S. Hanna and Gerald L. Wilson, *Communicating in Business and Professional Settings* (New York: Random House, 1984); Gerald M. Phillips, *Communicating in Organizations* (New York: Macmillan, 1982).

29. Larry E. Greiner and Robert O. Metzger, *Consulting to Management* (Englewood Cliffs, NJ: Prentice-Hall, 1983), p. 9.

30. William B. Cash and Robert L. Minter, "Consulting Approaches: Two Basic Styles," *Training and Development Journal* 33 (September 1979): 26.

31. Chris Argyris, "Explorations in Consulting-Client Relationships," *Human Organization* 20 (Fall 1961): 122.

32. Cash and Minter, "Consulting Approaches," p. 26.

33. Ibid., p. 27.

34. Greiner and Metzger, *Consulting to Management,* pp. 46–47.

35. Ibid., p. 48.

36. Jerome Fuchs, *Management Consultants in Action* (New York: Hawthorne, 1975); Larry E. Greiner and Robert O. Metzger, *Consulting to Management,* Howard M. Klein, *Other People's Business—A Primer on Management Consultants* (New York: Mason/Charter, 1978); Gordon Lippitt and Ronald Lippitt, *The Consulting Process in Action* (La Jolla, CA: University Associates, 1978).

37. Gerald Goldhaber, *Organizational Communication* (Dubuque, IA: Wm. C. Brown, 1983), pp. 360–362.

38. Ellis Hays, "A Behavioral Objectives Approach to the Development of a Code of Ethics for Communication Consultants," paper presented at a meeting of the International Communication Association, April 1972.

chapter *10*

Designing Successful Communication Training Programs

THE PERSUASIVE BASIS FOR COMMUNICATION TRAINING PROGRAMS

The Sophists of Contemporary America / Acquiring a Rhetorical Perspective on Training

TRAINING MODELS

The Selection Model / The Problem-Solution Model / The Process Model

ESTABLISHING A TRAINING PROGRAM

Stage 1: Assessing the Need for Communication Training
Initial Inquiries / Meeting the Training Director / Establishing Assessment Procedures / Making the Formal Assessment Report

Stage 2: Designing the Training Program
Establishing the Goals / Determining the Training Process / Organizing the Training Schedule / Developing Activities and Lecturettes

Stage 3: Implementing the Training Program
Constructing a Syllabus / Choosing Instructional Resources / Meeting the Class / Establishing the Ground Rules / Interacting with the Participants / Asking for Responses to the Program / Previewing/Debriefing Each Meeting / Making Assignments

Stage 4: Assessing the Effectiveness of the Training Program
The WGW Assessment Instrument / Conducting Oral Appraisals / Meeting with the Training Director / Redefining the Design of the Program

If you are asked to design a communication training program for an organization in your community, you can reasonably assume that (1) the organization is in trouble but it doesn't know why, (2) a powerful person in the organization thinks better communication is a good idea, (3) a particular type of communication training is not already available in public seminars, or (4) the organization has identified a communication behavior as part of competent job performance. You might want to say, "Stop. Wait a minute, what about assessment? How do you know you have a problem with communication and that training can do anything about it?" This is a very useful first question to ask any potential training client. Let's consider what you are likely to hear in response.

The organization in trouble may not have time for assessment, at least not for the formal auditing procedures described in Chapter 8. It might have already made its own assessment, which may be passed along to you. But to verify its appraisal of the situation, you still need to do some analysis of the communication skills at issue. As you establish the training program, you can still ensure that the training meets most of the organization's needs.

If a powerful person in the organization, the CEO or a vice-president, perhaps the personnel director, thinks better communication is a good idea, then assessing the type of communication development required is even more important. Your analysis of the situation can give detailed and precise objectives to satisfy the powerful while enhancing the organization. But that person may have already decided on a specific communication skill as the training objective. Assessment may then be more useful as an argument for a more complete communication development program.

The organization may specify training in a wide range of communication skills, many of which may not be available in public seminars. Recent research by Harris and Thomlison indicates that a wide variety of communication training are requested.[1] The stronger desire for training in communication skills such as motivating people and listening doesn't mean that these are more important forms of communication than is conference leadership, but instead, points out that previous education and natural talent are deficient in these areas. A training program in one type of communication skill is likely to stimulate awareness of other potential areas for communication development. A consistent and coherent program can integrate training in many specific communication skills around a central philosophy of the purpose of communication. Since many organizations recognize the power of communication to influence and persuade both within the organization and in public communication, we have taken a rhetorical perspective on communication training. After explicating this perspective, this chapter examines alternative training models and presents a four-stage plan for designing and assessing an effective training program.

THE PERSUASIVE BASIS FOR COMMUNICATION TRAINING PROGRAMS

Persuasion, in the sense of the investigation and production of goal-seeking strategies for inducing the cooperation in listeners or audiences, is a useful, artistic foundation for potential trainers and their audiences. Persuasion addresses the classic issue of management: How to accomplish tasks efficiently through an orderly method that is capable of gaining the desired result while making efficient use of available resources.[2] Persuasion theories are based on methods for assessing the needs of a target audience, investigating alternative ways and means of meeting those needs, planning a communication strategy, and carrying out the strategy smoothly, deliberately, and eloquently. Hence, persuasion theories should provide a focus for understanding communication training needs and organizing communication training programs.

Because persuasion works with science and technology[3] as the skill through which technical and scientific information is presented to various publics, persuasion training focused on skill development doesn't require in-depth knowledge of the subject at hand. Training can provide instruction in how to develop persuasive presentations, work cooperatively in decision-making groups, and reduce interpersonal misunderstanding and conflict without becoming experts in the relevant technical or scientific fields. Sussman has argued that the communication professional without technical expertise can harm a client by "muddling through" if she or he claims (1) technical expertise when there is none or (2) the capability to solve the client's problem rather than claiming only to provide training to permit the client to solve the problem.[4] But muddling through can be minimized by offering content-free training in communication formats using a persuasion-oriented approach to communication development.

Persuasion is an effective foundation for communication training programs. Tompkins has described the need for a communication-centered concept of the modern organization centered on the processes of exercising power and influence among an organization's members.[5] We maintain that since such a concept is persuasive in nature, it requires that attention be focused on training managers and executives in the arts and techniques of deliberation and formal presentation.

The Sophists of Contemporary America

As the focus of a communication development program, rhetoric becomes a productive "way of knowing" for the trainer and trainees who share the view that we should seek the most effective communication strategy in every situation. This attitude doesn't claim that all communication is argument, but that we should know and use rational suasive techniques to reach organizational communication objectives. The best arguments can thus be prepared and used as appropriate in decision making, group communication, and reports within the organization. Public communication has been more aware of the importance of well-reasoned appeals adapted to specific audiences. Our goal is to address goal-oriented, format-seeking needs of an organization, developing communication skills to make the organization aware of its persuasive potential. To the extent that this approach supplies organizations with formats and techniques suitable to their needs, trainers and trainees become the sophists of contemporary America. But just as Gorgias made his reputation and his living providing clients with arguments and delivery skills that won the day in court, so must trainers provide communication development programs to increase their clients' effectiveness in the business world. As we will later demonstrate, instruction and practice in making arguments is central to our approach to communication training. Not only are we engaged in teaching professionals how to make well-formed, well-adapted arguments, but we are also engaged in revealing the fallacies that persuade a less-informed consumer of persuasion.

Acquiring a Rhetorical Perspective on Training

One realistic objection to the claim of a rhetorically informed approach to training in American organizations is that managers and executives think rhetoric is either a strange term for impoverished ideas presented in embellished language or that rhetoric is more appropriate for the liberal arts than for the organizational sciences. We have found the opposite case to be true. First, we maintain that the professionals in technological and scientific organizations tend to be better educated and more appreciative of how persuasion functions in their business lives than their counterparts in traditional bureaucratic businesses and industries. Perhaps this is because fewer opportunities occur for persuasion in a bureaucracy than in more modern and flexible corporate structures. Second, the survival of our discipline requires that key concepts such as rhetoric should not be devalued or obscured when dealing with organizational employees. Increased familiarity with rhetorical ideas can aid audiences who have practical communication needs. Third, we have found that when the term rhetoric is carefully defined in terms of the experiences and goals of corporate life, employees use rhetorical concepts more willingly. The fear that rhetoric is inappropriate to business settings may stem more from an academic dispute between competing research paradigms than from the actual experience of communication trainers in organizations.

An organization's training needs don't rely on the same principles of education that inform university curricula. First, time constraints severely limit the scope of training activities; most managers simply don't have time for training unless they can justify the time lost from work by gains in productivity. Their actual performance on the job must improve because of the training they receive or the value of the training is questionable. Second, participants in managerial communication training programs already hold college degrees in their fields. What they demand from training is increased awareness of behavioral options that improve their job performance capabilities. Although theoretical awareness can be made a vital part of their increased awareness of communication, the trainer must not tip the scales toward irrelevant theoretical discussions. Third, the practicing professional manager brings to training acquired techniques that our academic theories and academic experiences often cannot readily explain. To force those in training to learn our language without in turn being willing to learn the language of their everyday experiences may produce tension that undermines the training. When time is a mutually shared constraint and the options for learning our theories or their experiences presents itself as a naturally occurring dichotomy, the trainer is wise to adapt to the needs and expectations of the audience.

These three points about the differences between university education and in-house training invoke the old disputes between sophists and academicians in ancient Greece.[6] Then as now, those who "took the show on the road" were ridiculed for failing to fulfill formal academic requirements while training patrons who lacked the interest or time to develop practical skills in a formal setting. Usually these skills were developed by formulas and proven techniques. As Hyde points out, "under this guidance (scientific criteria for technological progress) the development of techniques is given priority so that these techniques can aid in the explanation, prediction, and control of the ambiguous human condition. Technical understanding first, human understanding second, become the procedural steps of technological progress."[7] For trainers whose expertise closely involves human understanding, simplified techniques and formulas appear to be reductionism, a potentially dangerous method of instruction, but one necessary for a successful training program. We have found that the sophistic situation in the modern age is not nearly as dichotomous as it seems for issues of technical versus academic interests. For example, what communication instructor would argue against teaching basic rules for speech making, such as the use of a basic form to guide speech production, or the use of agendas to guide group problem-solving or decision-making activities? Are these not formulas? And when an instructor guides a discussion concerning the discovery and analysis of argument, are not Toulmin's model of argument or Ehninger's depiction of argument classifications useful? Again, are these not techniques? Our belief is that technical and academic interests can run parallel in a communication training program.

In attempting to adapt to our audience, practicing professional managers in high technology organizations, we have discovered a rhetorically informed, practical skills approach to communication training useful. Training can improve the communication competencies of managers in three interrelated areas of job performance: presentational speaking and writing, small group problem solving and decision making, and interpersonal skill development and conflict resolution. In each area we emphasize the coordination of active listening, rational argument, and persuasive strategies designed to motivate subordinates and peers. The techniques and formulas we provide serve as inducements for them to participate willingly in the training program. Once the program begins, these inducements to act can also become inducements to know, giving participants the potential to learn useful principles to design their own techniques. Hence, our advertisements and course objectives promise a pragmatic, skill-oriented program designed for the needs of managers. But as the sophists before us must have known, in practice the sound use of formulas and techniques depends on making informed choices of productive communication behaviors in a given case.

TRAINING MODELS

The relationship between the communication trainer and the organization can be modeled in three basic forms: the process model, the problem-solution model, and the selection model. These models are significant because they describe the various perceptions of the organization seeking help. In order to understand the expectations of the client more clearly, a training program designer should analyze and anticipate the expectations of potential clients. A specific model may describe the organization's attitudes completely. But more likely the organization's relationship with the communication trainer embodies a combination of models. We consider each model as a five-stage description of the relationship between the communication trainer and the organization. Each model varies according to (1) how the relationship is established, (2) how complete is the training program's prior development, (3) how the training program is adapted to the organization, (4) how training is administered, and (5) how the relationship is terminated.

The Selection Model

The most basic model of communication training is the selection model. In this model the organization selects the trainer and a training program after determining its needs. The relationship is established by either the trainer offering a program for purchase or the organization seeking a trainer with a known product. The training program is complete prior to the organization's contact with the trainer, which is prepared through use with prior clients who may have requested the training. In selecting a fixed form of training, the organization takes responsibility for diagnosing its communication needs. The trainer can only adapt the program to the organization if the program can be altered without changing its identity as a product. For example, training in group problem solving might be used in an organization run according to management by objectives because both are task-oriented, relatively objective concepts. Training in motivation techniques would be restricted to concepts that are consistent with the MBO management philosophy. According to the selection model, the organization expects training to be delivered in the form that it was purchased, with standardized application and transfer of skills. The relationship between the trainer and the organization is terminated at the end of the training program, to be renewed if another group of employees requires the same training.

The Problem-Solution Model

The problem-solution model describes a situation where the communication consultant is contacted by the organization when the organization perceives that it is in trouble. The communication consultant diagnoses the problem and recommends a solution. If training is required, the consultant may develop a training package for the organization or recommend an existing program. The consultant may then become the trainer or be asked to reassess the organization after training is complete. The relationship between the communication trainer and the organization is terminated when the problem is solved and the organization perceives its trouble to be over. If the training extends over enough time, continuing after the initial problem is forgotten or solved, the organization may terminate a potential long-term relationship with the trainer until the problem reappears.[8]

The Process Model

The process model represents the work of Schein in describing training as an ongoing, dynamic process of consultation. Training helps the client to perceive, understand, and act to resolve problems in processes like communication.[9] The organization and the consultant contribute to the training process by jointly establishing the relationship, analyzing the problem, and developing and administering training. The organization profits from the consultant/trainer's expertise by acquiring the capability of conducting its own assessment and training development in the future. Thus, the relationship is terminated when the consultant can contribute no further to organizational development, and when the organization can diagnose and resolve its communication problems independently. Now that we have discussed the organization's expectations for training, let's consider how you could establish a training program.

ESTABLISHING A TRAINING PROGRAM

Regardless of how the relationship between organization and training developer is established, a training program takes shape in four stages. The first stage assesses the need for communication training, a process of implementing assessment procedures and making an assessment report. In the second stage the results of the assessment are translated into a design for the training program by setting objectives and determining the details of the training sessions. The third stage implements these design details in a syllabus and class meetings develop according to the guidelines suggested by learning theory and experience. The fourth stage assesses the effectiveness of the training program with the WGW assessment instrument and oral appraisals, leading to program redesign. By the end of one training program, another session of the modified program may be required, or a new communication training need may have emerged. The four-stage development cycle can be started at any point as appropriate to move toward ongoing training needs.

Stage 1: Assessing the Need for Communication Training

Initial Inquiries   Initial inquiries about training are like any other solicitation of business—the harder the seller pushes, the more the buyer relies on trusted personal contacts to verify that the promises are true and the product worthwhile. Your distribution of 5,000 brochures may make a flurry in the mail, but heavy dependence on advertising produces a response that is most readily for seminars or workshops open to the largest market—the public. Smaller, more selective groups of consumers are best wooed with personal calls and visits following the brochure, which are backed up by cheerful offers to demonstrate your style to the management club.

A sharp presentation on the latest topic, however, is not good for long. Trends in every business community make certain training attractive as the latest way to meet a commitment to organizational development, but not all stylish techniques are always popular. An examination of training programs over time has shown that new ideas in training either fade if they don't meet expectations or are internalized as part of the repertoire of useful training concepts.[10] For example, cassette-tape learning to fill idle moments was never attractive enough to those seeking some well-earned rest, but videotapes produced in a professional and sophisticated manner are widely used as a convenient, cost-effective training format. Thus, if the trend toward computer-aided instruction continues, your expertise in that format may bring you business just because you offer the product. Continued success can only come from training programs that have useful content as well as stylish format.

Initial contact between communication trainers and organization-size clients is thereby based on a reputation in the community. Personnel development and training directors are naturally alert to communication-oriented workshops and seminars offered to the community at large. Scouts from interested organizations can preview the quality of your instruction and the content of a typical public program to assess your potential. If they indicate that their organization might be a client if other topics were covered, then you have already passed your first screening. The public seminar aimed at a general audience and an average skill level is a difficult type of training to handle well, since you have to adapt to those who show up on registration day. But trainers/consultants who establish a good reputation for their public seminars can soon move up to providing specific training for a known organization.

Meeting the Training Director   The training director who brings in a communication consultant or trainer is in a delicate position. By bringing in an outsider, the training director may be admitting an inability to deal with the organization's communication problems. If the training director's job is simply to locate and schedule appropriate training resources from the community, then you are likely to be as welcome as any consultant. But if you are there because the director is incapable of doing what the organization thinks is really an internal job, then you must tread lightly indeed. The training director is more than a liaison between you and the organization. The training practices established by that director have created an attitude toward training throughout the organization to which you will have to accommodate.

The training director's situation should be analyzed as you become familiar with the organization as a whole. You need to know how strongly your assessment and training activities will be backed up within the organization. The support for your activities might come from the training director if the training department has real power within the organization. But if there is no regular training director or if the training program is not respected, then you will need the support of the organization's CEO. If interest in changing organizational communication emanates from the CEO, both you and the training director will obviously be able to proceed with less difficulty.

Thus, meeting the training director is the first test of your compatibility with the organization. If you can convince the training director that you are there to help increase the effectiveness of the current training program, you can demonstrate that you are not a threat to the status quo. You may have to recommend changes in training at the end of the assessment stage, but by then you will have good reasons for what you recommend. As you meet the training director, you are still integrating yourself into the organization's power structure. Since training and development often have very little real power compared to more profitable departments, you might align yourself with department heads in other parts of the organization. Those relationships might give you the authority to conduct assessments, but you would have to go back to the training director to implement training programs. In many cases, the training director might have control over training expenditures for the entire organization.[11] Thus, you need to become part of the training-oriented network from the start by showing how your assessment can lead to better organizational development. You can help the training director maintain power while acquiring an essential liaison with the entire organization.

Establishing Assessment Procedures   Assessment procedures may be established through negotiation to determine who will do what form of assessment. You may not need to use full auditing procedures if exploratory interviews indicate that communication is ineffective in a specific part of the organization. The training director may have conducted some assessment prior to contacting a specialist in communication development. Any findings from this type of internal investigation should be confirmed to check on the director's objectivity.

Your greatest advantage, in addition to your expertise, is your relatively objective perspective on the situation. The assessment you conduct should capitalize on your ability to see the situation objectively. Thus, if assessment procedures are carried out by both you and the training director, you should do the exploratory interviews and the follow-up interviews since they are most objectively conducted by an outsider. The training director and selected assistants might administer questionnaires for network analysis after being instructed in their use. Computer facilities for data analysis might be arranged by the organization with your close supervision.

Procedures requiring trained observers might be used only if the observers selected from within the organization can demonstrate that they are free from bias and have strong interrater reliability. You can train them and check their observations' reliability during the training period, but you would have to trust their continued accuracy. Self-assessment procedures like communication diaries and communication experience descriptions might be coordinated by the training director. Less familiar assessment procedures like SYMLOG analysis of interpersonal relationships and work groups might be demonstrated in a workshop for supervisors or department managers and implemented by the training director with help from selected members of each department. These assessment procedures should involve both you and the training director as well as every part of the organization. The organization's participation in assessment should build awareness of communication issues and involvement with communication development training yet to come.

Making the Formal Assessment Report   The formal assessment report should be written according to the guidelines in Chapter 8. In making the report to the organization, you need to address two further issues. First, how can you include as much of the organization as possible in the audience for the report? Those involved in assessment may have some expectation of feedback. The report should reach those who will be impacted by training based on the assessment. Then they will understand the need for the training as well as the problems revealed by the assessment. The obvious issue here is whether everyone participating in assessment should get the results. The decision about who gets the report may be made for you, and the audience may be limited to change agents in management who will be implementing training in communication development.

Once the audience is known, you can proceed to the second issue. How can you adapt the delivery of the report to suit the attitudes and awareness of the audience? If your goal is simply to deliver your analysis and terminate the relationship with the organization, then your main concern will be that the audience believes what you say and takes your suggestions about future action seriously. This goal may be ensured if you back up every analysis of the organization with data to show that the problem exists on a significant level. Selected examples chosen from communication experience reports can give the data meaning and demonstrate what the problem looks like in practice. The audience's acceptance of your conclusions would also be heightened if you could show how the communication problems you have identified affect each member of the audience. By presenting scenarios of communication problems likely to occur in the future, you can involve and motivate the entire audience to do something about the problems at hand. If you intend to offer a training program to help the organization resolve its problems, then you can use the assessment report to motivate the audience to support future training. But before training can begin, you must design the training program.

Stage 2: Designing the Training Program

Designing a training program to meet the needs of the organization requires close coordination between the consultant and representatives of the organization. Once assessment is complete, management can assign selected members of the organization to assist the training director and the consultant in designing the training program. These additional participants in the design process increase the likelihood that the program's content will be useful to the organization. Although the consultant can coordinate these discussions, leadership in identifying goals for the program should originate with the client, in response to the assessment report. As a training process and schedule are developed by the program planners, the consultant may prepare activities and lecturettes to suit each communication topic included in the final program design.

Establishing the Goals   Establishing goals for the program uses information from two sources, the consultant and the organization's representatives. In a dialogue similar to negotiation, the organization may point to problems shown by assessment and demand a solution from the consultant. The organization focused on clear descriptions of job skills might wisely ask for training to produce behavioral skills according to a competence standard. For example, every supervisor who goes through the program should be able to lead a problem-solving group and conduct employee performance appraisal according to organizational standards. However, Lippitt reports that managers are more likely to require conditions rather than behaviors, results like reduced costs, increased productivity, better morale, and personnel who can be promoted.[12] The consultant can only provide training in communication competencies, and thus cannot establish goals that promise cost or productivity benefits. The manager has the responsibility of utilizing trained employees for the best possible impact on the organization.

The objectives for the training program should also distinguish between competence in communication practices and knowledge about communication. One of the hardest decisions for the program designers is to decide whether training should provide (1) formulas for effective communication practices without any understanding of the rationale behind the procedure, or (2) enough information about the rationale for a communication practice to allow an informed choice between several procedures for effective communication. The problem of integrating knowledge and practice has been clearly identified for over 20 years as one of the main concerns of training program design.[13] Unless this is settled before the program is planned, the consultant cannot prepare the appropriate blend of knowledge with practice in a set of behavioral objectives.

Determining the Training Process   The training process is part of the organizational development plan devised to train the right people in the right skills at the right time. Those responsible for coordinating the development of operations and personnel should receive their communication training before their department does in order to prepare for changes in communication practices. Acceptance of a training program requires that influential members of the organization receive training before those they influence. If key personnel are left out of the initial training program, they may resist implementing the practices learned by the rest of the organization. The best training process trains the entire organization in one communication competence before moving on to the next phase of the program, so that the organization can develop as a whole. Dividing the goals for the program into workable phases also allows the program to adapt to unexpected problems as each new phase begins.

Organizing the Training Schedule   The training schedule should disrupt the ordinary activities of the organization as little as possible. A manager required to send too many personnel for training at one time or during a peak work period may refuse to cooperate with the program rather than lose ground on a project. Organizations with facilities located far apart often have a significant portion of their personnel in transit, or someone scheduled for one location may go temporarily to another office. The basic goal of the training schedule is to use the training resources to their fullest extent and to move the organization through the program as quickly as possible. Given the constraints of the organization's activities, the schedule should permit catching up with missed sessions while still demanding some commitment to attend. If the schedule doesn't allow time during working hours, training can be scheduled during the weekend or at night. But the burden on the trainer to compete with the resulting hostility or fatigue may reduce the effectiveness of the program.

Developing Activities and Lecturettes   The program designers are wise if they permit the communication consultant to develop activities and lecturettes once the topics and objectives have been chosen. The consultant's expertise should include knowledge of many ways to use the training experience to reach the program's objectives. Learning theory has recently returned to the idea that teaching is comprised of five interrelated factors: the teacher, the student, the subject matter, the environment, and the time period.[14] Developing activities should take all five factors into account, adapting the teacher and the subject matter to the student, the environment, and the time period. The time factor is most important in developing lecturettes, since you are limited by the audience's attention span and ability to assimilate new ideas. The best training gives the trainees as much time as possible to practice and learn the communication skills of the day. Even though you may have decided to combine behavioral objectives with understanding based on knowledge, lectures should not exceed 20 minutes and should be reinforced and clarified by high-quality visual aids. Each lecturette should focus on one main idea, the topic of activities to follow. If the class has been given reading, the lecturette should not assume that the reading has been completed and internalized. Reading assignments should be discussed separately from the lecturette to keep the presentation orderly and within the planned time limit. The lecturette should also be adapted to the situation.

Adapting yourself and your subject to the situation calls for some consideration of learning modes and learning styles. Learning modes are commonly identified as feeling, thinking, watching, and doing.[15] Each trainee is likely to learn best from a slightly different combination of these activities, so the best training offers different types of activities presented in a wide range of teaching styles. Reporting on their work with learning style inventories, Smith and Renzulli found there is no one right teaching style to match all trainees' learning styles.[16] But trainers should plan for four basic learning styles, each revealed in the expectations of the trainees. Although labels for these styles vary according to the researcher, Ward's descriptions of adult learning styles best distinguish the types common in training.[17]

1. The idealistic learner wants to discover what skills constitute competency in a specific situation, resenting training that offers a highly structured, simple formula for communication competency. The trainer who does the thinking for the trainees is insulting their self-image by treating them like children rather than as analytical thinkers. Idealistic learners respond best to activities requiring them first to think and watch and then to feel and do. All modes of learning attract them, but the discovery process must occur in the correct order at their own pace.

2. The pragmatic learner is so convinced of the uniqueness of his or her work situation that your training cannot possibly apply unless he or she sees it working in the real world. The classroom is too different from the workplace for anything experienced in class to be transferable to the job. The learning mode most suitable for the pragmatic learner is doing, but only if the situation is the actual job setting or a close facsimile.

3. The realistic learner doesn't value discovery or evaluation of options in training, preferring to be told what to do. He or she tolerates practicing communication skills, but only for the purpose of perfecting the technique by learning a structured procedure with explicit goals. The realistic learners learn best by watching and doing. Feeling and thinking just complicate the task they are trying to perform.

4. The existentialistic learner doesn't believe there is one right way, but tries to learn how to respond to a specific situation. The existentialistic learners are concerned with alternatives in performing their duties and regard other trainees as resources for new ways of doing things, especially in complex behaviors like communication. They value training focused on feeling, thinking, watching, and doing if they're trying out someone else's way of communicating to learn new responses to a situation.

Your activities and lecturettes can be developed to suit the expectations of the principal learning style in the class. The pragmatic learner may clamor for more "real-world" applications, but that is a good excuse for exchanges of experiences among the trainees. You can often restore some interest in a topic by encouraging the class to exchange stories of communication problems or triumphs. You benefit by learning what is important to the trainees on an individual level, and they get a chance to satisfy their individual learning needs. Now that we have addressed the design of the training program, let's consider implementing the training program.

Stage 3: Implementing the Training Program

Implementing the training program is a seven-stage process in which you take control of the design for the program and translate the program's goals into a well-organized class. Preliminary planning involves constructing a syllabus and choosing instructional resources. Once you have met the class, you can develop the ground rules that produce effective interaction with the participants. In order to involve them in the class, you then must encourage their responses to the program within clearly organized meetings. Previewing and debriefing each meeting maintains the participants awareness of their progress, while making assignments keeps them involved in the subject between meetings. First, we turn to guidelines for constructing a syllabus.

Constructing a Syllabus   The syllabus has a simple function, to organize activities and lecturettes to match the available time in the training schedule. The syllabus can start from the time period allotted for training, alternating lecturettes, activities, discussion, and breaks until the time is exhausted. By organizing training for the entire program, the syllabus also informs the trainees about what they should expect, orienting them to the program as a whole and making their own planning much easier. You can rough out the syllabus by distributing major topics evenly over the time available, filling in with as many activities as the remaining time permits. Every hour of training usually includes a 10-minute break for refreshments and personal business, leaving 50 minutes in every hour for lecturettes, activities, and discussion. Lecturettes can introduce a topic, but often an activity producing the problem you hope to solve is even more effective. Once the topic has been established, the lecturette can expand the subject for 10 to 20 minutes. Whether the trainees are expected to take notes or follow an outline depends on the situation. The lecturette should be followed by an activity demonstrating the problem or practicing the skills to resolve the problem. The class will usually want to discuss their experience for at least 10 minutes, so a 15-minute lecturette and a 10-minute break leave 25 minutes in each hour for activities. Extra time should be allowed for the mechanics of setting up visual aids or feedback devices like videotape. Once you have written and distributed the syllabus, some trainees may regard it as a de facto contract, so the syllabus should be followed if at all possible. Adjust to unexpected events by dropping activities or discussion segments, but don't eliminate a main topic to get back on schedule, since you are accountable to the program design as presented to the organization.

Choosing Instructional Resources   The organization may offer you a variety of instructional resources, ranging from chalkboards to rear screen projection with synchronized soundtrack. Choosing instructional resources depends on your level of expertise in running your own show. If you have the time and the experience to develop professional grade videotapes or projections to complement lecturettes and activities, take advantage of that opportunity. But use only the resources that you can handle skillfully. For example, bad videos are unacceptable to audiences accustomed to professionally produced commercial TV programs. The best instructional aids are the simplest, a clearly legible set of flipcharts prepared ahead of time is quicker and more readable than hasty scrawls on a chalkboard. A well-planned set of visual aids on the overhead projector is much easier to produce and use than slides with or without a soundtrack. A useful guideline for choosing instructional resources is to seek the maximum degree of contact with the class by controlling the environment to keep trainees awake and involved in the program. The less you talk and the more they do, the more stimulated they will be by their experience, so choose your resources to maximize their involvement with you and the subject.

Meeting the Class   Meeting the class is much like making contact with the organization for the first time. You may have been planning the program for months but, as far as the class is concerned, everything starts with the first meeting. The first meeting has three goals: to orient the class to the syllabus and its goals, to establish an awareness of a need for the training, and to show how the training program outlined in the syllabus can meet that need.

Just as you had to show the organization how it could benefit from training, you also need to show the class that they can benefit from participating in the training program. Thus, meeting the class with clear reasons why they will benefit from training is essential to motivate them to get involved with the program. If you can identify their problems, they may agree to having those problems and be interested in the program. But if they identify their own problems and make a commitment to use the training to solve their problems, then their motivation to participate fully is much stronger.

Establishing the Ground Rules   Assuming that the class is eager and willing to participate, the training classroom is a new situation with ambiguous rules for conduct. You can resolve much of this ambiguity by establishing the ground rules for conduct during the first meeting, specifying what behaviors will be expected and what will not be tolerated. But even with such a clear start, the training class is a social and task-oriented entity like any other, capable of working out its own rules as the program progresses. How much you need to control this process depends on how close the natural evolution of class conduct matches your own expectations and requirements. Often, letting adults establish their own social structures is enough, as long as the authority you intend for the trainer is maintained. Mediating conflict in discussions rather than forbidding arguments may be much more encouraging to participation and a frank exchange of views. The fact that the training takes place in what is still a work environment gives you the option of referring back to the rules of the organization to control any potentially serious problems. But your authority ultimately derives from your expertise and potential to help the participants be more effective on the job.

Interacting with the Participants   Since you are valuable to the participants because of your knowledge, your interaction with them might be constrained by professional conduct on both sides. If you show sincere interest in the participants and their problems, and you also show how you can help them, they are more likely to risk a warmer, more trusting relationship. If you also show that you are similar on a personal level, with similar attitudes about politics, style, or sports, you might become friends. What could friendship do for the training program? Friendship might make the program more enjoyable, but you could also lose your professional identity and authority as the expert trainer, sacrificing your objectivity about the problems facing the organization. The most productive interaction with participants strives to be pleasant and entertaining while maintaining a focus on the job at hand, developing communication competencies.

Asking for Responses to the Program   Responses to the program may come immediately from individuals with a clear idea of what the program means to them. These are the people who love the program because it makes them into the persons they always wanted to be. Or, these are people who hate the program because they have decided they don't need the training, don't want the training, and won't like the training. Such participants are usually vocal enough to tell you how they feel without prompting.

The rest of the participants may not feel they have opinions or may not feel

Appropriate interaction with participants is an important ingredient of successful training.

free to express themselves. These participants are important to understand so you can design a program closer to their needs, and they must be encouraged to express their feelings about the program while it is in session. By asking for comments in discussion from those who don't come forward on their own, you can often involve some of the more thoughtful participants. By mediating conflicts so that all those involved have a chance to express themselves, you can encourage more participation and self-expression. As you show the class that everyone is expected to respond to the program and may be asked to do so at any time, more participants will prepare themselves for active involvement. Their responses benefit them by exerting influence on how the program is conducted while helping you adjust the program to the situation.

Previewing/Debriefing Each Meeting   The class attends each meeting with a general notion of what to expect from the syllabus. However, a trainer who wants participants to focus clearly on the subject at hand will make use of previews and debriefings. The previews set up expectations for the training session that the trainer can satisfy, identifying reasonable goals. The preview also channels the participants' thoughts toward the topics that will actually be covered, avoiding subjects to be covered in another session or to be avoided altogether. Whereas the preview sets the objectives for the session's work, the debriefing shows how these objectives have been met. The debriefing not only recapitulates the accomplishments of the day, it defines what has been accomplished in order to encourage the participants' continued involvement and motivation. If participants' skills are not yet at the level set as the objective for the session, the debriefing can indicate how the participants may reach their objective. By showing the class what their experience means, the debriefing gives substance to the otherwise confusing or disappointing events of the day.

Making Assignments   The debriefing is the natural point at which to make assignments for the next session. Participants have just been told what the day's activities have accomplished. They have the satisfaction of reaching some of their goals, and are motivated to continue their effort in the time before the next training session. Making assignments may present the task to be completed by the next session as a challenge and an opportunity for further development. Since training goes on in a work environment, you might be tempted to make assignments as if they were an additional part of the participants' jobs. This approach mixes work and training, ruining the momentum built up in the training session. Training assignments have their own purpose, to support activities and progress in the next training session. They may be used to apply skills acquired in class to the work situation by asking participants to try out their new competencies and observe the results. Cases for study may be brought into class from work to make the training more relevant to work needs. But compliance with assignments is not enough for training assignments to be useful. The participant must be motivated to take the ideas and procedures willingly from the classroom back to the "real" world to continue communication development in that environment. Once the training program has completed its requisite number of sessions and transferred skills and information to the participants, you must return to assessment to evaluate your success.

Stage 4: Assessing the Effectiveness of the Training Program

In the fourth stage of establishing a training program, we discuss assessment procedures like the WGW assessment instrument and the use of oral appraisals. We also consider some important issues in meeting with the training director and refining the design of the program to enhance the organization's communication development.

The WGW Assessment Instrument   In addition to repeating selected portions of the ICA and WGW audits after each training program to assess change in the organization, the training program itself can be assessed with the assessment instrument. This questionnaire (see Figure 10.1) is intended to elicit evaluation of the structure and content of the training program. Detailed responses are encouraged to give meaning to the numerical ratings. This questionnaire can produce very useful information about the success of a training program in satisfying its participants. Negative response to some topics or experiences may not be avoidable, but the questionnaire can help you tailor the next program to match the trainees' expectations more closely. This questionnaire should be accompanied by oral appraisals.

Conducting Oral Appraisals   Once the assessment questionnaire has been administered and the responses summarized, the redefinition of the training program may begin. If further feedback on troublesome or confusing issues is required, oral appraisals may be conducted formally and informally by you or the training director. If conducted formally, the appraisal of the training program

When asked for a numerical rating, use a 1–10 scale with 10 being the best possible score. Whenever possible, give examples in the space provided or on the back of the evaluation forms. Your response to these questions is a valuable part of training program development.

1. How much will the skills and knowledge gained from this training help you do your job?　　(1–10)　＿＿
2. What did you learn that will be useful?

3. Were the objectives of the training clear to you?　　＿＿
4. How well were these objectives met?

5. How well did the course content suit your needs?　　＿＿
6. What subjects were left out that you expected?

7. What subjects were included that you didn't need?

8. What topics were the most useful or interesting?

9. What topics were the least useful or interesting?

10. How would you rate your skills/knowledge before starting the program?
　＿＿
11. How would you rate your skills/knowledge now?　　＿＿
12. How well did the instructor communicate with you?　　＿＿
13. What were the instructor's strong points?

14. What should the instructor change or improve?

15. How well organized was the program?　　＿＿
16. How effective/useful were the instructional materials?

17. How informative were the activities in class?　　＿＿
18. How could the activities be improved?

19. If a co-worker asked you to rate this course, how would you rate it?
　＿＿
20. Do you have any further comments on the program?

Figure 10.1　WGW assessment instrument instruction.

should take the form of an interview probing into the significant issue. For example, if some participants rated the program high on usefulness in their jobs (question 2) but would rate it low when asked by a co-worker (question 19), some inquiry would be required to find out why co-workers would not be encouraged to take the course.

Oral appraisals may also begin to assess the impact of the training program by examining communication practices once the training has been put into practice. If new communication skills and communication-related benefits are not reflected in the daily conduct of the organization, the training program may have to be redesigned. Whatever the results, a meeting with the training director is certainly in order to plan for the future.

Meeting with the Training Director   Meeting with the training director after your program has been completed and evaluated is a time for reassessing your relationship. After seeing what you can actually do, the training director has a better idea how you and your training program can fit into the organization's overall planning. You may be encouraged to develop other training programs or to offer the same program to other units of the organization. Once you have demonstrated the professionalism and effectiveness of your training ideas, the training director may become more cooperative and supportive of future collaborations.

At this time, you should make sure to reinforce this working relationship in two ways: (1) Plan to redefine the design of the program to meet the organization's needs even more effectively in the future. (2) Make sure that the organization's managers are informed of the training program's results. Your letter to the appropriate officer may remind the organization that you and the training director have made a significant contribution to the firm's communication effectiveness. This may seem like needless publicity, but once the problem that led to training abates, management may easily forget your role or minimize your program's worth.[18] In order to maintain your relationship with the organization, you can now turn to redefining the design of the program.

Redefining the Design of the Program   The redefinition process starts with the assessment of the organization's communication needs and compares those needs to the results achieved by the training program. If you have met the organization's needs while satisfying the participants' expectations, all the better. The training program usually needs to be adjusted in three ways. First, the content of the activities and lecturettes can be adjusted to match the typical learning modes and styles of the next group of trainees.

Second, the style of presentation can be discussed and adapted to suit the expectations of the next audience. Organizational culture establishes some unique expectations for style. Some organizations may favor a hearty, humorous approach, whereas others may respond best to a serious, no-nonsense presentation. Generally, it takes some experience of the organization to learn how to entertain the audience while you are training them. They expect a show worth missing work for.

Third, the program often must be changed to suit another type of trainee or a different environment. The material in a conflict resolution program for quality circle participants would be quite different from conflict resolution for supervisors. Different groups in the same organization frequently have different requirements because of their duties. You cannot expect them to apply the same set of ideas and procedures to a different situation. At the risk of offending some idealistic learners, you usually need to match the training as closely as possible to the job situation.

The environment for the program may also change with a move to another site. New facilities such as video or computer hardware can be integrated into the program to take full advantage of organizational resources. Refining the program design should take advantage of all the information gained in teaching and evaluating the course. If you refine your training program as the situation evolves, you will find your performance becoming more appropriate for the audience while maintaining your interest by trying new ideas.

SUMMARY

This chapter has examined three main topics, all parts of designing successful communication training programs. We presented arguments for the rhetorical basis of communication training, defining the role of sophists in contemporary America. After showing the importance of acquiring a rhetorical perspective on training, we described the three basic training models, the selection model, the problem-solution model, and the process model.

These theoretical issues were followed by a discussion of the four stages of establishing a training program in an organization. The first stage included making contact with the organization and the use of assessment procedures to produce an assessment report. The second stage described how to respond to the assessment by designing a training program in terms of organizational goals, a general training process, organized in a schedule of lecturettes and supporting activities. The third stage focused on implementing the program according to a seven-stage process, taking the trainer from constructing a syllabus through making assignments. Stage four evaluates the quality of a training program with a WGW assessment instrument and oral appraisal interviews, leading to a meeting with the training director to refine program design. The purpose of this chapter has been to introduce readers to some of the issues and questions faced by any communication consultant trying to develop a successful training program. In applying these principles, you may feel great satisfaction in helping an organization improve its communication practices. You may be even happier when you see how communication training benefits participants who find such training enables them to realize their personal and career goals.

ENDNOTES

1. T. Harris and T. Thomlison, "Career-bound Communication Education: A Needs Analysis," *Central States Speech Journal* 34 (1983): 257–267.

2. J. Baird, Jr., and P. Bradley, *Communication for Business and the Professions* (Dubuque, IA: Brown, 1980). See also P. Tompkins, *Communication and Action* (Glenview, IL: Scott-Foresman, 1982).

3. J. W. Wenzel, "Some Uses of Rhetoric in a Technological Age," paper presented to the Speech Communication Association convention, Louisville, KY, November 1982. See also M. Hyde, ed., *Communication, Philosophy, and the Technological Age* (University, AL: University of Alabama Press, 1984), pp. 1–12. See also T. Goodnight, "The Personal, Technical, and Public Spheres of Argument: A Speculative Inquiry into the Art of Public Deliberation," *Journal of the American Forensic Association* 18 (1982): 85–91.

4. Lyle Sussman, "OD as 'Muddling': Implications for Communication Consultants," *Communication Quarterly* 30 (1982): 85–91.

5. P. Tompkins and G. Cheney, "Unobtrusive Control, Decision-Making, and Communication in Contemporary Organizations," paper presented at the Speech Communication Association Convention, Louisville, KY, November 1982. See also G. R. Salancik and Jeffrey Pfeffer, "Who Gets Power and How They Hold on to It," *Organizational Dynamics* (Winter 1977): 3–21. See also Jeffrey Pfeffer, "The Ambiguity of Leadership," *Academy of Management Review* (January 1977): 104–112.

6. George Kennedy, *Classical Rhetoric and Its Christian and Secular Tradition from Ancient to Modern Times* (Chapel Hill, NC: University of North Carolina Press, 1980), pp. 18–24, 133–154.

7. Hyde, *Communication,* 1–12.

8. G. Wigglesworth, "The Training Whirl (And How to Keep It from Sucking You Under)," *Training* 21(5) (1984): 70–80.

9. E. H. Schein, *Process Consultation: Its Role in Organizational Development* (Reading, MA: Addison-Wesley, 1969).

10. R. Gordon, C. Lee, and R. Zemke, "Remembrance of Things Passé," *Training* 21(1) (1984): 22–42.

11. L. Winters and J. Dimino, "Power Brokering in Training," *Training* 21(5) (1984): 49–56.

12. G. L. Lippitt, *Organization Renewel* (Englewood Cliffs, NJ: Prentice-Hall, 1982), p. 320.

13. L. This and G. L. Lippitt, "Learning Theories and Training-Parts I and II," *Training and Development* 33 (June 1979): 12–13.

14. R. Hyman and B. Rosoff, "Matching Learning and Teaching Styles: The Jug and What's in It," *Theory into Practice* 23(1) (1984): 39.

15. David Kolb, *Learning Styles Inventory* (Boston: McBer, 1977).

16. L. Smith and J. Renzulli, "Learning Style Preferences: A Practical Approach for Classroom Teachers," *Theory into Practice* 23(1) (1984): 49.

17. L. Ward, "Warm Fuzzies Versus Hard Facts: Four Styles of Adult Learning," *Training* 20(11) (1983): 31.

18. Wigglesworth, "Training Whirl," 70–80.

five

ORGANIZATIONAL COMMUNICATION AND CAREER DEVELOPMENT

chapter 11

Organizational Communication Career Development

THEORETICAL APPROACHES TO CAREER CHOICE

> Trait-factor Theory / Developmental/Self-concept Theory /
> Personality Theories / Situational Theory / Explaining
> Occupational Choice

ORGANIZATIONAL COMMUNICATION CAREER CHOICES

> The Nature of Organizational Communication Careers / Position
> Titles of Communication Professionals / Position Descriptions of
> Communication Professionals

STAGES IN ORGANIZATIONAL CAREER DEVELOPMENT

ISSUES IN CAREER DEVELOPMENT

ORGANIZATIONAL CAREER DEVELOPMENT PROGRAMS

> Guidelines for Organizational Career Planning / Implementing
> Career Planning

Are you planning for your career? Do you know what kind of job you will seek upon graduation? Where are you heading? Are you taking the right courses? What do you want? How do you get it? Can you get it?

Do you know the answers to these questions? Have you begun the process

287

of career planning? These are serious questions. Most people are counting on a good job upon graduation from college; they want to become successful; they realize that success requires planning. If you and others believe these statements, then why do so many people plan inadequately? Of course, we have no way of knowing for sure, but we speculate that part of the problem is inadequate information and counseling of those facing career decisions.

Career planning is something you can begin right now. But it is much more than settling on a job title that you intend to take upon completion of your training. It is a process involving a career choice and a plan to pursue a career path. The information in this chapter will help you achieve these tasks.

Career planning is another activity communication specialists are called upon to help the organization do for its members. You may be asked to be responsible for such a program in your organization. Here, too, this chapter can be helpful.

This chapter focuses on the career planning process. First, we present several theoretical approaches to career choice, which suggest what is involved in this important decision. This discussion leads to a consideration of organizational communication careers. This same section helps to narrow your interest to a particular area of the communication field. Next, we address the idea of stages in career development. People follow predictable stages that can be understood and utilized in planning. Third, we pose several major issues confronting the professional in early, middle, and later career life. Anticipating these issues can be a key factor in your success. Finally, we provide assistance for the person facing the task of creating and/or working in an organization's career development program. Here we provide guidelines and activities for such a task.

THEORETICAL APPROACHES TO CAREER CHOICE

Research into career development has been undertaken to answer one of two questions: (1) What factors in people are related to career choice? (2) How do people arrive at career choices? The first question deals with traits. The second deals with process. We address these issues in this section.

Trait-factor Theory

The factor most frequently measured to discover career options is *interest*. A well-known test to achieve this end is the Strong Vocational Interest Blank (SVIB), developed by Edward K. Strong.[1] For Strong, an interest was represented by a liking of some particular thing, whereas an aversion was a disliking. Strong measured vocational interest by asking a person to respond to particular activities, occupations, or other objects with either liking (L), indifference (I), or disliking (D). Strong compiled interest scores from each person's responses to the SVIB items.

Strong administered his interest inventory to members of various occupational groups. From their responses he derived a profile that he assumed represented particular occupations. He then compared this profile to that of people in other occupations as well as scores representing the general public to see how the occupational group differed. He used the resulting profile—the items differentiating the occupational group from others—to specify interests specifically associated with particular occupations. Using these data, Strong could tell a person who completed the SVIB which occupational groups had interests similar to his or hers.

Developmental/Self-concept Theory

This second kind of theoretical perspective makes use of a person's image of him or herself—his or her self-concept and developmental psychology. Donald Super[2] is mainly responsible for the developmental self-concept theory of vocational behavior. Super seems to be influenced by two major areas: self-concept theory and developmental psychology. E. S. Bordin[3] suggests the idea that a person's response to a vocational interest inventory represented a projection of that person's self-concept with respect to stereotypes the individual might have of certain occupations. In other words, a person likes or dislikes certain occupations based on how they fit with the person's self-concept.

Charlotte Buehler,[4] a developmental psychologist, proposed that life can be seen as stages. For her, the first, the growth stage, begins at birth and lasts until about age 14. The next one is an exploratory stage from 15 through 25 years of age. This is followed by a maintenance stage, until about age 65. Beyond age 65, the person is considered to be in the decline stage. Super, too, follows such stages. He believes that vocational stages are tied to life stages, with specific tasks taking place during each period.

Super[5] suggests that the self-concept forms as a person recognizes him or herself as a distinctive individual, but also as similar to others in certain ways. The adolescent, who is in the process of discovering who he or she is, requires comparisons and testing of talents. At the same time, the youth is identifying with others. At first this is a general identification, perhaps identification with a same-sexed parent. Later the identification moves to more specific models. The adolescent female identifying perhaps with a neighbor or a teacher, depending on whom she or he might find attractive as a model.

Super suggests that the role-playing of these models leads to consequences that have vocational implications. Samuel H. Osipow[6] presents a particularly good example of how this role-play leads to vocational decisions:

> Similarly, the adoption of a role may lead directly to a career, but it is more likely that role playing will have an immediate consequence which may eventually influence vocational decisions. Talents explored will often lead to talents in new fields that have not been acknowledged previously. Thus, in playing the role of journalist, a student may join the school newspaper staff and meet a teacher who inspires him or her to become a writer. This decision, in turn, may lead to joining a literary club, reading Sinclair Lewis' *Arrowsmith,* and eventually becoming a research scientist.

Super's process of vocational development occurs by completing five vocational development tasks:

1. Crystallization of Vocational Preference (14–18 years old)
2. Specification of Vocational Preference (18–21 years old)
3. Implementation of Vocational Preference (21–24 years old)
4. Stabilization of Vocational Preference (25–35 years old)
5. Consolidation of Status and Advancement (36–45 years old)

So the person moves through stages calling for different behavior. The adolescent is exploring; the young adult is taking action through education and job search; the middle adult is finding a particular place within the vocation; and the older adult is settling into a career.

Personality Theories

There are several theoretical approaches to understanding career choice based on personality. John Holland[7] has presented a theory based on personal orientation. He bases his theory on the assumption that personality and environment interact in such a way as to cause people to move toward environments that are congruent with their personal orientation.

Holland bases personal orientation on a person's likes and dislikes. The individual is asked to rate 160 occupations on the basis of like or dislike. The theory assumes that this task represents a projection of the personality with respect to vocational types. The result is scored in relation to six occupational environments:

1. *Realistic.* Characterized by aggressive behavior; interested in activities requiring motor skill, strength, and coordination. (Examples: architecture, farming, forestry)
2. *Investigative.* Characterized by thinking rather than acting, organizing, and understanding rather than dominating or persuading; prefer to avoid close interpersonal contact. (Examples: mathematics, biology)
3. *Social.* Characterized by seeking close interpersonal relationships; avoid situations such as intellectual problem solving and exertion of physical skill. (Examples: clinical psychology, social worker, diplomat)
4. *Conventional.* Characterized by concern for rules, regulations, self-control, subordination of personal needs, and identification with power and status. (Examples: accountant, finance officer)
5. *Enterprising.* Characterized by verbal skill used to control and manipulate others; aspire to power and status. (Examples: manager, lawyer, public relations)
6. *Artistic.* Characterized by self-expression, creativity, individualism, and expression of emotions. (Examples: artist, musician)

Occupations were assigned to each of these categories, largely on an intuitive basis.

The central notion in Holland's theory is that a person's Vocational Preference Inventory score (VPI) is a good predictor of that individual's present career aspiration and later career choices. For example, enterprising people will tend to select careers in management or some related field. Holland through several longitudinal studies has produced convincing evidence that this hypothesis holds.[8]

The orientations toward careers were found to be related to each other in a predictable pattern.[9] Holland conducted a factor analysis of data derived from the VPI scores that plotted into a rough hexagon pattern. These relationships are displayed in Figure 11.1. The model shows similar orientations as adjacent categories (realistic-investigative, artistic-social) and dissimilar orientations as diagonally opposite (conventional-artistic, realistic-social).

You can identify an occupational type by observing the category and its adjacent categories. For example, let's consider the occupation of a manager that falls into the enterprising category. This category describes a verbally skilled person who is persuasive, controlling, and aspires to power. Now, if you look at Holland's model you see that the adjacent categories are social and conventional. A social manager would be an individual who is supportive of people and interested in interpersonal relations. These traits are often associated with the human relations school of management. Or, the manager might be conventional, concerned with roles and regulations, having a strong identification with power and status. These are traits associated with the scientific management school.

Holland has produced an instrument that can be used by an individual who wishes career guidance. The self-directed search can be scored by the individual and a profile can be computed from the scores. The test describes the meaning of the scores and directs the individual to a range of occupations that are compatible to the profile.

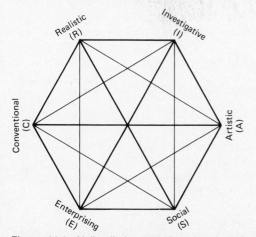

Figure 11.1 Holland's hexagonal model of relationships among occupation types. (*Source:* John H. Holland et al., "An Empirical Occupational Classification Derived from a Theory of Personality and Intended for Practice and Research," ACT Research Report No. 29. Iowa City: The American College Testing Program, 1969.)

Situational Theory

Peter Blau and his associates[10] were among the first scholars to try to integrate the various situational factors into a model of career choice. They see occupational choice as a function of social experiences and social and economic conditions. The social experiences of the person influence personality development (needs, self-concept, orientation, interests, and values). The social and economic conditions affect occupational opportunity, thereby facilitating or detracting from the person's aspirations. Blau and his colleagues constructed the model, displayed in Figure 11.2, to show the factors and their relationships.

The model is divided into two columns: the left represents the individual, the right represents the selection agency. The bottom half of the model represents what is brought to the career choice situation. The top of the model represents situational factors affecting the choice. You can gain an appreciation for the complexity of the choice situation when you follow from the box in the lower corner labeled "biological conditions" to the box at the top labeled "immediate determinants."

Explaining Occupational Choice

This discussion of career choice theories suggests that there is not much agreement concerning how people may undertake making a good fit between themselves and career choices. The disagreement concerns which personal characteristics a person matches in order to match the work situation. Figure 11.3 displays the characteristics suggested by each theoretical orientation.

Of the models presented, Holland's personality model has the most support. Perhaps personal orientation is the most important personal characteristic in occupational selection. His theory for the most part has led to more successful predictions of career choice than the others we presented. Yet, most of us recognize that economic and social conditions may help us narrow the options we see as being a viable fit between our personal orientations and the choices we might make.

ORGANIZATIONAL COMMUNICATION CAREER CHOICES

"What can I do with my education when I graduate?" This is a question that we find is frequently asked by communication majors. This is a legitimate question since much of the course work in communication studies doesn't focus on a particular career path. There are three studies that are especially helpful in answering this question for those wishing to begin planning their career paths more specifically.

The Nature of Organizational Communication Careers

A 1977 report by Goldfine and O'Connell[11] provided the results of a national survey of members of the Industrial Communication Council. The study sought

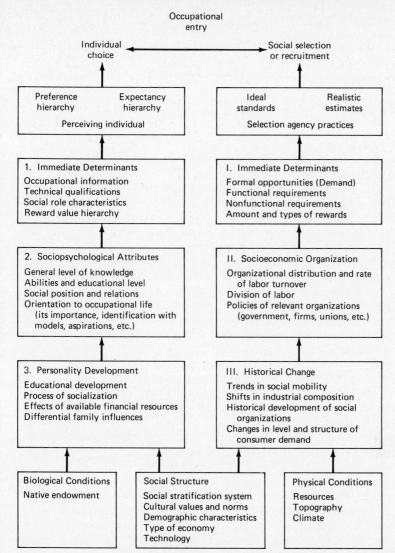

Figure 11.2 The Blau model of occupational choice. (*Source:* Peter M. Blau, John W. Gustad, Richard Jesson, Herbert S. Parnes, and Richard Wilcox, "Occupational Choices: A Conceptual Framework," *Industrial and Labor Relations Review* 9 (1956): 534.)

to discover the nature of the members' jobs, their salary ranges, and the differences between men's and women's jobs and salaries. Here are their major findings:

1. Seventy-five percent of those responding were working in manufacturing, finance, insurance, consulting, petrochemical, or pharmaceutical firms.
2. The balance in employment between men and women was particularly striking in certain kinds of organizations. Men outnumbered the women in manu-

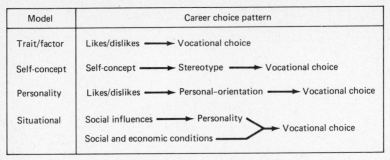

Figure 11.3   Models of career choice.

facturing and petrochemical industries nearly two to one. On the other hand, women outnumbered the men in pharmaceutical organizations five to one.

3. The responsibilities of members of communication departments were employee publications, company newsletters, consulting, upward communication, audiovisuals, employee benefits, public relations, annual reports, speeches, training, and multimedia presentations. The responsibility most often indicated was written communication.

4. The communication professionals most frequently had a bachelor of arts degree and held the title of manager or director. Their first position within the profession was in one of these areas: writing, recruitment, and interviewing, or training.

5. The median salary for the men responding was $31,400, while it was $24,000 for women. This salary difference may be accounted for by the place the men and women found themselves in the organization. The men were usually three levels away from the chief executive officer and the women were four levels away.

6. The respondents were asked to indicate the communication skills required daily on their jobs. The central skills were writing, editing, interviewing, oral communications, and communication diagnosis.

7. Satisfaction with their careers differed for men and women. Men were more satisfied with their current position and desired to remain in it. Women were less satisfied and wanted to change positions. Twice as many women wished to change their jobs than men. But, men believed that they were better able to be active in career development—shape their careers, obtain information about careers, and change career direction—than women.

Position Titles of Communication Professionals

Gerald L. Wilson and Philip A. Gray[12] surveyed departments of communication to collect data about their graduates. Two kinds of information about the graduate's employment were requested. First, data were collected to discover career positions communication majors actually take upon graduation. The four most frequent career positions were: public information/public relations/promotional (15 percent of the students took this kind of position), marketing (11 percent), teaching (11 percent), and sales (10 percent). Careers were taken by fewer graduates in the areas of: media production (7 percent), writing (7 percent), personnel (6 percent), on-air media (5 percent), advertising (5 percent), training (5 percent), graduate school and government (4 percent each), counseling and consulting (3 percent each). The remainder of the students found jobs in research, with airlines and in the church.

Specific job titles were the second kind of information sought. You can see the kind and variety of jobs taken by inspecting the list in Table 11.1.

Position Descriptions of Communication Professionals

Job descriptions were collected by Charles Petrie and his committee[13] for the International Communication Association's Organizational Division in 1975. They gathered descriptions for various kinds of job assignments, then presented the most common descriptions for each. You might look at your areas of interest and consider the kinds of skills and course work you would need to be a competent professional in that area.

Internal Communications

Provides consultation, assistance, and guidance to management on matters relating to employee and management communication; coordinates employee communication programs and activities; coordinates publishing of regular employee media; advises, coordinates, and conducts attitudinal and other polls among employees; provides editorial and publishing services; produces, edits, and distributes special publications.

Develops and maintains informational unit to serve the needs of senior management and the communication department.

Develops, coordinates, and implements small group, face-to-face communication programs to facilitate team building, problem identification, and problem solving.

External Communication

Is responsible for full range of external public relations activities: corporate advertising; community, shareholder, financial, and government relations; produces corporate literature, sales promotions, and special productions.

Directs and coordinates all activity in the development, implementation, and administration of a corporate identification system covering all aspects of visual communication, material, and media.

Has administrative responsibility for public relations and development departments.

Is responsible for internal communication, communication with employees' families, and community relations.

Plans and directs public information and community relations programs.

Assists executive officer in the public aspects of his or her position.

Table 11.1 POSITIONS TAKEN BY RECENT COMMUNICATION GRADUATES

Career category	Position/title
Management	Trainee Business analyst Branch manager Property manager
Sales	Marketing/Sales Buyer Insurance underwriter Sales/Promotion and public relations Sales representative Realtor Account representative
Personnel	Director Customer service representative Training director Coordinator, labor relations
Public relations	Field representative Fund raiser Intern Communications director Industrial relations Director Specialist
Media	Advertising Reporter/Photographer Broadcaster News director Producer Executive trainee Copy editor Copy writer Account executive Researcher
Research	Research associate Procedure analyst Budget advisor Development and social research Assistant director for marketing research
Counseling	Counselor Director Crisis specialist
Education	Teacher Coach Assistant to the dean

Source: Gerald L. Wilson and Philip A. Gray, "A Survey of Practices and Strategies for Marketing Communication Majors," *ACA Bulletin* 45 (1983): 35.

Publications

Supervises staff which produces internal and external publications; makes and distributes films; produces booklets, displays, and exhibits; answers complaint letters; and handles other writing assignments.

Supervises writers responsible for writing, editing, and publishing in-house publications.

Is responsible for acquisition, development, and production of books in the communication fields; also responsible for presenting books to sales staff and working with the advertising staff on promotional materials.

Writes and edits news releases, publications, special projects, and recruiting brochures; maintains archives, mailing lists, and biographical files.

Produces monthly employee newspaper: gathers news, coordinates news staff, takes pictures, edits, prepares layout, writes, and proofreads.

Media

Responsible for development of coordinated programs in the photo-audiovisual area.

Research

Responsible for development of research program to support the policy programs activities of the branch; organizes conferences, symposia, and meetings.

Directs research projects.

Assists in the technical administration of the department and undertakes special assignments in relation to planning and coordinating education, extension, and research services, communications, staff development, and training.

Consultant

Consults with and assists clients in planning, organizing, implementing, and measuring communication to employees, managers, and key publics.

STAGES IN ORGANIZATIONAL CAREER DEVELOPMENT

Edgar H. Schein[14] provides a useful model to illustrate the relationship between the career experiences of a person and an organizational definition of career development. He sees the organization as representing a three-dimensional cone. (This design is drawn as a cone to represent an organizational model where the number of organizational members decreases as the individual moves higher in the organization. If the structure were such that there were more members at higher levels, then the model might be represented by a cylinder.) The outer surface of the cone represents the external boundary, whereas the core signifies the "inner circle" of the organization. Figure 11.4 illustrates this model.

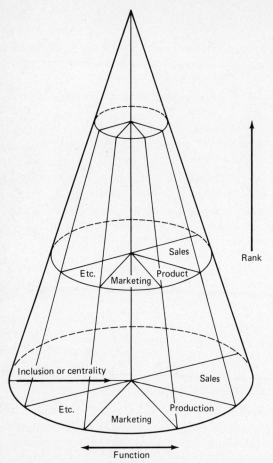

Figure 11.4 Schein's three-dimensional model of an organization. (*Source:* Edgar H. Schein, "The Individual, the Organization and the Career," *Journal of Applied Behavioral Science* 7 (1971): 404.)

The three dimensions of the cone—vertical, radial, and circumferential—represent the various kinds of movement you might make in the organization. A vertical move, moving up or down, represents a promotion or demotion, changing of rank or level in the organization. A radial move, moving into or out of the cone, suggests becoming more central in the organization. This may be a result of your becoming more important to the organization or acquiring increased influence or some other reason. Of course, a move away from the center would suggest the opposite. A circumferential move, traveling around the cone without moving up or down, translates into a lateral move within the organization. A move from marketing to sales would be such a change.

Three kinds of boundaries correspond to each of these movements. (1) Hierarchical boundaries separate the various hierarchical levels in the organization. There are as many of these as there are levels. (2) Inclusion boundaries also correspond to radial movement. These separate individuals or groups who differ in their centrality. (3) Functional boundaries separate departments, or groups that perform different functions.

These boundaries can vary in three ways. The number and type of boundaries will differ from organization to organization. They may also vary on the dimension of permeability. For example, if it is difficult to move from sales to marketing or from production to research, then the boundaries would be described as relatively impermeable. Finally, the boundaries may vary on the basis of the type of filtering process used; for example, who decides on promotion and how many people are involved in the decision. As you can imagine, all of these boundary factors have an effect on your movement through an organization. In addition, the overall shape of your organization will affect career development. If the cone is steep, there will be more competition promoted. If the cone is relatively flat, then there will be fewer promotions with less competition. On the other hand, if the shape is cylinderlike, then there will be more promotion of lower-level members.

Schein sees the person coming to the organization with basic personality characteristics that are relatively unchangeable. Change occurs as the person constructs various social selves as he or she moves from social situation to social situation within the organization. Your social self will change, for example, when you move from outside the organization into your first job in the organization. Schein[15] describes these changes:

> These changes which occur in a person during the course of his career, as a result of adult socialization or acculturation, are changes in the nature and integration of his social selves. It is highly unlikely that he will change substantially in his basic character structure and his pattern of psychological defenses, but he may change drastically in his social selves in the sense of developing new attitudes and values, new competencies, new images of himself, and new ways of entering and conducting himself in social situations. As he faces new roles which bring new demands, it is from his repertory of attributes and skills that he constructs or reconstructs himself. . . .
>
> When we think of organizations infringing on the private lives of their members, we think of a more extensive socialization process which involves changes in more stable selves. Clearly it is possible for such "deeper" influences to occur, but in assessing depth of influence in any given individual-organizational relationships, we must be careful not to overlook adaptational patterns which look like deep influence but are only the activation of changes in relatively more labile social selves.

Stages of a career within an organization are linked to passage through the various boundaries. Schein describes the stages a person generally follows in a career with those in an organization: preentry/entry, basic training/initiation, first regular assignment, second regular assignment, granting of tenure, termination and exit, and postexit. Table 11.2 presents the stages, positions, and transactions between the individual and the organization.

Table 11.2 STAGES, POSITIONS, AND PROCESSES IN AN ORGANIZATIONAL CAREER

Basic stages and transitions	Statuses or positions	Psychological and organizational processes: Transactions between individual and organization
1. Preentry	Aspirant, applicant, rushee	Preparation, education, anticipatory socialization.
Entry (trans.)	Entrant, postulant, recruit	Recruitment, rushing, testing, screening, selection, acceptance ("hiding"); passage through external inclusion boundary; rites of entry; induction and orientation.
2. Basic training novitiate	Trainee, novice, pledge	Training, indoctrination, socialization, testing of the person by the organization, tentative acceptance into group.
Initiation first vows (trans.)	Initiate, graduate	Passage through first inner inclusion boundary, acceptance as member and conferring of organizational status, rite of passage; and acceptance.
3. First regular assignment	New member	First testing by the person of his or her own capacity to function; granting of real responsibility (playing for keeps); passage through functional boundary with assignment to specific job or department.
Substages a. Learning the job b. Maximum performance c. Becoming obsolete d. Learning new skills, etc.		Indoctrination and testing of person by immediate work group leading to acceptance or rejection; if accepted further education and socialization (learning the ropes); preparation for higher status through coaching, seeking visibility, finding sponsors, etc.

Table 11.2 (*Continued*)

Basic stages and transitions	Statuses or positions	Psychological and organizational processes: Transactions between individual and organization
4. Second assignment Substages	Legitimate member (fully accepted)	Processes under number 3 are repeated.
5. Granting of tenure	Permanent member	Passage through another inclusion boundary.
6. Termination and exit (trans.)	Old-timer, senior citizen	Preparation for exit, cooling the mark out, rites of exit (testimonial dinners, etc.).
7. Postexit	Alumnus emeritus retired	Granting of peripherial status.

Source: Edgar H. Schein, "The Individual, the Organization and the Career," *Journal of Applied and Behaviorial Science* 7 (1971): 416.

Schein[16] makes several predictions about organizational careers and the socialization process. These should be useful to you in understanding how to make predictions about the process:

Hypothesis 1. Organizational socialization will occur primarily in connection with the passage through hierarchical and inclusion boundaries; efforts at education and training will occur primarily in connection with the passage through functional boundaries. In both instances, the amount of effort at socialization and/or training will be at a maximum just prior to boundary passage, but will continue for some time after boundary passage.

The underlying assumption behind this hypothesis is that (1) the organization is most concerned about correct values and attitudes at the point where it is granting a member more authority and/or centrality, and (2) the individual is most vulnerable to socialization pressures just before and after boundary passage. . . .

Hypothesis 2. Innovation, or the individual's influence on the organization, will occur in the *middle* of a given stage of the career, at a maximum distance from boundary passage.

The person must be far enough from the earlier boundary passage to have learned the requirements of the new position and to have earned centrality in the new out-culture, yet must be far enough from the next boundary passage to be fully involved in the present job without being concerned about preparing for the future. Also, the person's power to induce change is lower if he is perceived as about preparing for the future. Also, the person's power to induce change is lower if he or she is perceived as about to leave (the lame duck phenomenon). . . .

Hypothesis 3. In general, the processes of socialization will be more prevalent in the early stages of a career and the process of innovation late in the career,

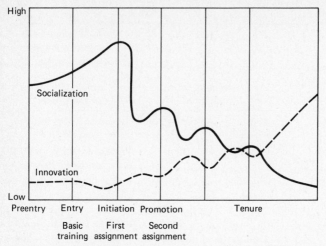

Figure 11.5 Socialization and innovation during the stages of an organizational career. (*Source:* Edgar H. Schein, "The Individual, the Organization and the Career," *Journal of Applied and Behavioral Science* 7 (1971): 422.)

but both processes occur at all stages. [Hypotheses 1, 2, and 3 are illustrated in Figure 11.5.]

Hypothesis 4. Socialization or influence will involve primarily the more labile [changeable] social selves of the individual, while innovation will involve primarily the more stable social selves of the individual, provided the individual is not held captive in the organization. . . .

Hypothesis 5. A change in the more stable social selves as a result of socialization will occur only under conditions of coercive persuasion, i.e., where the individual cannot or does not psychologically feel free to leave the organization. Conditions under which coercive persuasion would operate can be produced by a variety of factors: a tight labor market . . . ; an employment contract which involves a legal or moral obligation to remain with the organization; a reward system which subtly but firmly entraps the individual through stock options, pension plans, deferred compensation plans, and the like.

Schein views organizational careers as a two-way process. The organization socializes (influences) the person; the person innovates (influences) the organization.

ISSUES IN CAREER DEVELOPMENT

If you were asked, "Who are you?" one of your answers will probably be "I am a student." You identify with how you spend most of your time, so at this point in your life you see yourself as a student. Once you are graduated and take a professional position, you might answer "An organizational developer, training director, teacher, marketing professional, public relations practioner," or whatever occupation you chose. Most people identify closely with the work they do, and particularly the status of their position.[17] Because of this close identification with a career, managing career issues successfully is an urgent matter. Issues related to your career are central in your lives.

Edgar H. Schein[18] has suggested that a person's career is dominated by issues that depend on the stage in the career. Early in your career you are adjusting from being a student to being a professional. You are probably in either a formal training program or your first assignment. You might contrast your former role with what you expected organizational life to be like. You will probably encounter surprises and engage in what M. R. Louis[19] calls "sensemaking." That is, you attempt to figure out these surprises and reduce their impact by examining and comparing past experiences with current situations. You look at the surprises in relation to their context, and seek interpretations from others.

In addition, you probably are concerned with determining your area of contribution—discovering how you fit into the organization, becoming productive, and seeing a viable future for yourself in your chosen career. These, too, are the organization's goals for a new employee. If the organization is successful in attempting to socialize you, you will discover the role expectations and job relevant skills necessary to achieve the motivation and commitment needed to help you realize your goals.[20] Your self-concept as a professional is an issue during this period. Your on-the-job experiences provide some understanding of knowledge and skill levels you actually possess. You are beginning to develop what Schein[21] calls a "career anchor." A career anchor is the values, abilities, and motives you use in order to guide and constrain your career decisions. The trial and exploration characteristic of this stage begins the formulation of this anchor.

This first period of a career is important. The individual's potential is first being realized. Howard and Bray[22] have even suggested that it is during these first few years that potential for advancement is clear. It is a crucial time in which to find a mentor relationship and develop a career strategy.

Midcareer brings new issues. A major issue is completing the development of your career anchor. The strength of your career anchor is important for future growth. Further specialization is also a mark of midcareer, that is, when you become truly skilled in your area of expertise. Charting this course is a major activity and frustration of this period, since it involves a reevaluation of career goals. If you haven't reached your goals by this time, you are confronted by the realization that you may not. If you have reached your goals, you may be wondering "was it worth it" or "is that all there is to it?"

Also there may be a growing sense of becoming obsolete. Frequently the young people entering the organization from universities and colleges are armed with the latest developments and techniques in their particular area. They are anxious to make their mark and the contrast between their knowledge and yours can be disconcerting.

Finally, many people in midcareer believe they are no longer marketable. A 40-year-old man or woman may be viewed by organizations as too expensive to hire when comparing the salary a 40-year-old person would expect versus the salary offered a younger person. For many midcareer people there is a feeling of "being stuck." A midlife crisis is clearly not a myth for some people.[23]

Late career poses different concerns. One issue is that of becoming a mentor. The question becomes, "How can I best use my experience and talent to help Phil (or another new person) become a productive professional?" Other issues deal with letting go and retiring. As you begin to reflect on the idea that your career is nearly over, your concern is that you haven't realized all your expectations. In fact, you will also face at this stage the uncertainty of retirement, knowing what your place will be in life. Will there be enough income to live comfortably? What can be done with the free time, previously spent working?

ORGANIZATIONAL CAREER DEVELOPMENT PROGRAMS

You are not alone in your interest in managing your career development effectively. Organizations see career development programs as furthering their aims, too. J. W. Walker and T. G. Gutteridge[24] surveyed 225 companies to discover why they valued career development. The researchers found that over 80 percent of the companies responding said that their development program was a response to a desire to develop their work force in order to promote from within. A related issue was the realization that such a program would overcome a shortage of promotable talent (63 percent). In addition, 56 percent of the firms cited a desire to help employees in their individual career planning.

Guidelines for Organizational Career Planning

Manuel London and Stephen A. Stumpf[25] present an excellent set of guidelines for a career planning program. We describe the elements they suggest are essential to achieving a successful program. These are establishing career paths, providing feedback, fostering realistic expectations, managing information, and matching jobs and people.

Establish career paths. The first step in a career planning program is to define work activities. Next, the personal requirements are established. Finally, families of jobs representing career paths are identified. These families include jobs that follow a logical progression so that they develop for the employee the necessary skills at the lower level to enable the person to move to the next position.

Communicating career path information should provide specific step-by-step objectives for you to follow. It also identifies potential role models in the organization that can be observed as you look toward advancement. Those on top in the organization, recognizing your potential, can help you develop. So, career path information can assist in establishing mentor-protegé relationships.

Provide feedback on performance and potential. Research literature on performance appraisal suggests that awareness of your behavior enhances learning and yields better performance.[26] Feedback also helps you to understand what kind of behavior is likely to be rewarded. With this knowledge, you have a greater

Career counselors are provided by organizations to assist new employees in understanding appropriate career paths.

opportunity for reward and thus feel a sense of accomplishment. Moreover, feedback is useful in planning your own personal career path.

Foster realistic expectations.   London and Stumpf[27] recommend four particular considerations to help you as an employee develop realistic expectations. First, you need to recognize that the most realistic career plan, in terms of motivation, is one that is achievable, but moderately difficult.

Second, realistic expectations are more likely to be generated if you and the supervisor participate in the career planning process together. The supervisor knows you and can coach you in realizing your expectations. A session with the supervisor should focus on the supervisor sharing standards of evaluation and helping you select a job family.

The third suggestion is that the manager should convey at what level of performance you can expect a reward and what it might be. The manager must analyze the incentive system in order to do this. Managers must be able to specify what rewards are under their control, which of them are valued, and follow through by providing these rewards for good performance.

Finally, the manager must deliver the rewards equitably. Overrewarding or underrewarding can present serious problems. The person who feels overrewarded may continue the effort, whereas the underrewarded person may be resentful, decrease performance, or leave the organization.

Delineate individual and organizational responsibility.   There is evidence that role ambiguity can stifle goal-directed behavior.[28] The organization should clearly state its policy on taking responsibility for providing specific career-related information. On the other hand, you need to know your responsibility in developing a personal career plan.

Manage information.   The ability to problem solve is intimately tied to the kind and quality of information available for the activity. In order to solve the problem of selecting a career path, both you and the organization have an obligation to gather relevant information carefully, make it available, and use it in the process.

Those in the organization who are responsible for assisting with career planning should keep records that include:

- Biographical characteristics
- Your skills
- Past and current performance evaluations
- Assessment center results
- Career interests and aspirations
- Supervisor's impressions of you
- Next assignment recommended
- Company plans for new hiring
- Statement of policies and procedures for filling positions
- Statement of policies on obtaining transfers
- Number of management positions filled during the year by job title
- Available training programs
- Information on career paths[29]

Your part in this information management process is willingly to provide information necessary for the organization to keep records of this type. You must also be prepared to receive this information and evaluate it objectively.

Match jobs and people.   Information management and matching jobs to people are clearly related. By carefully collecting relevant information, an organization can create category systems that will facilitate placement. Computer programmers can help those responsible for career planning to create a personnel data base or skill inventory system. Maintaining personal profiles on each employee is also much easier when a system is computerized.

If you work for a smaller company, computers may not be accessible. An alternative system is to use a mechanical card file to achieve a similar end. Miret[30] describes such a system that France's Euroquip Corporation implemented for the 800 executives. This system includes a card for each executive and a card for each job. Information about job requirements and personal qualifications are coded

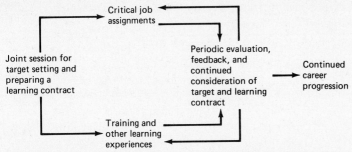

Figure 11.6   A model of career development. (*Source:* Manuel London and Stephen A. Stumpf, *Managing Careers*. Reading, MA: Addison-Wesley, 1982, p. 164.)

into about 100 groups. These groupings make it possible to discover career paths as they show similarities. The system is not completely mechanical since the person involved in the process needs to realize when the fit is somewhat imperfect. Here there is a training requirement rather than a disqualification for the position.

Implementing Career Planning

The implementation of career planning requires joint planning sessions with the supervisor, critical job assignments, training and learning experiences, regular evaluation and feedback with respect to employment goals, systematic rewards, and thorough, timely career progression. This sequence grows out of the guidelines for organizational career planning proposed by London and Stumpf. They illustrate this sequence in a model for career development, displayed in Figure 11.6.

The career development counselor can implement this model by keeping in mind certain guidelines and engaging in activities that provide the movement of the employee on a career path. If you follow this model, you see that this involves target setting (understanding the skills required, having detailed job descriptions, providing clear communication of the job requirements, setting targets), providing developmental activities (training, role models), experiencing critical job assignments (challenging, but doable, with clear expectations), providing feedback (periodic review of goals, a learning contract), and evaluation and reassignment. Beyond these tasks, the model works best when commitment by the supervisor to career development is ensured. One method of ensuring this is to make the program part of the supervisor's performance objectives. Guidelines and activities for implementing a career development program are displayed in Table 11.3.

SUMMARY

A number of factors influence career choice. A person's interests, self-concept, personality, and social situation are major influences. Strong's Vocational Interest Blank asks a person to indicate likes and dislikes to determine for what career the person may be best suited. Super views career choice as a function of a

Table 11.3 GUIDELINES AND ACTIVITIES FOR A CAREER DEVELOPMENT PROGRAM

Guidelines	Activities
Ensure understanding of target job skills and abilities.	Prepare well-documented job descriptions. Supervisors clearly communicate job requirements.
Provide developmental activities reflecting individual strengths, weaknesses, preferences, and goals.	Use learning contracts specifying a logical sequence of training experiences.
Set target jobs and time frames for reaching these.	Discuss and establish as part of career planning.
Provide challenging job assignments as early as possible.	Identify jobs and projects with components critical to the individual and the organization. Redesign jobs and projects along critical dimensions.
Assign effective role models who can provide enabling resources.	Assign individuals to supervisors who are known to be good role models.
Provide performance feedback.	Train supervisors to give meaningful feedback.
Ensure accurate and realistic expectations.	Clearly communicate expectations. Encourage job visits.
Ensure a variety of experiences.	Vary assignments along such dimensions as line-staff, technical-nontechnical, working with others and alone. Take advantage of variation between jobs within departments for easy transfers.
Encourage commitment and involvement of top management and participants.	Involve supervisors and subordinates in designing and carrying out the program. Reward supervisors for developing subordinates.
Allow evaluation and redirection of career plans.	Annual examination of career progress. Rewrite learning contract and reset targets.

Source: Adapted from Manuel London and Stephen A. Stumpf, *Managing Careers* (Reading, MA: Addison-Wesley, 1982), p. 167.

person's self-concept and developmental stages. He believes that a person likes or dislikes certain vocations based on how well they fit the person's self-concept. Self-concept with respect to vocation for Super is developed through role-playing certain occupations. Holland, on the other hand, believes that career choice is related to personality. The person presumably has a personal orientation that fits particular vocational areas. Holland tests likes and dislikes to discover a person's orientation and matches this to a set of potential careers. Blau and his colleagues suggest that the process of career choice is more complex, being affected by both personality and a number of social and economic conditions.

We described the nature of organizational communication careers, and outlined the skills needed, titles of jobs frequently taken, and position descriptions for the various career areas.

Careers develop in stages. Schein presents a model suggesting that the shape of the organizational hierarchy affects how a person moves through these stages. An organization is constructed of three boundaries: vertical, radial, and circumferential. These correspond to the hierarchical "inner circle" and departmental boundaries. Movement through these boundaries is facilitated or retarded by the relative permeability of the boundaries and the shape of the organization. If the organization is shaped like a steep cone, there will be more competition for promotion; if like a flat cone, there will be fewer promotions with less competition; if like a cylinder, there will be more promotions available at the upper level. Schein also suggests that stages are related to a variety of statuses and transactions between the individual and organization. These were summarized in Table 11.2.

Movement through a career presents a number of critical issues. In early career the theme is adjustment. Here the issue is role identification. The individual engages in sensemaking as an attempt to cope with surprises related to role. The person also begins to form a career anchor—the motives, values, and abilities he or she finds useful in guiding and constraining career decisions. In midcareer, when the person moves to an area of expertise and specialization, the career anchor is completed. Often, however, this period brings a reevaluation of career goals and the setting of new goals. For some people there is also a sense of becoming obsolete. Late career poses new issues and concerns—such as becoming a mentor for some new person and preparing to "let go." Retirement is nearing and fears of decreased income and too much time are real problems confronting the person at this stage.

London and Stumpf suggest that a successful organizational career planning program involves establishing career paths, providing feedback, fostering realistic expectations, managing information, and matching jobs and people. The responsibility for such a program is jointly shared by the organization and the employee. Career guidance can be offered by the subordinate's supervisor. Such help should involve joint target setting, providing developmental activities, finding the appropriate job assignments, and providing feedback, evaluation, and reassignment.

ENDNOTES

1. Edward K. Strong, Jr., *Vocational Interests of Men and Women* (Stanford, CA: Stanford University Press, 1943).
2. Donald E. Super, *The Psychology of Careers* (New York: Harper & Row, 1957).
3. E. S. Bordin, "A Theory of Interests as Dynamic Phenomena," *Educational and Psychological Measurement* (1943): 49–66.
4. Charlotte Buehler, *Der menschliche Lebenslauf als psychologiches Problem* (Leipzig: Hirzel, 1943).
5. Donald E. Super, "Self-concepts in Vocational Development, in *Career Development:*

Self-concept Theory ed. D. E. Super et al. (New York: CEEB Research Monograph No. 4, 1963).

6. Samuel H. Osipow, *Theories of Career Development,* 3d ed. (Englewood Cliffs. NJ: Prentice-Hall, 1983), p. 156.

7. John L. Holland, "A Theory of Vocational Choice," *Journal of Counseling Psychology* 6 (1959): 35–45.

8. John L. Holland, "Explorations of a Theory of Vocational Choice and Achievement: II. A Four-year Prediction Study," *Psychological Reports* 12 (1963): 547–595; John L. Holland, "Explorations of a Theory of Vocational Choice: IV. Vocational Preferences and Their Relation to Occupational Images, Daydreams and Personality," *Vocational Guidance Quarterly* 11 (1963): 232–239; 12 (1963); 17–14; 12 (1964): 93–97; John L. Holland, "Explorations of a Theory of Vocational Choice: VI. A Longitudinal Study Using a Sample of Typical College Students," *Journal of Applied Psychology, Monograph Supplement* 52 (1968): 1–37.

9. John L. Holland, *Making Vocational Choices: A Theory of Careers* (Englewood Cliffs, NJ: Prentice-Hall, 1973), p. 23.

10. Peter M. Blau, John W. Gustad, Richard Jesson, Herbert S. Parnes, and Richard Wilcox, "Occupational Choices: A Conceptual Framework," *Industrial and Labor Relations Review* 9 (1956): 534.

11. M. Goldfine and S. O'Connell, "Beyond Communication," a paper presented at the meeting of the Industrial Communication Council, San Francisco, 1977.

12. Gerald L. Wilson and Philip A. Gray, "A Survey of Practices and Strategies for Marketing Communication Majors," *ACA Bulletin* 45 (1983): 32–35.

13. C. Petrie, E. Thompson, D. Rogers, and G. Goldhaber, "Report of the Ad Hoc Committee on Manpower Resources." Report prepared for the Division IV meeting of the International Communication Association, Chicago, April 1975.

14. Edgar H. Schein, "The Individual, the Organization, and the Career: A Conceptual Framework," *Journal of Applied Behavioral Science* 7 (1971): 401–426.

15. Ibid., pp. 308–309.

16. Ibid., pp. 314–316.

17. Daniel Yankelovich, *The New Rules: Searching for Self-Fulfillment in a World Turned Upside Down* (New York: Random House, 1981) found that people identify with the status of the organization (e.g., IBM, CSC, Harvard) more so than with occupational categories.

18. Edgar H. Schein, "Increasing Organizational Effectiveness Through Better Human Resource Planning and Development," *Sloan Management Review* (Fall 1977): 1–20.

19. Meryl Reis Louis, "Surprise and Sensemaking: What Newcomers Experience in Entering Unfamiliar Organizational Settings," *Administrative Science Quarterly* 25 (1980): 226–251.

20. John P. Wanous, *Organizational Entry: Recruitment, Selection and Socialization of Newcomers* (Reading, MA: Addison-Wesley, 1980).

21. Edgar H. Schein, *Career Dynamics: Matching Individual and Organizational Needs* (Reading, MA: Addison-Wesley, 1978).

22. A. Howard and D. W. Bray, "Today's Young Managers: They Can Do It, But Will They?" *The Wharton Magazine* 5 (1981): 23–28.

23. Abraham K. Korman and Rhoda W. Korman, *Career Success/Personal Failure: Alienation in Management* (Englewood Cliffs, NJ: Prentice-Hall, 1980).

24. James W. Walker and Thomas G. Gutteridge, *Career Planning Practices: A AMA Survey Report* (New York: AMACOM, 1979).

25. Manuel London and Stephen A. Stumpf, *Managing Careers* (Reading, MA: Addison-Wesley, 1982), pp. 137–147.
26. D. R. Ilgen, C. D. Fisher, and M. S. Taylor, "Consequences of Individual Feedback on Behavior in Organizations," *Journal of Applied Psychology* 64 (1979): 349–371.
27. London and Stumpf, *Managing Careers,* pp. 142–144.
28. M. Van Sell, Arthur P. Brief, and Randall S. Schuler, "Role Conflict and Role Ambiguity: Integration of the Literature and Directions for Future Research," *Human Relations* 34 (1981): 43–71.
29. Ibid., pp. 144–145.
30. P. Miret, "The Creation of a System of Personnel Management Forcasting: Technology or Sociology," in *Manpower Planning and Organizational Design,* ed. D. T. Bryant and R. J. Niehaus (New York: Plenum, 1978).

Name Index

Subject Index

editing, 186–187
evaluation, 188–189
interviews, 187
press conferences, 187
producing, 186–187
research, 188–189
speakers, 188
special events, 187–188
writing, 186–187
definition of, 172–173
effect of
importance of, 189–190
methods of evaluation, 191–195
questions for evaluation, 195–197
stages of evaluation, 190–191
function of, 172
models of
coorientation, 175–177
public-information, 174
publicity, 173–174
two-way asymmetric, 174–175
strategies for, 185–186
Public Relations (Bernayr), 175
Public relations auditing, 188
Public Relations Society of America, 254

Quality circles, 33, 153–154
Questionnaires, 207–208
Questions, evaluation
agreement-disagreement, 196
closed, 195
multiple-choice, 195–196
open, 195
ranking, 196–197
semantic differential, 196

Random samples, 193
Receivers, 13–14
Reciprocity of exchange, 81
Relational approach, 40–41
Relationships. *See also* Behavior; Motivation;
Needs
and communication, 7
and competition, 138
competitive, 124–125
and culture, 8, 8
friendly, 123–124
in groups, 164–167
analyzing members, 165
analyzing setting, 165–166
effective, 164–165
goal-setting, 165
predicting outcomes, 166
preparing discussion, 166
resolving conflicts, 166–167
and maintenance of organizations, 91
and managers, 31
and message, 82
and networks, 98
in organizations
analysis of, 139–140
functions of, 138–139

problems of, 136–137
and productivity, 137–138
and power, 136, 139
superior/subordinate, 125–126
and WGW communication audit, 220
and work flow, 136–138
Research
position descriptions in, 297
of public communication, 188–189
qualitative, 191–192
quantitative, 192–195
Responses. *See* Feedback
Responsibility, 48
Rhetoric, The (Aristotle), 9
Rituals
arrival, 108
belonging, 109
exclusion, 109
importance of, 107–108
learning, 107–108
participation, full, 108
Rumors, 106–107

Sampling, 193–194
Sapir-Whorf hypothesis, 94
Selective perception, 12
Self-disclosure, 140
Shannon/Weaver model, 11
Situational approach, 37–38
Situational theory, 292. *See also* Grunig's
situational theory
Smoothing, 145
Social auditing, 188
Social control, 106–107
Sophists, 265–266
Sound, 10–11
Sources, 9–10
Speaking, 188
Staffing, 246
Statistical Package for the Social Sciences
(SPSS), 229
Strategic ambiguity, 83
Strong Vocational Interest Blank (SVIB),
288–289
Surveys, 192–193
Syllabus, 275–276
SYMLOG
and analysis of data, 229
and group communication, 157
and group performance, 221, 226–227
Systems, 33–34. *See also* Organizations
Systems school, 33–34

Target system, 235
Technological school, 34–35
Technology
and communication, 34–35
and networks, 104–105
Theory X, 31–32
Theory Y, 31–32
Theory Z, 33
Thoughts, 21